Contested Coastlines

Contested Coastlines

Fisherfolk, Nations and Borders in South Asia

Charu Gupta
and
Mukul Sharma

Routledge
Taylor & Francis Group

LONDON AND NEW YORK

First published 2008
by Routledge

2 Park Square, Milton Park, Abingdon, Oxfordshire OX14 4RN
52 Vanderbilt Avenue, New York, NY 10017

Routledge is an imprint of the Taylor & Francis Group, an informa business

First issued in paperback 2019

Transferred to Digital Printing 2008

Copyright © 2008 Charu Gupta and Mukul Sharma

Typeset by
Bukprint India
B-180A, Guru Nanak Pura, Laxmi Nagar,
Delhi 110 092.

British Library Cataloguing-in-Publication Data
A catalogue record of this book is available from the British Library.

ISBN 978-0-415-44905-2 (hbk)
ISBN 978-0-367-17610-5 (pbk)

For our Parents

Shashi Kala Sharma
Damyanti Gupta
Lalit Mohan Gupta
Saryu Prasad Sharma

Contents

Acknowledgements

Writing this book has been a protracted journey. Covering four nations of South Asia and guided by our activist, journalistic and academic inclinations, it was difficult to synthesise this project. This daunting task would have been impossible without those who helped us achieve this work and they deserve greater thanks than these pages can convey. These acknowledgements are but the most public of our profound appreciation to so many.

The research and writing of this project was supported by various bodies. A grant was received from the United States Institute of Peace to do substantial fieldwork for this work. Fellowships and Visiting Scholarships from Panos South Asia; the Asia Scholarship Foundation, Thailand; Social Science Research Council, New York; Teen Murti Fellowship and Rama Watamull Visiting Scholarship at the University of Hawaii at Manoa enabled the work to develop. Sunimal Fernando and the organisation INASIA, Herman Kumara and National Fisheries Solidarity, J. John and Centre for Education and Communication became like fellow travellers during fieldwork in Sri Lanka and India. Lok Shakti Sangathan and SSVK and their convenor Deepak Bharti provided the much needed organisational support. The biggest thanks for many of the ideas and arguments used in this book goes to all our interviewees, particularly the fisherfolk and their families, without whom this book could never have been written. Fisherfolk organisations and individual activists, especially late Premjee Vhai Khokhari, Harekrishna Debnath, Thomas Kocherry, Steve Creech, A. Vijayan, V. Vivekanandan and Karamat Ali helped us enormously in trying to understand the various dimensions of the issues at stake. Discussions with fellow scholars and friends and their comments on various issues, including authoritianisms of the 'national' and ambiguities of our identities, constantly contributed in sharpening the arguments presented here. They include Itty Abraham, Rita Manchanda, K. Sivaramakrishnan, Jeremy Seabrook, S. Shankar, Sankaran Krishna, Monisha Dasgupta, S. Charusheela, Mahesh Rangarajan, Sudhir Chandra, Souparna Lahiri and Aditya Nigam. A warm thanks to

Nalin Bharti, Noni Meetei and Ritu Bajaj, who helped with the research and fieldwork for chapters on Bangladesh, Indian Ocean and Law, respectively. Akbar Zaidi used his contacts in Karachi to procure a large amount of material on fisherfolk of Pakistan, and we express our appreciation.

We have written and presented earlier, different versions of some of the issues and arguments here. Special mention needs to be made of articles published in the *Economic and Political Weekly*, 39, 7 (3 July 2004); *Frontline*, 21, 3 (3–16 January 2004); *Himal*, 11 (November 1998) and in Rita Manchanda (ed.), *Media Crossing Borders* (South Asia Forum for Human Rights, Nepal, 2004). Papers were also presented at the Annual Spring Symposium on Margins and Migrations: South Asian Diasporas Across the World, organised by the Center for South Asian Studies at the University of Hawaii; at the Annual Fellows' Conference on Asian Constructs of Social Change organised by the Asia Scholarship Foundation at Bangkok and at the South Asia Conference of the Pacific Northwest (SACPAN), held at the University of British Columbia, Vancouver. The comments received have greatly enriched our arguments. The suggestions and observations of Routledge's anonymous reader were also of great help in reconfiguring the manuscript. A very warm thanks to Omita Goyal, who was a delight to work with and responded with enthusiasm to the manuscript. We would also like to thank Jyotsna for all the help she rendered with copyediting this manuscript.

Finally, working as a team made us realise our professional/ personal weaknesses and strengths, and made the experience of writing this book a deeply meaningful one. We were entering arenas hitherto unexplored by us, as none of us had any background of international relations, coastal studies, migration studies or fisherfolk per se. There were many scholars much more versed in these areas. We felt unsure of ourselves, about where the work was heading and some of those anxieties still remain with us. We hope that our sensibilities as a feminist historian and as a developmental journalist, both working from the margins of our disciplines, have enabled us to provide a slightly different take on issues raised in this book. Further, a combination of academic and journalistic mindsets made the writing more complicated, with different emphasis and styles, often leading to heated arguments, but in the end we hope also making our experiences and focuses richer and more nuanced. All errors and idiosyncrasies are of course our own. Our son Ishaan provided immense moments of joy and relief, teaching us not only how to enjoy small things in life but also our differences. Our parents have given constant encouragement and unquestioning support, and it is to them that we dedicate this book.

Charu Gupta
Mukul Sharma

1

Introduction

'We're Prisoners of War', Chacko said. 'Our dreams have been doctored. We belong nowhere. We sail unanchored on troubled seas. We may never be allowed ashore. Our sorrows will never be sad enough. Our joys never happy enough. Our dreams never big enough. Our lives never important enough. To matter.'
—Arundhati Roy, *The God of Small Things*[1]

Who was I? Where did I belong? In Kolkata or in the tide country? In India or across the border? In prose or in poetry?.... Where else could you belong, except in the place you refused to leave.
—Amitav Ghosh, *The Hungry Tide*[2]

This book examines the troubled and tragic journeys of South Asian coastal fisherfolk, who are victims of defined and undefined boundaries and borders in the seas and are arrested and kept in foreign jails by various countries for having entered each other's territorial waters.[3]

Most of the studies on marine coastal fisherfolk of South Asia have been ethnographic descriptions, concentrating on their social life, rituals, knowledge, fishing organisation, kinship structure and patterns.[4] There have been some studies which have reflected on the growing tensions and conflicts between fishermen of the region, especially between traditional fishers and mechanised trawler owners.[5] Further, studies on wars, conflicts and tensions between countries of South Asia, which have attracted a vast number of scholars, have been focussed on 'big', 'visible' issues like Kashmir, nuclear politics, Liberation Tigers of Tamil Eelam (LTTE), terrorism, Hindu/Muslim conflict and ethnic tensions.[6] There is scant mention of the less spectacular, everyday conflicts, which perhaps are equally damaging. This book brings these two streams together by probing not high moments of conflict, but everyday clashes, which may be called 'routine violence', to borrow the term from a recent work.[7] We do so by focussing on the coastal fisherfolk and the ubiquity of their behaviour and movements which govern their travels and transactions. Disputes in South Asia today are not only about soldiers and wars; they have permeated daily lives and suffused border areas, where the majority of casualties have been ordinary people. Coastal fisherfolk particularly, have been embroiled in these daily conflicts between countries of South Asia.

This book further illuminates the dynamic interplay between ecology and conflict in such struggles. It argues that there is a need to rethink questions of peace and security in the context of people, environment and resources. Strife is directly related to environmental degradation and struggle over natural resources. In fact, in recent years, many social scientists too have argued that scarcity of renewable resources (e.g., land degradation, deforestation and fisheries depletion) is increasingly becoming a factor in the creation of political conflict. Scholars suggest four channels through which this tends to happen: a decline in economic performance, ethnic clashes due to population movements, a weakening of political institutions, and a general exacerbation of existing socio-economic-political cleavages.[8] At the same time, however, this book moves beyond seeing environmental crisis as the sole reason for discord among coastal fishworkers and their countries in the South Asia seas. Rather, it makes the link between scarcity of renewable resources with other areas of society, especially economics, law and politics. In the case of South Asia, the Indian Ocean and coastal fisherfolk, various examples of these linkages are visible.

The focus of this work is the coastal states of South Asia and the fisherfolk movement pertaining to them. Thus, it covers India, Pakistan, Sri Lanka and Bangladesh, which share the resources of the Bay of Bengal, the Indian Ocean and the Arabian Sea. They have shared and practised sustainable use of resources in the region for centuries. However, the last three decades, in particular, have witnessed growing tensions between countries of South Asia. Communication among them has broken down and has hampered the task of opening and sustaining supple, heteroglossic dialogues. The governments of India, Pakistan, Sri Lanka and Bangladesh have attempted to remould the recalcitrant clay of plural cultures and civilisations into lean, uniform, hyper-masculine and disci-plined countries, where borders have become sacrosanct. While in the case of land they have been mostly successful in drawing clear-cut lines, there is great anxiety about the seas, where lines of demarcation are blurred. Due to the haziness of lines on the seas, historical affinities and unities, and close geographical locations of the region, fisher people have traditionally crossed sea borders, but they are increasingly believed to be creating grave instability in territorial boundaries of ethnically, religiously and ideologically defined countries. This has spilled into everyday tensions and conflicts.

Our book implicitly also calls into question the usage of 'South Asia' as a homogenous, intact entity, as has often happened in the US academy. While it is true that a large part of South Asia was one till recently, with shared cultures, we do need to take into account that after partition, the countries in the region have also followed diverse and divergent trajectories, away from any assumed unity. For us, South Asia represents a space which shares a lot, but which has also witnessed massive tensions, conflicts and wars. It is an arena demarcated by porous borders, some drawn across seas, made leaky by the material imperatives of everyday movements. This permeability has compelled us to look at the movements of coastal fisherfolk between South Asian countries. Studies on transnational migrants have also usually focussed on international movements of people across borders, usually from the east to the west. Less, however, has been said on movements within South Asia as they are usually not seen as transnational. Our concern, however, is precisely such movements between coastal countries of the region.

The continuous arrest and detention of coastal fisher people when they cross maritime boundaries is a growing threat to the lives and livelihoods of fisherfolk. Literally and figuratively on the margins in the national imaginaries, they have been victims of a discursive process whereby all the involved nations have sought to obliterate the fuzziness of these coastal fisher communities, and produced clear-cut categories like insider and outsider, safety and danger, domestic and foreign, and self and other.

While highlighting the anxieties of the state regarding these coastal fisherfolk, this book also attempts to understand the various reasons for their movement across sea borders. Here we are influenced by a recent work which talks of illicit movements that take place across national borders on a daily basis. These transnational activities are widespread in the case of coastal fisherfolk of South Asia, and to term them as criminals, to arrest and even sometimes kill them, would be to take a very narrow, state-centric view of their movements.[9] In the process, the book also troubles migration studies, as the bulk of the work on it has concentrated on 'legitimate' and 'illegitimate' long-term migrants. Coastal fisherfolk, however, are short-term, temporary migratory subjects on an everyday basis. For them crossing the sea border is a part of their daily existence, where the coastal areas of another country are often like neighbourhoods, to be ventured into without licences or permits. These fishermen represent a world of transnational realities of subaltern existence, exposing the porosity of sea borders, and the fluid terrain of migration and daily movement. Anxieties of borders co-exist with the unconcerned daily rhythms of everyday material life on the sea borders, as for these fisherfolk it is simply a question of livelihood.

However, these fisherfolk are subject to constant arrest for breaking maritime boundaries. While their stories are of tremendous hardship and suffering for no fault of their own, they are also stories of emancipatory possibilities that could emerge from the spatial freedoms which they have practised. They are a tribute to human resilience, to a positive outlook and creativity under oppressive and humiliating conditions, and to the indomitable spirit of the defeated and the forgotten. At the same time, there are also some contradictory voices, where some of these fisherfolk have started articulating the very same language which is used to suppress them.

This book tries to understand the journeys of these fisherfolk and coastal conflicts in South Asia from several overlapping but distinct perspectives. While broadly divided into studies of various South Asian countries, this introduction first reflects on the ecological malaise afflicting the coastal region, and the role of capitalist growth in the marine fishing sector, linking it to increasing everyday conflicts. Second, it explores the cartographic and border dilemmas of various South Asian nations, especially in connection with the coastal fisherfolk. Third, it focusses on the ambiguous identities of these fisherfolk. Finally, it talks of the tremendous human suffering involved in these arrests, and the constant violation of human rights. Various chapters that follow expand these concerns through empirical evidence and specific case studies, while also highlighting the interconnections between them.

This book combines an activist intervention with certain academic concerns, placing the subaltern coastal fisherfolk at the very core of the work. Broadly, it argues for a humane, pro-fisherfolk politics, involving an understanding of the historical context in which all national and ethnic identities have been structured and become fixed, as well as envisioning a future in which coastal fisherfolk of South Asia are able to live peacefully, with a right to livelihood and fairness in the worlds they inhabit.

Ecology, Capitalism and Conflict

Third Fisherman: Master, I marvel how the fishes live in the sea.
First Fisherman: Why as men do a-land the great ones eat up the little ones.

—William Shakespeare, *Pericles*[10]

It has been argued effectively that traditional analyses of conflict which rely primarily on ethnic, religious and cultural explanations are inadequate, since these do not take into account the increasingly obvious links between a growing scarcity of renewable resources and violent conflict. This is especially true in developing countries as they are more vulnerable to environmental changes.[11] Ecological threats may be less dramatic than clearly identified military threats, but they can be as pervasive. Further, security is being shaped by environmental factors, where it is asserted that large-scale human-induced environmental pressure may seriously affect national and international security. The theoretical literature on security studies has encouraged this new thinking, whereby conventional arguments of state secrecy, nuclear and military power have given way to ecological concerns, placing them on top of the agenda of policy-makers. As one scholar states: 'Conventional models of national security have not considered access to resources and the degradation of global environmental services, a central problem of international politics and security'.[12]

Environmental degradation raises the levels of stress within national and international society and increases the likelihood of many different kinds of conflict, impeding the development of cooperative solutions.[13] The links between environment and security also illuminate the complexity of the environmental crisis.

The emergence of environmental politics is a recent phenomenon. Environmental degradation aggravates existing faultlines and often creates new ones with their potential to erupt into violent conflict. However, the debate over the links between environmental security and conflict has been intense. Stephen Libiszewshi is of the view that an environmental conflict is a conflict caused by the scarcity of a resource produced by man-made disturbance of its normal regeneration rate. Environmental scarcity can result from the overuse of a renewable resource or from over-straining the ecosystem's sink capacity, that is, pollution. Both can reach the stage of destruction of the living space.[14] In this debate, however, some of the most articulate and influential arguments have been advanced by Jessica Mathews. In her widely cited article 'Redefining Security', she endorses 'broadening [the] definition of national security to include resource, environmental and demographic issues.'[15] Pointing to the interrelated impact of population growth and resource scarcity, she portrays a bleak future of human suffering and turmoil.

In his groundbreaking work, Thomas Homer-Dixon builds a powerful case for linking ecology with security by elaborating an environmental conflict model. In this endeavour, he lists the decline in coastal fisheries, a renewable resource, as one of the reasons for conflict.[16] The Food and Agriculture Organization (FAO) estimates that 100 million metric tonnes of fish can be sustainably caught each year from the world's oceans, lakes and rivers. In 1993, humans were catching about 86 metric tonnes per year.[17] As human extraction approaches the limits of sustainability, there are signs of a worldwide fisheries crisis. The FAO now estimates that 69 per cent of marine fish stocks are 'fully exploited, over-exploited, depleted, or in the process of rebuilding as a result of depletion.'[18] In many places around the world, overexploitation has caused a dramatic decline in the productivity of regional fisheries. These events have not only harmed ocean ecosystems, but have produced widespread human hardship and unemployment. Moreover, they can be a cause of violent conflicts. In this light, the crisis in marine resources, the increasing decline of fisheries and its link to tensions and conflict becomes crucial, especially in the context of South Asia.

However, while acknowledging the role that ecological crisis and environmental degradation play in increasing conflicts, it is not enough to understand the plight of coastal fishworkers in South Asia merely in environmental terms, or in terms of 'biology' and 'nature'. Moreover, most of the cited works are influenced by neo-Malthusian approaches, which evoke spectres of terrible calamity. Such approaches also lay excessive stress on population explosion as the main reason for environmental problems.[19] Although we should not underestimate environmental scarcity, people have also shown a tremendous capacity for overcoming it, finding alternative methods, and even at times exercising self-control for the larger benefit. This suggests that we need a more nuanced approach. Insofar as security is premised on maintaining the status quo, it runs counter to the changes needed to alleviate many environmental problems, because it is precisely the status quo that has produced the problems. Inequities in the use of resources are a major problem in the current economic crisis, where the developed world makes disproportionate use of resources. Moreover, as in the case of fisheries, mechanised trawlers are increasingly displacing traditional fishing people and methods.

It is partially true that too many people and overfishing have both created scarcity of this renewable resource and also contributed to the growing conflict between the South Asian countries. In conditions of scarcity and overcrowding, people fight each other, and in this case there has been increasing competition among the fishermen themselves. Growing levels of pollution, mechanised fishing and aquaculture have contributed greatly to the ecological crisis. However, the environmental malaise afflicting the Indian Ocean is not the sole reason for scarcity of sea resources and the growing conflict. A rhetoric that primarily stresses ecological scarcity as a central cause of conflict is partially flawed. Both scarcity and conflict are also socially and economically induced.[20] Scarcity is also about preserving the concentration of wealth and power in the hands of a few. This is not to deny the role of environmental scarcity, but to state that socially and economically generated divisions in the marine sector have also contributed to growing conflicts over resources. Thus, unequal distribution of resources has exacerbated ecological crisis as well as conflict. Further, people whose livelihoods have been 'degraded' by various processes cannot be expected to take seriously the idea of conservation.

We also seriously need to question our very defintions of national security, and obsessions of states in the name of security. We need to ask—security for whom? For the people or for the nation? After all, it is the poor who are the most vulnerable to environmental crisis and ecological threats. To a large extent, those who currently benefit from the existing modes of development and political order are those least likely to take environmental arguments seriously or to wish to initiate dramatic changes. They are also most likely to construct political arguments in terms of environmentalism as a security threat when suggestions of limits on resource uses or wasteful lifestyles are advocated. And, to a large extent they are also capable of using military force to maintain the status quo. Actually military action puts the preservation of the state above any concerns for environmental stability, or even the survival, of large numbers of people.[21]

The decline in marine resources in South Asia too is profoundly linked with a complex of interrelated issues: unequal economic distribution of wealth and capitalist relations in the coastal areas,[22] political relations between the countries and exaggerated anxieties of security and border preservation. There have been increasing conflicts thus, within and without, between small-scale fishers and the mechanised fishers, between fishermen and boat-owners, between one region and another, and most critically between one nation and another, which is the main concern of this book.

Tyranny of the National: Disciplining Bodies

It is not necessary that war be waged only on borders
Wherever there is war there are borders
                                        —Snehmayi Chaudhry[23]

One of the primary goals of the modern state is to create and maintain an illusion of a single nation-state, where assimilation and conformity acquire fundamental importance.[24] As has been recently pointed out, there is a constant search for clarity and 'purity' in the midst of blurring, mixing and uncertainty that is the actually existing condition of all nations. The nation seeks to carve out a core or 'mainstream', the unhyphenated national, the real obvious natural citizen, where minorities and marginal groups might be a part of the nation but 'never quite'.[25] The telos of the state and the nation seek to deny that differences are constitutive of our social life. For this reason, the state clearly attempts to demarcate between what is, and what is not, legitimate. The creation of a 'legible people'[26]—a people open to the scrutiny of officialdom—has become a hallmark of this modern statehood.

To establish its omnipotence, the state considers it has a right to intervene in the everyday life of its people, their employment and their bodies, especially if this is perceived as coming into conflict with its power. It also incorporates cultural and political forms, representations, discourses, practices and activities, and specific technologies and organisations of power that, taken together, help to define public interest, establish meaning, and define and naturalise available social identities.[27] The agreed-upon identities imply closure on other modes of being by disrupting, diluting, sometimes even denying the possibility of alternatives and obliterating pre-existing cultures. There is a disproportionate advantage given to the majority community, with a marginalisation of minority groups. Further, 'nations form against one another as competing instruments in the service of the core's domination of the periphery'.[28] There is, thus, a redefinition of notions of sovereignty and security.

At the same time, in the present context of international capitalism, open markets and globalisation, it has often been remarked that nation-states are under tremendous pressure; pressure which contradicts the idea of the omnipotent state and challenges its power in important ways. 'Global financial integration, dense global networks of trade and migration, a global communications infrastructure bearing an incipient global mass culture, the global reach of transnational corporations'[29] have made many writers agree on the growing irrelevance of national boundaries and geopolitical rivalries. It would seem that the nation-state has 'lived its time' in this century of globalisation, and no longer remains the dominant entity in the interpretation of contemporary events. This claim has been extended to an argument of erosion in territorial boundaries and control. Thus, Lawrence A. Herzog argues: 'The internationalization of the world economy… has led to an inevitable reshaping of boundary functions. The most obvious change has been the shift from boundaries that are heavily protected and militarized to those that are more porous, permitting cross-border social and economic interaction'.[30]

However, nationalism and globalisation actually seem to be strengthening each other in paradoxical ways. Globalisation seems simultaneously to integrate and to fracture, include and exclude, national identities. This world of expanding deterritorialised boundaries is also a world of more numerous, and in some cases, stronger states.[31] There is a simultaneous debordering and rebordering of the state. In fact, the nation-state has long been the vehicle, the ideological justification and the political legitimation for liberal, rational forms of political and cultural unity and economic convergence. Certainly, the ideal of nationhood today is a ubiquitous phenomenon which refuses to go away. It continues to exert its hold over the political imagination; it continues to be reproduced as a cause worth more than individual life; and it frames the practice of political democracy.[32]

Even if there is conflict between some of the claims made in this age of globalisation[33] and the nation-states, the political realities of the present world, show that the legal right to cross borders and frontiers is still controlled by the states. The globalisation process has not been accompanied by the opening of borders. In fact, global interconnectedness notwithstanding, the propensity of many societies, including formerly 'cohesive' ones, to define themselves on the basis of their ethnic, national or spatial origin, of religion, as well as of culturally and ethnically distinct regions, by excluding those they consider as 'others', has never been greater. Thus, place still remains a major repository of rights and membership. The assumption that identities are deterritorialised and state territories are readily there for the taking, regardless of place and national origin, has no objective existence outside the minds of its proponents. Territoriality provides an emblem of the power of the nation.[34] Regulative geographies of nationalism continue to contain and maintain the space and place of the national state.[35] The case of coastal fisherfolk particularly proves the point, since not only land, even sea territories are considered 'sacrosanct' by the nations.

Globalisation has resulted, particularly in developing countries, in an even more urgent concern for accurate representations and markings of borders and maps. The indeterminate boundaries of the global map rest alongside the determined and 'fixed' boundaries of the national map. It has been pointed out that borders are the markers of identity and have played a role in this century in making national identity the pre-eminent political identity of the modern state.[36] In fact, the principle of a border as the ultimate marker of national security has remained firmly in place. Timothy Mitchell has noted how border controls have helped define our conception of the state and have given it the appearance of autonomy, authority and power:

> By establishing the territorial boundary and exercising absolute control over movement across it, state practices define and help constitute a national entity. Setting up and policing a frontier involves a variety of fairly modern practices—continuous barbed-wire fencing, passports, immigration laws, inspectors, currency controls, and so on. These mundane arrangements, most of them unknown 200 or even 100 years ago, help manufacture an almost transcendental entity, the nation state.[37]

South Asian countries, in the process of decolonisation, have mostly inherited artificial boundaries, fragile national unities, brittle political systems and distorted economies. Thus, one of the ways to claim the legitimacy of the existing state is by insisting on fixed mappings. Maps represent national anxieties. They contribute to the definition of that which roots people in specific localities. Benedict Anderson has updated his famous work by a chapter on mapping and maps, pointing out the ways in which maps become potent symbols of nations and are turned into logos that stand in for, and represent, the nation.[38] Creation, maintenance and protection of maps, borders and boundaries, be it over land or sea, has thus become a central concern of many countries, including those of South Asia; indeed, even more so here, given the nature of prevailing tensions and a mentality obsessed with security. Also, since India, Pakistan and Bangladesh were till very recently one, they have felt the need even more to mark their borders firmly, to establish a clear national identity. Even though marking of borders has failed to deter illegal flows, it is seen as essential to construct the appearance of a more secure and orderly border. The border is depicted not as a novel, fragile, contingent creation, but as something ancient, robust and real. A border, which is always difficult to define, is portrayed as having a fixed definition. It is defined as containing a homogeneous population and an unalterable political demarcation. This notion glosses over, or essentialises, identities, often obliterating the actual problems and concealing the variety of human behaviours and cultures, especially in a region like South Asia, which is marked with many social and economic similarities.

There has thus been a rapid expansion of policing of sea borders and rising tensions over prohibited cross-sea border flows of fishworkers. Maritime borders are increasingly protected and monitored, not to deter naval armies or impose tariffs on sea trade, but to confront a perceived invasion of these 'clandestine', 'undesirable' fishermen, conducting cross-sea border economic activity. Concerns over these activities have been increasing in the security agendas of the states of South Asia. The border regulatory apparatuses of the states are thus being revamped, with increasing restrictive controls over the movement of fishermen. As has been noted, despite the relaxation of barriers to the flows of goods, information and capital, when it comes to regulating the movement of people the nation-state claims its old splendour in asserting its sovereign right to control its borders.[39] The state restrictions on the cross-border movements of coastal fisherfolk expose the augmentation of national identity through border setting.

Further, the foreign and defence policies of various South Asian countries presuppose a given spatialisation of the world in terms of 'us and them'. As has been remarked, in this game of us and them, histories are told and retold, traditions invented and denied, statuses ascribed and challenged, allegiances forged and broken, and identities claimed and rejected.[40] In the process, it is not enough for these countries to have its heroes of the nation; equally fundamentally they must have a foe, an enemy, the 'other', which not only sustains the nation, but gives it further authority. If there is none, one has to be constructed and nurtured. Myths and anxieties of the 'other' are taken here as realities.[41] The presence of the 'other' justifies the use of violence and suppression by the state against the people assumed to be 'other'. In countries of South Asia today, the existence of an evil 'other' has become a routine part of public discourse. The 'other' becomes more enduring here as it is anchored in the immediate neighbourhood, where common borders are disputed. Thus, Pakistan is often represented as the 'other' for India and viceversa. Both countries attempt to 'fix' India and Pakistan as mutually antagonistic identities. It is no exaggeration to suggest that Indian nationalism cannot be nurtured without the existence of the Pakistani enemy and viceversa. Most writings succumb to this. As remarks Anil Kumar Singh, 'Pakistan has been a perennial source of threat to Indian security.... growing Sino-Pakistan nexus has further heightened India's sense of insecurity'.[42] From nuclear explosion to cricket matches, to the 'less dramatic' arrest of coastal fisherfolk—everything is neatly fitted into this syndrome. Historical narratives of suspicion, ethnic fragmentation, hostility, stereotypes and mutual recriminations abound. Past and present collective histories of partition (India and Pakistan), ethnic strife (India and Sri Lanka) and migrations (India and Bangladesh) have become intermeshed and united with the biographies and livelihoods of fisherfolk, determining their sense of self and space.

Border histories are incomplete without an ecological component. Environment and nature emerge from the backround and play a leading role in the defining of borders. Mountains and seas have signified 'natural borders' for India historically. However, the seas have been seen as producing unstable borders, leading to a disturbing fluidity. Borders, which delimit state boundaries and are transformed into national identity, are particularly unclear in the seas, thus posing a potential threat to everything that is identified with the nation. In India too, sea has been seen as a major point of vulnerability. K. M. Panikkar remarks:

It is necessary to emphasise that from that historic day when Vasco da Gama with his fleet of warships arrived at Calicut, India has ever been under the relentless pressure of sea power, steady and unseen over long periods, but effectively controlling our economic life and political life. In fact, since 1498, India has been blockaded... While the threat from land side is sporadic and is effective only under given conditions, the threat from the sea is ever present and perpetually effective.[43]

His geopolitics ends with a reminder, 'The only practical remedy to this permanent geographical weakness of India, its exposed position in regard to powers operating from the sea, is the strength of her own internal political and economic structure.'[44] At another place, he states:

While to other countries, the Indian Ocean is only one of the important oceanic areas, to India it is the vital sea. Her life lines are concentrated in that area. Her future is dependent on the freedom of that vast water surface. No industrial development, no commercial growth, no stable political structure is possible for her unless the Indian Ocean is free and her own shores fully protected. The Indian Ocean must therefore remain truly Indian.[45]

Various steps have been taken to organise a blue water navy to secure the Indian coastline, and also to define the sea border as accurately as possible and in the greatest detail. In fact, sea border control has increasingly gained importance, and there is a whole body of coast guards, sea customs and sea border patrol units who are responsible for security at maritime borders. The expenditure on these bodies has seen a substantial increase in almost all countries, and it is believed that a display of strength on the sea borders is essential to discourage clandestine, illegal and unlawful entries by fishermen. The perception of the state is that these crossings cannot be controlled unless sea borders are made more secure, which means more and more policing.

While most coastal fishworkers have shown a lack of concern for such markings, some of them, too, have been influenced by this ideology of the state. The ruling elite of various South Asian countries have attempted to orchestrate or compel popular consent, mould minds and legitimate their ongoing nation-building projects. Fishermen have responded to this vocabulary in unexpected ways by selectively adopting, reinterpreting, or discarding parts of it. The ideology of nationhood is so dominant at times that combined with the ecological malaise and the declining fish catch, some of the fisherfolk have started speaking the same language as that of the state. They too sometimes regard the 'other', the 'outsider', belonging to a different nation, as impinging on their national rights over the seas, and taking away the catch, which is 'legitimately' theirs. This explains the escalating tension between fisherfolk themselves, particularly of Sri Lanka and India, especially in the recent past.[46] Thus, while most coastal fishworkers transgress boundaries, some of them, although a minority, also help in reconsolidating them. There has thus been a constant play of collaboration with, and resistance, or rather, an indifference to, the state that the fisherfolk have engaged in, revealing a complex mix.

Today, the rhetoric around security in South Asian countries has acquired exaggerated dimensions. Security has often been assumed to be synonymous with protection from external threats

across borders to a state's vital interests and core values.[47] Priority
is given to perceived security threats also due to the mainstream
established domains of security studies and international relations.
South Asia today has become a highly militarised region, sharing
disputed borders and locked in political and military competition.
The sociological axiom underlying this view about security is that
of single, individualised and unitary national interests competing
with each other. The question of people's security as an independent subject of inquiry does not arise here. The use of coercion
decisively, to establish the supremacy and indivisibility of the
juridical state, has become a part of this security package. It has
been remarked that these constructs of border threats and national
security are nothing other than one more in an endless series of
attempts to corral the future and subject various people to yet
another arbitrary discipline.[48]

Fisherfolk Flows: Ambiguities of Identities

humari jaat machimaar
humari naat machimaar
hum sab machimaar ek

(our caste is fishing,
our occupation is fishing,
we all fishermen are one)
    —A popular saying among fishworkers of Vanakvada village in Diu.

The anxiety of the state, however, comes into fundamental con-
tradiction with the lives, livelihoods, needs, demands and desires
of the majority of coastal fisherfolk, who in any case are on the
peripheries of the state, both physically and metaphorically. These
fishermen are citizens only in the most tenuous sense, and their
liminal existence belies simple dichotomies. Movement of fisherfolk in the seas has been an age-old phenomenon, which has
continued in traditional and new ways. The physical geography
and constructed omnipotence of the state is challenged and con-
tradicted by the cartography of fishworkers' identities, who engage
in deterritorialising journeys on a daily basis. They query the tyranny

of the national, challenging the image of the nation as a spatially contiguous entity. Their movement signifies, as has recently been argued, the difference between organised crime and innumerable illicit acts that take place across national borders everyday.[49]

Historically, too, lands have separated communities; oceans have brought them together.[50] In his classic work, Braudel negates the image of the ocean/sea as a geographical barrier; instead he views it as a factor of communication, linkages and unity among diverse communities.[51] The seas thus signify a unity for the fisherfolk communities, where crossing of borders and entering each other's territory is a daily phenomenon; it is natural and inevitable. These fishermen are like 'nowhere men', surfing a 'nowhere ocean'. These coastal fishworkers are part of what Homi Bhaba calls the 'wandering peoples who will not be contained within the *Heim* of the national culture and its unisonant discourse, but are themselves the marks of a shifting boundary that alienates the frontiers of the modern nation.'[52] They, in a way, represent negations of the proper working self, as their daily lives and lifestyles violate the fundamentals of the state and notions of security and borders. As the state attempts more and more to reaffirm a given vision of borders and security, the fisherfolk disorder and reorder established arrangements. Aggression of the state goes hand in hand with the transgression of the fisherfolk, rupturing both conceptual and physical boundaries. There is a pervasive paradox here: the more the border defines and controls, the more the fishworkers infringe it. Despite a variety of social, economic and political constraints, the bodies of these fisherfolk exhibit a remarkable flexibility and resilience. The dynamic journeys of these subaltern subjects challenge the idea that nations are hermetically sealed. The legitimising tools of cohesion and unity of the nation-state become blunt in the face of complexities of these movements.

What is the national identity of these coastal fishworkers? Are they one of 'us' or 'them'? They represent a national fragment that symbolises the inter-state tensions of the moment. They have multiple trajectories of identity, challenging any claims of a unified nation. The territorially bounded practices of national citizenship and inert international relations are too leaden-footed to match the dexterous movement of these coastal fishworkers. 'Identity' is not a static set of attributes that characterises them. Their identity changes, flows, reverses and reinvents itself. It is a constantly living practice, based in part on historical experiences of past encounters, but also upon flexibility and fluidity according to changing circumstances. Nuances and inflections of that experience surface from time to time according to the shifting conditions and impulses. The identity of these fisherfolk is a pluralist construct that denies the dominant, morally transcendent mode of national becoming. Their movement reframes the question of identity in less territorially bounded and more mobile and mediated ways.

The very notion of citizenship, as we will see, is problematic for these subordinated fisherfolk living on the borders of say India and Bangladesh or India and Sri Lanka. For them, the choice between proving one's 'pure' nationalist credentials, of being a 'true' citizen, and that of livelihood, survival and daily life is practically an impossible one. Both their national identity and their spatial limits in terms of political boundaries are marked by haziness and fluidity. In fact, many coastal fisherfolk, particularly of India–Bangladesh or even India–Pakistan, have familial and marital ties across borders, making such lines even more problematic for them. This transgresses given and fixed identities and disrupts the spatial imagery of countries. The construction of a singular boundary is complicated here by ground realities, where legacies, boundaries and identities overlap. The state has been unable to eradicate these links across sea borders.

The crossing of borders by these fishers on a daily basis can partially be seen as hidden voyages of resistance, whereby these fishworkers defy boundaries.[53] Their actions may not explicitly be a critique of the nation but neither do they encompass the nation. As subalterns, they are perhaps 'incapable' of imagining a nation. It may thus be more useful to see these acts as representing an unconcern for state and national anxieties, and an exercise in asserting their customary fishing rights.[54] These fishermen are more concerned with their economic survival, their livelihoods, and the maintenance of familiar and functional everyday practices of social life, rather than notions of citizenship or borders.

These fishing communities mark an ambiguous space, located on the edges of various South Asian countries, precariously balanced between the flow and the contained, legality and illegality, inside and outside. Thus anxieties of borders co-exist with the unconcerned daily rhythms of everyday material life on the sea borders. They are usually very short-term, temporary migrants into each other's territories.[55] They represent a world of subalternity, of another universe of values, attitudes and outlook. These two worlds—from top 'cartographic anxieties', from below 'ironic unconcern'—make up the twilight zone in which sea borders and fisherfolk of South Asian countries exist.

The lives of the coastal fishworkers and their relationship with the seas create a locus where divergent, even antagonistic, national identities intersect. Their consciousness is theoretically against incompatible entities and antagonisms. It offers a third viewpoint, which is multiperspectival and tolerant of ambiguity and ambivalence. As marginal subjects and interstitial artisans, these fishworkers are stranded between legality and illegality. They produce ambiguity and doubt about the taken-for-granted values of home and the nation. Bodies of coastal fisherfolk in South Asian countries are metaphors for questioning and contesting fixed notions of citizenships and nations. Their bodies are shaped by their very mobility, movement and motion in the ocean, representing 'bodies in contact'.[56] They serve as social and cultural intermediaries, navigating intersections of ocean borders, and helping in creating networks linking people of different nations, religions and ethnicities.

On the Fisher's Body: Human Rights and Suffering

And the death of the people was as it has always been:
as if no one, nothing had died,
as if they were stones falling
on the ground, or water on the water
—Pablo Neruda, *Canto General*[57]

The transnational movements on a daily basis and the fluid identities of coastal fisherfolk actually result in even more anxieties for the state, which feels that the border needs to be protected at all cost, and any crossing by the fishworkers, even if unintentional, must be prevented. These fisherfolk become deviants and suspects in the eyes of the state as they resist established identities and undermine stated boundaries. The state thus has to discipline, manage, contain, control and regulate their bodies at all cost, bringing them under constant surveillance. Statements of security are inevitably inscribed upon, and made through, the body of the arrested fishermen. The body of the fisherfolk is tortured in an attempt to avenge the daily affronts to the might of the state, whose borders they have permeated. The result has been the use of physical force, threat, violence, arrests, and even killings, justified in the name of sovereignty of the state. Since these fishermen refuse to conform to the ideological and political identities of the state, they are persecuted and pushed out by the aggressive state. As always, political violence here too plays a central part in the preservation and hegemony of the state.

All these South Asian countries, while claiming respect for human rights, defend the arrest of fisherfolk of another country as both an unavoidable and a necessary measure to forestall security threats and ensure order and respect for the law. As has been suggested, documents of civilisation are at the same time documents of barbarism.[58] 'Unthinkable' and 'unpresentable' acts of the state, like use of torture, violence and arrests, are justified and made recognisable and tolerable by representing them in acceptable discourses like patriotism, retaliation for real and imagined acts of the past, terrorism, smuggling, violation of maritime acts, need to preserve the state's territorial integrity, protection of coastal borders and requirements to safeguard the nation. The state in one and the same breath talks of protecting the nation and indulges in inhuman practices. Documents of so-called protection of borders and security of nations, perhaps noble causes in their own right, are also documents of human suffering and violence conducted on the bodies and souls of fishermen and their families. The arrests and torture inflicted on the fishermen is inseparable from the hidden violence and nationalist jingoism of these South Asian countries. Territoriality of the state becomes a privileged medium for forcibly controlling the movement, lives and livelihoods of fisherfolk within the state's material and physical space. An illegitimate act thus acquires legitimacy.

Arrests of fisherfolk circulate and cross boundaries. All countries are equally culpable of such actions. Arrests have become embodied in various practices, institutions and icons of the state, be it coast guards, jails or courts. The goal of these human rights violations is not just to protect the borders or inflict pain on an assumed 'other', but also to create punishable categories of such fisherfolk, forging and maintaining boundaries among them, enforcing behavioural norms among them and forcing them into conformity. Arrest is combined with a myriad of disciplinary procedures damaging to the body and spirit of the fisherfolk. Various mechanisms of control of fishermen are seen by the state as protection from both political and economic threats.

What happens to the arrested fisherfolk in this scenario? They are confined to jails of another country for years together through no fault of their own. We hear a 'forest of narratives' from these victims of arbitrary arrests, detention and torture, engendering multiple conceptions of reality. Their bodies are sites of suffering, violence and trauma. Although suffering is unique to each individual, the testimonies of many of the arrested fishworkers are remarkably similar. All the arrested fishworkers undergo the psychological trauma of uprooting. Across borders, they share the same nostalgic memories and stories of home, village and soil, not often articulated in terms of the nation. Most of these fishermen relate to familial, local, regional and even religious identities much more than to national identities. Home is sanctified as a place of protection, safety and sanctuary. Their neighbourhood and community back home provide points of reference, daily rhythm and meaning to their existence. The jail, on the other hand, symbolises exile, creating claustrophobia, confinement and control. It represents a loss of identity and a physical uprooting. In the jail, they live in crowded conditions, sharing highly inadequate facilities, poor sanitation and lack of privacy. They suffer anxieties due to uncertainties over their release, and feel helpless and powerless. But more than anything else, there is a deep sense of loss of everything—of dignity, of hope, of self-esteem. They are scarred forever.

The suffering and traumatised fisherfolk are so broken by the ordeal that they often speak of a sense of guilt, shame, failure, moral inadequacy and embarrassment. They persistently question themselves as to what they had done to get themselves arrested in the first place.[59] Just as Jews have been held responsible for anti-Semitism,[60] women for misogyny,[61] so too these arrested fishermen blame themselves and are blamed by others for their own oppression. Some of the surviving fishermen that we interviewed suffered deep social, political and psychological isolation while in jail. They frequently contemplated suicide. The suffering is not restricted to the imprisoned individuals. The situation of those who are left behind, of the families of these fisherfolk, is no better. They repeatedly express their loss of a loved one and their helplessness in getting them released. Wives of arrested fishermen undergo particularly profound suffering. They are completely isolated in such times, and often become targets for reprisals by the larger community and by authorities. While various trade union bodies and citizens' initiatives have from time to time taken up this issue,[62] the lack of will on the part of many countries has proved to be the greatest impediment to the release of the arrested fishworkers. The situation continues to be grim, and acquires even more grave proportions when tensions between countries escalate.

Conclusion

The political and social issues here are complex and resist easy solutions. However, what can broadly be said is that it is essential to transcend the unfettered processes of capital accumulation as the development metaphor. Its single-minded and unidirectional trajectory is destructive of diversity, place and ecology. We need to take our fisheries out of the hands of the relatively few large companies that control them, and hand them over to the coastal communities of small-scale fishers, and 'reinvent' sustainable fisheries. We need to simultaneously question the homogenising political systems of nation-states, which neither recognise diversity nor distribute power equally. As Partha Chatterjee remarks, we need to confront the central question of the modern state and its mechanisms of normalization that seek to obliterate the fuzziness of communities, and that marginalise those who do not conform to the chosen marks of nationality.[63]

We need to contest, interrogate and reverse state anxieties. We need to rethink the very terms in which we discuss security, the very language we use to articulate our 'realities', problems and dreams.[64] It calls for a drastic rethinking and revisiting of questions of peace and security in the context of ecology, resources, and above all, people. The attention of the state has to shift from the security of the borders to the security of the people. This involves a belief in the heterogeneity of the people. The desire of a country to be sovereign and strong should not contradict or come into conflict with the rights of the people living in that country. This requires a fundamental shift in the basis of political legitimacy—from efficacy to the active consent of the governed. Separating security from state security will allow the working out of strategies, visions and horizons for a more humane treatment of fisherfolk. Coastal fisherfolk provide us with an opportunity for constructive interaction between peoples across boundaries, reducing constructs of exclusivist identities. They negotiate with national borders and security concerns in ways that demonstrate their autonomy and livelihood needs. They are symbols of continuing resilience in the face of constant oppression. Their lived experience expresses both identity and meaning; who they are is reflected, as with all human beings, in the stories they tell of themselves.

2

Beyond Borders: The Indian Ocean Region in South Asia

Writing the histories of oceans has often been a difficult task when the overwhelming weight of historiographical pressure is in the direction of writing the history of nations.

—Sanjay Subrahmanyam, *Maritime India*[1]

Oceans and nations stand in tension vis-à-vis one another. Oceans are part of the global commons. They mark liminal, leaky and fluid spaces. They signify interconnections and mutual dependence, standing as symbols of unity and bonds. Nations are bounded, inscribed and confined by the artificial limits of boundaries. They have come to signify fixed borders, insular land pieces, and relatively fixed territorialities, much less permeable than oceans. Decentring lands and nations and focussing on oceans makes one go beyond the tyranny of the national and examine the integrative power of networks and increasing contacts. At the same time, the relationship between oceans and nations cannot be denied, as nations are more and more determining ocean spaces and establishing their control over water through maritime boundaries.

Both lands and oceans are an integral part of our geographical spaces and are often together treated as 'given' natural realities. But they cannot be implied with meanings, unless there is an interaction between nature and people. This interface inherits the varied, associated meanings of geographies. The territoriality of a geographical expression has been continuously mapped throughout human history on multilateral dimensions, including economic, political, ethnic, socio-cultural and strategic. Physical geography is also constantly shaped by concepts and political relations in specific contexts of space and time. Oceans today serve as identity markers of emerging global cultures and environmental consciousness, also underlining that environmental discourse cannot be

confined to borders. They are central to human welfare and existence. Blanketing 71 per cent of the earth's surface, they provide
the human race with food and recreational opportunities, serve
as highways for world commerce, and cover immense sources of
usable energy and other non-living resources.

The Indian Ocean Region (IOR) of South Asia, in the context
of this book, has been a witness to increasing contacts[2] and simultaneously increasing coastal conflicts, where questions of ecology,
fishermen and nations have intersected. This chapter attempts to
study the IOR, examining the historicity of constructing ocean as
boundary, in terms of economic, political, strategic and cultural
realities. This chapter also briefly overviews the historical profile
of the region, and studies the resources available here and their
relationship to ecology, crisis in fisheries and fishworkers.

It has been recently remarked that there is a paradox in the
idea of an ocean as being at the basis of a cultural complex of
resemblances and counterpoised differences. Its distinctiveness
as an entity may be claimed by those with an interest in doing so,
yet it is rarely complete in any one people's view: what some see
as its socio-cultural horizons are what others may see as its centre,
and so on in the manner of a latticework of contacts and influences. The Indian Ocean rim might be thought of as too widespread
for there to be sufficient ongoing co-ordination of maritime activities to constitute significant unity. And yet there has been a density
in the Indian Ocean interaction, and it seems legitimate to refer to
this ocean as a socio-cultural area of considerable significance.[3]

The Indian Ocean is the third largest ocean in the world, con-
stituting a fifth of the world's total maritime surface and domi-
nating the sea-face of Asia. Its physical geography encompasses
the body of water between Africa, the Southern Ocean, Asia and
Australia.[4] The maximum depth of the Indian Ocean is 7,209
metres, with an average depth of 3,711.[5] Geographically, it is an
area from the latitude 40° south to the Gulf of Oman and the
head of the Bay of Bengal on the north, and from the South African
Coast on the west to the coastline of Myanmar, Thailand, Malaysia
and Western Australia on the east.[6] It includes the Red Sea, the
Persian Gulf, the Arabian Sea and the Bay of Bengal. The Indian
Ocean 'region' is understood to refer to both the rim and the
hinterland states, the latter being those dependent on the Indian
Ocean. The geographical solidarity of the Indian Ocean also brings

the concept of the region as a distinct 'community'. This maritime space connects no less than 37 countries inhabited by a third of the world's population.[7] According to some, the community comprises as many as 60 states, including those not even remotely connected to the Indian Ocean.[8] Further, its frontier is marked by a chain of islands criss-crossed by narrow straits and channels.[9] In short, the geographical extent of the Indian Ocean expresses the beauty of a heterogeneous civilisation.

The South Asian region covers half of the Indian Ocean, extending from the Persian Gulf to the straits of Malacca.[10] It occupies an important strategic location in an area that has been the hotbed of international politics and conflicts for decades. The region is inhabited by almost one-fifth of the human race in about 3 per cent of the world's land surface, whose magnitude of deprivation is matched only by their desire to have a place under the sun. South Asian countries are marked by a distinct identity, as they share a common history of modern colonial subjection by the West. The geographical entity of South Asia comprises Bhutan, Bangladesh, Maldives, India, Nepal, Pakistan and Sri Lanka. The coastal countries are only five, excluding Nepal and Bhutan (see Table 2.1). It physically dominates the northern part of the Indian Ocean, which serves as a vital link between the West and the East, connecting Europe through the Middle East, with South-East and East Asia.[11] The region is traversed by important sea-lanes of international trade and vital oil supplies from the Gulf. India has more or less a central position among the countries of the Indian Ocean, particularly in the South Asian region,

Table 2.1: Geographical Profile of South Asian Seas Region

Country	Area (sq. km)	Coast-line (km)	Year of Sovere-ignty	GNP US $ (Per Capita)	Total Popu-lation ('000)	Popul-ation Growth Rate	Density (Per km)
Sri Lanka	65,000	1,340	1984	400	17,619	2.1	273.4
Pakistan	803,000	1,046	1947	350	122,802	4.2	154.3
Maldives	298	644	1965	300	205	3.8	799.9
India	336,500	7,003	1947	300	870,000	3.1	264.7
Bangladesh	142,000	580	1971	160	111,400	2.6	754.9

Source: The Europe Year Book 1995: A World Survey, Vols 1 & 2, Springer, 1995, London. *The Ocean Year Book 3,* University of Chicago, 1983.

geographically, culturally, politically and even economically. Four countries share a common land border with India, whereas Sri Lanka and Maldives share a maritime border.

Histories, Memories, Movements in the South Asian Indian Ocean Region

The South Asian IOR is filled with histories of cultural encounters, webs of trade, slavery, colonisation, knowledge and migration, where till very recently Pakistan, India and Bangladesh were one. It was the centre of a series of interlocking commercial networks that reached far and wide. It is not difficult to find broad uniformities with respect to political, administrative, legal, economic and cultural structures in the region, largely because of a common history of colonial subjugation and later their emergence as independent developing states. It has been an interregional arena of deep interactions. The people here have various deep, common and unique bondings on grounds of historical ties, religions, cultural traditions, linguistic affinities, social norms, and political and economic issues. The history of movements across the Indian Ocean proves these ties even further.

There exists sufficient evidence to show that sailing in the Indian Ocean began from very early times.[12] Freedom of navigation was the norm in this region, which witnessed flourishing maritime trade links. Even Vedic texts point to a history of sea voyages; there appears to have been an active coastal trade in ancient India and South Asia in general. Historical studies have pointed out that the Egyptians began to send their marine expeditions to the Indian Ocean in search of precious gold and incense in 2,300 BC.[13] It has also been said that the people of the Indus Valley and Mesopotamia frequently sailed across the Indian Ocean. Iconographic representations, such as graffiti on potsherds, clay models, illustrations on seals and clay amulets dating to the Harappan period indicate the nature and diversity of boat-types used in the western Indian Ocean in the third millennium BC.[14] Many historians also endorse that their expertise in navigating the Indian Ocean shores had made the Phoenicians one of the earliest masters of trade and trade routes in the region.[15]

The history of navigation became clearer when the Greeks began their marine expeditions on the waters of the Indian Ocean. Alexander was the first Greek to think of establishing international trade routes, which was the basis of his dream of a universal Empire.[16] Evidence suggests that in 326 BC Alexander's naval officer, Admiral Nearchus, made a voyage of nearly 1,500 miles from Indus to Ormuz in Indian boats, in the face of gales and rough seas. The boats, some of which were 30-oared, were made by a Panjabi tribe, Ksatri (Xanthroi), and they showed that Indians at that time were well versed in navigation and shipbuilding. After Alexander, the maritime activities of the Greco–Egyptians increased and culminated in Eudoxus' voyages, who visited India in 119 BC, and established a direct maritime link between India and Egypt.[17]

This process of navigations went on. From the 5th century BC to the 6th century AD, Indian emperors enjoyed naval supremacy in the South Asian IOR. There were alternate successions of this maritime power domination. From the Mauryas and then the Satvahana dynasty in AD 575, the mastery of the eastern seas passed to the Andhras and then to the Pallavas.[18] The Pallavas were then replaced by the Chalukyas, who became a great maritime power from AD 600 to AD 642. From the 9th to 10th centuries onwards there are increasing references in inscriptions to fishing rights, duties levied on commodities brought through water-routes and to revenue being obtained from taxes on fishing. This was also a period of expanding maritime networks in the Indian Ocean.[19] South Indian dynasties particularly had extensive maritime involvements. During the rule of Cheras, Pandyas and Cholas, Indian sea power extended its sway beyond the South Asian part of the Indian Ocean.[20] The Chola inscriptions, for example, refer to the expeditions undertaken by Raja Raja Chola to the vast fragments of Maldives islands between AD 985 and AD 1014,[21] whose people, it is claimed, were contemporaneous to the people of Indus Valley and Shang Civilisation.[22] Raja Raja Chola even dispatched naval expeditions to conquer Burma, Malaysia and Indo–China. His successors won several naval battles and strengthened the Chola power in Ceylon (present day Sri Lanka), Malaysia, Java and Sumatra. This reveals the presence of Sri Lanka in the politics of ancient maritime affairs.[23]

Parallel to this was the cultural interaction of societies in this region, which is till today a part of the cultural and religious life of many of these communities and societies. Vestiges of Indian culture are discernable in the coastal provinces of far away China, for example in Fukein. Similarly, remnants of Chinese life are found in Nagapattinam on the eastern coast of India, and Quilon and Calicut on the western coast. The Malayan archipelago too was in close contact with the Coromandel Coast because of trade relations in the region. Ancient maritime commercial interactions left indelible imprints in India and Malaysia. Gujarati influence can be significantly felt in Zanjibar, Melinde and other coastal regions of East Africa. Areas like Veraval, Janjira, Danda–Rajpuri, and some parts of Karnataka on the north-western coast of India were safe havens for the Abyssinians or the Habsis, who held mastery over the Arabian Sea for a long time before the Europeans established their sway. The Siddis or the Habsis were gradually integrated into the life of the subcontinent. The Siddis, an Islamic community hailing from various parts of Africa, especially Abyssinia, were found in the coastal regions of Gujarat, Maharashtra and Karnataka, much before the arrival of Portuguese on the western coast of India. They held high positions in the army, navy and civil services under the Bahamanis, though they were originally brought to India as slaves. In the course of maritime interactions, a host of Indians settled in South Africa, Mauritius, Madagascar and Maldives. Sri Lankan mariners were engaged in voyages to western parts of India since the days of Alexander.[24]

A study of economy and civilisation in the IOR from the rise of Islam to 1750 shows this was a period of unity and disunity, continuity and discontinuity, ruptures and thresholds.[25] Scholars have pointed to instances of unity during the Mughal rule in the IOR, when a vibrant relationship existed with the Indian Ocean.[26] For example, Akbar organised his imperial navy, stationed at Dacca, to protect the Bengal coast from the onslaught of pirates.

With the beginning of the modern period, the entire South Asian region was caught in the colonial web of Western European powers like the Portuguese, the Dutch, the French and the British, with intensive power rivalry among them. The arrival of Vasco da Gama on the Indian coast in 1498 marked a significant turn.[27] By the last quarter of the 18th century, the Americans and the Russians too started navigating the Indian Ocean. The colonial history of South Asia witnessed a series of power changes in the region. The Portuguese lost their supremacy to the Dutch, the Dutch to the French and the French to the British. The English emerged as the undisputed masters of the Indian Ocean after the Third Carnatic War. Since then, the British constantly increased their naval power, and their hegemony remained unquestioned till the middle of the 20th century. However, the assumption that the organic unity of the Indian Ocean rim was completely ruptured with the establishment of European domination has been seriously and effectively challenged in a recent study, which shows continuous exchange and various flows of culture, economy and most important, people in the colonial period.[28]

This brief overview of the history of the IOR and the South Asian maritime world reflects a theatre of civilisational, cultural, and religious interaction and transfusion.[29] Like all oceans, it has performed two important functions: as a medium of communication and as a reservoir of resources. Movements across it have not only been about trade, wars and military histories; they have also shaped the everyday life of the people, particularly in the coastal regions of South Asia. The history of the Indian Ocean also reveals that mostly there have been safe passages across it—a bit like travel across a desert—from one place to another without large colonisation of oceanic spaces occurring, as human beings have mostly concentrated on colonisation of lands. The borders of the Indian Ocean were not marked and there was relatively free movement of fishermen, who had traditional fishing rights. However, the modern nations of South Asia are attempting to colonise or rather 'nationalise' as much of the ocean as possible.

Natural and Human Resources in the Indian Ocean

There is a conventional way of defining oceans as storehouses of varied resources, both living and non-living. With the modernisation of ocean resource engagement, the pressure on ocean ecology has mounted. It is estimated that at the bottom of the oceans, there are mineral deposits, which are large enough to supply all humankind for centuries to come. With the growth of modern technologies, various approximations have been made to map out the resources in the seabed of the Indian Ocean. Its basin is rich in minerals and accounts for 32.5 per cent of the world's crude oil, 80.7 per cent of gold mined, 56.6 per cent of tin, 39 per cent of antimony, 28.5 per cent of manganese, 25.2 per cent of nickel, 18.5 per cent of bauxite, 18 per cent of lead, 13 per cent of iron ore and 12.4 per cent of zinc. Besides these, the IOR produces 77.3 per cent of world's natural rubber, 76.2 per cent of tea, 42 per cent of wool, 26.7 per cent of cotton yarn and 19 per cent of coffee.[30]

As far as fisheries are concerned, according to estimates, 2 MT of fishery reserves are available in the oceans. It is said that there is enough fish which, if exploited scientifically and efficiently, can satisfy the protein needs of the whole world. In fact, fisheries are considered the world's fifth largest food resource and account for 7.5 per cent of total global food production. According to the FAO, the value of world fishery products exports in 1998 stood at US $49 billion. The net foreign exchange earnings of developing countries in 1997 from fish and fish products stood at about US $16 billion which, as per the FAO, is much higher than the combined net export earnings from coffee, tea, rice and rubber.[31]

After the Pacific Ocean, the Indian Ocean accounts for the largest number of commercial marine species and the biggest share of full-time fisher population in the world. In fish diversity too, it is second only to the Pacific Ocean. Between 1950 and 1998, the population of the IOR doubled from under 1 billion to 2 billion. Over the same period, marine fish production increased eightfold—from less than 1 million tonnes to about 8 million tonnes. It is significant that while the Indian Ocean population remained at 40 per cent of world total during this period, the share of the Indian Ocean marine fish catch to world catch increased from under 5 per cent to about 10 per cent. The potential of the fishery to contribute to the overall well-being of the IOR is, therefore, evident. It produces significant quantities of fish, both for the domestic and the export markets.[32] Among the littoral states, India stands as the leading producer of fish in the IOR, also accounting for the largest number of fisherfolk.[33]

The IOR also has the largest small-scale, artisanal fisheries in the world and the wide variety of craft-gear combinations employed to catch hundreds of marine species is the hallmark of the region, where fish is a culturally important food as well as a source of employment, income and foreign exchange. About 100 million people in the developing world depend on fish as their primary source of protein.[34] Tuna and tuna-like species form the bulk of fish production in the Indian Ocean, with about 19 species contributing to about 20 per cent of the total fish catch. According to the FAO, a quarter of the world's tuna production is from the Indian Ocean and its adjacent seas. Half the catch is believed to come from the artisanal and small-scale fisheries, while in other oceans most of the tuna catches are netted by industrial vessels. The region also produces large quantities of shrimp and cephalopods. These are mainly exported, accounting for an important source of foreign exchange. The smaller pelagics, which form the largest bulk of production, are in general locally consumed and are the most important source of vital nutrition for the poor.

The role and dependence of coastal fisherfolk communities on fisheries implicates the availability of fish resources. It has been remarked that the first mariners were drawn from the coastal fishing communities. It is they, along with travellers, merchants, labourers and migrants, who have forged a unity in the ocean. Fishworkers of both genders are a special brand of brave, intelligent individualists with a romantic association with their boats, the sea and adventure.[35] However, even more than their peasant counterparts, fisherfolk have remained the lost people of history and silent actors, despite the fact that they provide a vital pool of labour and maritime skills. Historically, fisherfolk have been subjugated politically and economically by more articulate and dominant groups such as the merchants and the ruling elites.[36] In the studies of oceans too, coastal fisherfolk have been relatively less 'visible' in comparison to say sailors, merchants and pirates. High politics and large-scale commercial activities have drawn much more attention than the daily fishing by the coastal fisherfolk, who have usually remained on the peripheries. This may have occurred due to a number of reasons. In the initial years of maritime explorations, there appears to have been no occupational specialisation. However, with the development of occupational divisions, marginalisation of fisherfolk also began. Dominant economic and political roles were assumed by those who controlled the agricultural and fish markets. Ports became more central to economic activities than fishing settlements. This often put the fisherfolk on the fringes of urban civilisation.[37] Further, they perhaps have no mention in the recorded maritime histories of South Asia because they have been too ubiquitous and embroiled in everyday life to merit special attention or mention. Their relative absence from maritime, ecological or even subaltern histories has made it difficult to see the agency of these fisherfolk in transnational movements and processes. Since they move on a daily basis, being usually short-term temporary migrants, they have also not found any place in migration studies.

At the same time, in the South Asian IOR, the bulk of the supply of fish for domestic consumption comes from the traditional/artisanal fishers. These fishers have been children of the sea, where fishing is not only an occupation to them, but also a way of life. Countries in this region share a long heritage of coastal fishing, seafaring and maritime trading, which continues in the present day as well. Observation, experimentation, empiricism, tradition and knowledge have allowed the fishermen to live a life dependent on fishing. Traditional marine fishing communities in India live on the geographic, economic and social fringes of the society. Fishing as a substance occupation for these communities has had a long tradition in the country. They constitute an 'ecosociety' that has ecologically tuned itself to the coastal ecosystem that they have been living in.[38] In fact, there have been many references to the fisherfolk in folk literature and the epics of India. Fishing as an occupation and livelihood has been mentioned in texts like Kautilya's *Arthashastra* and some of the *Smritis*.[39] Initially, it appears that most of the fisheries sector was traditional, small-scale and largely community-based and some remnants of it have remained in fragmented form. There was a small craft-owning class and a larger worker class, but economically there was little distinction between the classes. The difference in income between the owners and the crew was not great enough to set them apart from one another. A sharing system prevailed, which ensured an equal share for all those who participated in the fishing operation, plus shares for craft and gear. The main fishing gear were shore seines, boat seines, lift nets, hooks and lines and tidal barriers. They were operated throughout the year to catch the available fish. Overall, it seems subsistence fisheries dominated, in which there was of course exchange and trade, but on a small scale.[40]

However, we do not wish to romanticise this state of affairs or celebrate the earlier period uncritically as harmonious and eco-friendly. Access to fish had always been contested, with unequal relationships of power very much prevalent even at that time, determining who benefited most. We are not *a priori* either in favour of or against development or modernisation. Our concern, however, is to see how distorted development and modernisation processes have exacerbated existing problems. We recognise that many fishermen would not want to 'go back' to these conditions, even if given the opportunity, and wish to enjoy the fruits of modernity. As has been recently argued, no matter how gigantic the costs or how unsettling the consequences of development, its proponents do not seem to have any difficulty in persuading people that they must not be left behind in its pursuit.[41] It has also been reasoned that development did not 'invent' Third World poverty, and that it actually became—for a period historically coincident with the Cold War, decolonisation, and modern nation-state building in many Third World locations—the dominant way of looking at and managing inequality.[42] But we do want to question the developmental model, which has evolved in the fishing sector particularly. It has not been the lack of development that has caused ecological malaise or increasing difficulties to the fisherfolk; rather, it is the very process of bringing development of a particular kind, of capitalism gone wild,[43] that has caused them in the first place.

Fishing Industry, Unequal Distribution and the Blue Crisis

Our sea is sick because of man, this superindustrialised and superabundant *Homo sapiens*.

—Andre Siegfried

Previously, fish to an extent was obtained freely by custom, but these days it has become an important commercial commodity. With conscious policies and institutionalisation of capitalist relations in fishing, combined with the growth of a global capitalist fish economy and culture, there have been significant changes in structures of power, which have proven to be advantageous for the rich and disadvantageous for the poor fishworkers. These policies have been more appropriative and exploitative than earlier ones. A homogeneous unfettered capitalist growth in the fisheries has jeopardised the traditional variety in the sector. However diverse regions of the world may have been brought into contact, and however production may have been rationalised and consumption increased, these processes have more drastically homogenised culture by spreading the civilisation of endless production and consumption across all national bounds. The growth of fishing reveals a harrowing tale of growing com-mercialisation of everyday life of fisherfolk, forced on them by a callous and insensitive capitalist order and state. Laws and controls have been implemented that are designed to make fish a purely marketed commodity that generates high rates of tax. In the process, the wide-scale popular traditions of fishing have been rendered marginal. These measures, combined with an ecological crisis, have had a profoundly impoverishing implication for a large number of coastal fisherfolk, dispossessing them of their chief resource base.

State policies with regard to coastal fisheries have deprived people of their livelihood. To err is human—to err constantly is policy-making. The marine fishing policies of the countries of South Asia are not geared towards the needs of the fishworkers and people in general but are oriented towards generating maximum profit for a few. They have accelerated the destruction of the coastal and marine ecosystem, without contributing in any way to an ecologically sound use of a fragile renewable resource. They have enhanced the flow of food from the needy to the affluent, ignoring the nutritional needs of the under or malnouri-shed sections of the population. In fact, policy-making related to coastal areas of the Indian Ocean and to fisheries development throughout this past century is characterised by an evangelical zeal to do away with the traditional systems and replace them with 'modern technology'. Thus a major change that a century of fisheries development has brought about is a radical transformation of a traditional, subsistence-based, livelihood activity into a cor-porate, commercial, business venture, where risks are outweighed by profit, which inevitably leads to overexploitation.[44]

It has been remarked that there have been broadly four phases of fisheries policy-making in India.[45] The late 19th century, with the establishment of the Department of Fisheries, saw the begin-ning of organised fisheries development. However, the colonial rulers viewed the existing fishing industry as extremely primitive and undeveloped, lacking in any of the modern methods and allied industries, and saw themselves as having a much wider knowledge and a certain degree of initiative to take this sector forward.[46] In the post-Independence period, the state adopted a modernisation-growth oriented model of development in the fisheries sector. Thus the second phase began in the 1950s, with the tripartite agreement between the United Nations, the USA and the Government of India, which resulted in the Technical Cooperation Mission (TCM). Under the TCM, India got costly equipment like fully equipped fishing vessels, ice plants, freezing and canning equipment, fishmeal plants, nylon nets and twines, fishing hooks, diesel engines, winches and gurdies at an affordable cost and it was then that policy-makers enthused over sophisticated fishing equipment.[47] This can be seen as the first phase of globalisation of the Indian seafood industry. The fisheries development philosophy was reduced to a more prosaic and easily digestible doctrine of 'growth and foreign exchange'. 'People' were more generally defined to include a broad category of individuals, whose qualification to enter the sector was their ability to invest in the new technology. Seeds for the industries of the future—trawling, industrial fishing and aquaculture—were sown during this phase.

The next phase began sometime during the late 1970s and it lasted until the early 1990s. This was the period of flowering, the 'golden age' of Indian fisheries, which was supposed to continue indefinitely. There was increasing specialisation and diversification of fishing technology. Virtually everybody, including the small-scale fisheries, flourished as a result of more technology. For the fishing communities, it was an era of prosperity. Many remarked that motorisation and mechanisation was the need of the time as traditional fishing, which was a manual operation, required much harder labour. It is significant that unlike other traditional occupational sectors, the marine fishing sector was one in which unbridled market forces, modern technology and export orientation were introduced without any opposition by an organised working class.[48] This was the most active period of the 'Blue Revolution', with industrialisation and internationalisation of fisheries. A survey of the fishery sector of India conducted for the World Bank in 1990, which influenced a great deal of fisheries development throughout the 1990s, showed the way forward: increasing inshore fish production by mechanised fishing boats; acquisition of deep-sea fishing vessels; fishing, processing and export of tuna, squid and cuttlefish; and establishment of new fishing harbours and strengthening and expanding existing ones.

Development of brackish water aquaculture, cold chain for fish marketing, individual quick-frozen plants, processing of by-catch into frozen, canned and artificial dried products, setting up ice plants, etc. were some of the other projects suggested.[49] Even during this period there was degradation, but it was concealed by the noise of bulldozers mowing down mangrove forests, making way for aquaculture ponds, and the high horsepower engines taking boats faster and faster. Of the people themselves, very little is heard. In fact, a book published by the Indian Council of Agricultural Research states the following about the fishers:

> The community, as a whole, is extremely conservative and largely illiterate. The craft, gear and other equipments used are, by and large, primitive, and, consequently, according to modern standards, the return per unit of effort is relatively small. Being economically and socially backward, comparatively ignorant and ill-educated, most fishermen fall victims to the many evils in society.[50]

The last phase began in the early 1990s, coinciding with the second phase of globalisation that was ushered in with more vigour, wider reach and greater impact for the country as a whole. Thus the process of mechanisation of the Indian marine fisheries, which began in the post-Independence period, continued ceaselessly. The total number of mechanised boats, which numbered 1,800 at the end of the Second Five-Year Plan in 1961, increased to 9,300 by 1974 and by 1984 they rose to 22,000. By 1991, the number rose to 22,292 and further acquisition of the ultra-modern Deep Sea Fleet (DSF) began. The number of DSF operating along the Indian coast was 75 during 1984–85. By 1991, their number went up to 180. In comparison, the strength of non-mechanised boats was 154,000 in 1985 and went up to 164,103 in 1991.

What has all this 'development' led to? There has indeed been a remarkable growth. Fish production has increased by leaps and bounds. Aquaculture, exports, foreign exchange—all have increased. But then, why do fishing fleets spend more time in harbour than at sea? Why do the huge aquaculture ponds look, for all practical purposes, like deserts? Why have mangroves become ghosts of what they were? Why are the fishers facing more and more hardships? Why has the duration of each fishing trip gone up? Why, after the initial boom, has there been a persistent decline in fish-catch? Why are many forced to abandon their traditional occupations, or become merely labourers, or risk their lives by crossing the sea borders and getting arrested?

It cannot be denied that this very period of 'development' has seen a sharp degradation of the coastal resources and marine environment, which is increasingly besieged by natural calamities, destruction of mangroves, irresponsible tourism, chemical pollution from land and sea, non-selective and destructive fishing practices, privatisation of fishery resources, coastal aquaculture and deforestation.[51] Coastal waters, important as a buffer between land and sea and a 'unique ecological heritage', have been increasingly degraded in the whole of South Asia. The age of prosperity and expansion is slowly coming to a halt. Large-scale fisheries have ruined the marine commons. The impact of this is enormous pressure on fishing, and has led to declining quantity and variety of fish catches, decreasing fishing days, increasing durations of fishing trips, increasing conflicts with other fisherfolk, and the largest ever number of destitute women and old people in the fishing villages.

Although even today the artisanal and small-scale fishermen provide the mainstay of the fisheries sector, both in terms of employment and catches, there is an evident depletion of resources and overcrowded inshore fishing all over the IOR. The open-access nature of the marine fishing ground has led to the overexploitation of fisheries resources within three nautical miles in almost all IOR countries. One reason is increasing availability and use of modern fishing technologies such as outboard engines, fibre reinforced plastic boats and hand-held Global Positioning System (GPS) receivers. These have contributed to several small fishers moving out of their traditional fishing grounds.[52] In the South Asian seas, opening up of all sectors of economy in the context of globalisation has led to a virtual rampage by modern harvest technologies in the marine fisheries, impacting fisherfolk in the whole region. The overall modernisation of fisheries has resulted in large-scale displacement of the fisherfolk in terms of their employment and settlement. Simultaneously, illegal, unregulated, unreported (IUU) fishing activities, especially by non-riparian nations or fishing entities in the IOR have significant implications for the development of fisheries of the riparian nations, particularly on the status of dependent stocks. This encroachment threatens the space of fisherfolk in terms of fishing mobility and livelihood of the fishing villages.[53]

The fisherfolk have been made to feel the power of the capitalist classes and the state in fishing in various ways. The 'modernisation' of common property resources like marine fisheries has proved dangerous to the coastal ecosystems, depleting resources, marginalising large sections of the coastal population and displacing fisherfolk from their traditional occupation, thereby increasing their insecurity. Modernisation of fisheries has also raised important questions about marine ecosystems. The degraded marine ecosystem poses a health risk to both fishers and fish consumers. According to the FAO, about 16 per cent of the marine ecosystem is overfished and another 6 per cent appears to be depleted. This results in economic losses and excessive fishing pressure.

With the modernisation of fishing, there has been an extensive neglect of ecological parameters, which is demonstrated by considering two important modern methods of fishing—trawling and purse-seining—which have been adopted in India through the 'planned development of fisheries'. Trawling is done by dragging heavy weights and beams on the seabed in order to squeeze the prawns out of the seabed. Trawling kills millions of undersized fish, benthic life, seaweed, and other sea vegetation on the seabed, which have the function of purifying the sea water by renewing the oxygen content. The purse-seining method involves quickly encircling shoals of pelagic fish species, before they grow and proliferate. These processes have made the life of fisherfolk very difficult. While all the maritime countries in the IOR face similar problems and policies, the scale of the modern mechanised sector varies depending on the articulation capacity of affected sections.

The magic formula of 'growth-created welfare for all' has proved unworkable.[54] Fishermen have realised in the past 15 years that motorised fishing involves much more capital and that by using smaller and smaller mesh sizes they are ultimately the sufferers. Also, mechanised boats seldom fish beyond a stone's throw from the shore, using mesh size of less than 10 mm at the cod end, often overrunning traditional nets and capturing huge quantities of juveniles, which go to poultry feed mills and aquaculture ponds. The average number of fishing nets per boat and the engine horsepower has increased in an inverse proportion to the catches. There is an increasing exposure to the vagaries of catch and price fluctuations. The debts to the local moneylenders and the fish trader-financers have multiplied. Very little of the profits and foreign exchange generated by fish export markets have benefited the local fishers and fishing communities. As fish stocks have declined and control over marine resources increasingly concentrated, the lives and livelihoods of fisherfolk have become ever more precarious. There has been a marginalisation of the small-scale artisanal fishers. Today they are greatly weakened from increasingly unsustainable livelihoods, from alienation, from lack of use rights, from loss of common property resources and from an absence of easy alternatives.

However, not all have suffered. The developments in the marine fishing industry have been lopsided, leading to heavy financing and liberal subsidies aimed at one species, one market and a handful of exporters. Market-based regimes and increasing industrialisation of fisheries has meant that control over resources has passed to actors outside the fishing community. The owners of mechanised trawlers and aquaculture farms and those who have economic and political power in society have actually grown stronger. The state and powerful private interests monopolise resources and control the markets. The elites of the fishing industry deny the fisherfolk control over the resources, markets and decision-making, on which their livelihoods depend.

Ironically, however, it is the fishermen who are mainly asked to pay the price for ecological degradation. The solutions suggested often minimise any disruption to the status quo. These are mainly prohibitions on fishing in the mangroves, on entry into mangroves themselves, on shrimp seeds, on fishing during certain parts of the year and in certain areas around the year. In effect, every problem is met with either a ban, or a regulation of access to everything that the coastal people have depended on for their livelihoods for centuries. In practice, regulations have meant a reduction of dependence of the coastal people on the natural resources like fish, mangroves and shells, and an erosion of their community rights over the water bodies. It appears that while the mechanised trawler owners and the aquaculture practitioners have been given the responsibility of increasing foreign exchange, the responsibility for conservation of resources and curtailing overexploitation of environment has fallen on the shoulders of the poor fishermen. It is they who are asked to adopt austerity measures. Thus solutions suggested are frequently simplistic, technocratic, oppressive and gender-blind—all of which ultimately reinforce the very structures that create ecological crisis.[55] There appears a distinct lack of ethics while pursuing the sustainability questions as part of ocean governance. According to Rajni Kothari:

> In the absence of an ethical imperative, environmentalism has been reduced to a technological fix, and as with all technological fixes, solutions are seen to lie once more in the hands of manager technocrats. Economic growth, propelled by intensive technology and fuelled by an excessive exploitation of nature was once viewed as a major factor in environmental degradation; it has suddenly been given the central role in solving the environmental crisis. The market economy is given an even more significant role in organising nature and society. The environmentalist label and the sustainability slogans have become deceptive jargons that are used as convenient covers for conducting business as usual.[56]

The depletion of fish stocks is also linked to wider ecological issues.[57] Various polluting industries like those of fertilisers, nuclear power plants, and fossil fuel extracting and refining units have grown in the coastal areas of the Indian Ocean. The consistent use of ocean as a theatre for experimenting with nuclear weapons and dumping of a huge mass of domestic sewage, waste, industrial effluents, oil spills and thermal power generation has led to large-scale pollution of the oceanic waters, as hardly 50 per cent of the total population in the IOR is with proper sanitation arrangements (see Table 2.2). Due to its pollution, the sea level has been rising and marine fishes, coral reefs and mangroves have been declared as endangered ecosystems (see Table 2.3).[58] A mere 1 metre rise in sea level may cover 14 per cent of Bangladesh, displacing 10 per cent of its people and 14 per cent of its agricultural land.[59] This alarming situation of rising sea levels will also lead to sinking of coastal boundaries and displacement of coastal communities. Oil shipping across the region, coupled with increasing emphasis on offshore oil exploration in many countries of the IOR, makes the northern Indian Ocean also very vulnerable to oil pollution.[60]

Though the Indian Ocean is one of the few oceans with untapped marine resource potential, it is also a region with one of the most poorly managed fisheries in the world, reflected in the progressive decline in fish production in the region.

Table 2.2: Discharge of Oil Pollutants

Seas, Beaches and Coastlines	Estuaries, Harbours and Docks	Rivers, Canals and Inland Water
Bilges	Bilges	Fuel Oil
Crude Oil	Crude Oil	Lubricating Oil
Dirty Ballast	Fuel Oil	Refined Distillates
Fuel Oil	Lubricating Oil	
Tank Washings	Coal Tars and Products	

Source: Abhijit Mitra and D. P. Bhattacharya, *JIOS*, Vol. 6, No. 1, November 1998.

Table 2.3: Impact of Oil Pollution on Marine Life

Community or Population Type	Expected Degree of Initial Recovery	Expected Recovery Rate
Plankton	Light to moderate	Fast to moderate
Benthic Communities		
1. Rocky Intertidal	Light	Fast
2. Sandy or Muddy Intertidal	Moderate	Moderate
3. Subtidal, Offshore	Heavy	Slow
Fish	Light to moderate	Fast to moderate
Birds	Heavy	Slow
Marine Mammals	Light	Slow, if population is seriously affected

Source: Same as Table 2.2.

Towards Sustainable Seas?

The IOR in South Asia is burdened with increasing depletion of ocean resources, severely affecting, particularly, the traditional coastal communities. Their problem has been exasperated, as the introduction has shown, by increasing conflicts between countries of South Asia, which have not even seriously taken up the idea of making the Indian Ocean a Zone of Peace (IOZP). Though the issue of IOZP has many dimensions and is a complex one, its spirit endorses an overall universal concern for peaceful inter-state power relations, which can have a direct impact on coastal fishing communities. However, IOZP is differently and contradictorily perceived by the different countries of South Asia, depending on their own foreign policies, bargaining interests and security perceptions. The self-acclaimed attitude of becoming 'a regional policeman' has remained an antithesis to IOZP.[61]

Alongside, various South Asian countries, particularly the coastal ones have been deeply concerned about determining their maritime boundaries in order to exploit maritime resources to their maximum advantage. India began the difficult task of demarcating boundaries with its maritime neighbours in the early 1970s (see Box 2.1). This was also perceived necessary in order to peacefully resolve disputed and overlapping claims of maritime jurisdiction. In November 1981, the Maritime Zones of India (Regulation of Fishing by Foreign Vessels) Act came into force. It laid down conditions under which foreign fishing vessels could operate in Indian maritime zones, clearly prohibiting fishing by other countries in its territorial waters. Fines and other punishments were to be imposed on those violating its provisions.[62] Pakistan too evolved its Maritime Acts. However, various disputes have continued and have become areas of serious contention, directly impacting the lives of the fisherfolk, as the subsequent chapters will show.

Box 2.1: Maritime Boundaries of India

The Indian coastline (including island territories) of 7,516.5 kilometres being [sic] the fifteenth longest in the world, the country possesses a vast EEZ.... It often comes as a surprise to many that India has maritime boundaries with a larger number of states than those with which it shares land borders. Whereas India's maritime boundaries necessitate delimitation with seven states on adjacent and opposite coasts—Pakistan, Maldives, Sri Lanka, Indonesia, Thailand, Myanmar, and Bangladesh—its land borders are shared with six states (Pakistan, China, Nepal, Bhutan, Bangladesh, and Myanmar). Due to considerable political and diplomatic efforts since the 1970s, virtually all of India's maritime boundaries have been demarcated. The exceptions primarily remain those with Pakistan and Bangladesh.

Source: Rahul Roy-Chaudhury, *India's Maritime Security*, Institute for Defence Studies and Analyses, New Delhi, 2000, pp. 49–51.

At the international level too, there have been various efforts and negotiations to deal with apprehensions about the danger of overexploited marine resources and to work towards sustainable seas.[63] The most important development in this arena has been the 1982 Third United Nations Convention on the Law of the Sea (UNCLOS III), which has often been regarded as a landmark international agreement that took the side of the developing countries, coastal states and the small islands, by providing them vastly extended maritime zones. It conclusively established a new international order by including the extension of territorial sea to 12 nautical miles (1 nm = 1.85 km), contiguous zone to 24 nautical miles, an exclusive economic zone (EEZ)[64] of 200 nautical miles and continental shelves that could even extend to more than 200 nautical miles. In the EEZ, the coastal states had sovereign rights for the purpose of exploring and exploiting, conserving and managing the marine resources, whether living or non-living. The aim of EEZ was also to ensure that legal and other rights in the ocean zone were properly codified and authorities enforced various laws on fishing rights, mining surveillance and research. The Convention thus, entitled the coastal states to exercise juris-diction over a larger part of the sea. For example, India obtained a wide EEZ of about 2.172 million square kilometres in the sea, all along its 7,500 kilometres coastline. This equalled two-thirds of the total area of its land, along with the potential addition of 1.5 million square kilometres of continental shelf by the year 2004. The living and non-living resources in this zone are exclusive to India, so also the trading and transport facilities navigated through this area. India thus contributes about 46 per cent of the total exploited living resources from the Indian Ocean.

Besides EEZ, the question of sustainable fisheries has been much talked about at various international conferences of the FAO. The 19th session of the FAO Committee on Fisheries, held in March 1991, recommended that the FAO should develop the concept of responsible fisheries and elaborate a code of conduct towards this end. The Code of Conduct of Responsible Fisheries finally came into being on 31 October 1995 at the 28th session of the FAO Conference in Rome.[65]

While all these measures have been important, they have often proved to be double edged, with severe limitations and even lacunae, particularly from the perspective of traditional fisherfolk. The crisis in marine resources has not been resolved, bringing increasing complexity to the world of fisheries. A significant manifestation of this complication is when fishermen of different nationalities begin to compete for a single fish resource, fairly close to the shores of one of the nations. Disputes also occur when one wishes to extend the apparent economic life of that particular fish stock, by introducing conservation measures.[66] Contentions fall into two major categories.[67] The first one is between countries that occupy opposite shores of comparatively narrow areas of the sea. The second category involves disputes between domestic and distant fishing fleets. Any solution to the fishery disputes has to be settled after taking into account a large number of factors. Fisheries limits are being reached as fish stocks are finite in character but countries of South Asia are increasingly pushing to exploit the productive potential of coastal and oceanic ecosystems to their advantage. The coastal fisherfolk too have been embroiled in this process and are facing the brunt of increasing conflicts over fish resources.

Conclusion

The historical and contemporary saga of the Indian Ocean reveals a theatre of colonial expeditions, power struggles, political sub-jugations, economic interactions and cultural transfusions. As inter-state relationships in the region have become more strategic, power equations between countries like Pakistan and India have been one of the greatest cause of worry in the region. One of the results of this has been that the fisherfolk of the region have been seriously threatened in their quest for livelihood. Their frequent arrests in the region reveal that they have been largely victims of bitter international relationships. The declining ecological status of the ocean is a matter that requires immediate action. There is a need to take the fisheries out of the clutches of the relatively few large companies that control them, and hand them over to the coastal communities of small-scale fishers who are dynamically evolving new capabilities.[68] Fishing activities have to be co-operative, not competitive, and the distribution of the common resource has to be equitable as otherwise, co-operation would disintegrate. A common resource, co-operatively managed and equitably distributed, will not be destroyed, whether by overfishing, which is a consequence of competition, or by pollution, which is a waste.[69] Countries are caught in the trap of power rivalries and making peace in the IOR is a distant reality. However, it is a dream that has to be cherished and the movement of fisherfolk across the region can provide partial answers to this dream.

3

Fisherfolk as 'Prisoners of War':*
India and Pakistan

Water and air have their own free will. How do we know that this is Pakistan's water or India's?
—Shamji, a fisherman from Vanakvada village, Diu[1]

The fisherman is like a yogi, an ascetic, who worships the sea. He spends a large part of his life in the sea, away from his family. There are no borders for him. He is the son of the ocean.
—Late Premjee Vhai Khokhari, National Fishworkers Forum (NFF)[2]

The people of India and Pakistan form one-sixth of humanity, and the incessant conflict between them concerns the destiny of more than 1 billion people. The irony is that the two countries know most about each other, differ least from each other and yet are most intolerant of each other. They are closest—geographically, ethnically, and in many other ways—but are also the most divided.

'Spectacular' issues like the nuclear tests, Kashmir, Kargil and various Indo-Pak wars have repeatedly drawn the attention of social scientists and researchers and much has been written and continues to be written on them. Yet, equally, if not more damaging are the everyday conflicts, which have directly impacted the lives of many. High points of any conflict are clearly visible and easily draw attention. The 'invisible', the 'marginal' and the 'everyday' may be banal, common and almost unnoticeable, but can be equally insidious.[3] The arrests of fisherfolk on both sides of the border, is a classic example of this everyday conflict.

These coastal fisherfolk of India and Pakistan have inevitably been drawn into the ambit of rivalry and antagonism, and repeatedly pay a heavy price for it. They, like others, have a right to freedom, to food and to livelihood. However, the concept of sea borders is difficult for them to comprehend as they are often blurred and in any case are largely immaterial for them. Further, less than 60 years ago, no such borders divided them. Today, most coastal fishermen on both sides of the border represent qualities of syncretism, openness, pluralism and tolerance. Their love for the sea and their passion for fishing bring them together. However, be it Indians or Pakistanis, Hindus or Muslims, these fishermen are repeatedly arrested and jailed for several years for transgressing the maritime boundaries between the two countries while engaged in fishing, and are treated almost as a threat to national security. The arrests began with intensity in the 1980s, and continue till date. These fisherfolk, already disadvantaged due to ecological malaise, declining fish catch, increasing mechanisation and government onslaught, have been further torn due to the specific nature of relations between India-Pakistan. The toll of this purportedly low-intensity conflict is no less than that of any conventional war. Here gross violations of human rights have been justified through acceptable clichés. Arrests are described as acts of nationalism; innocent fishermen are jailed in the name of border protection. In fact, as compared to Sri Lanka or Bangladesh, the scale and ramifications of this imbroglio are most acute in the case of India-Pakistan.[4] This chapter analyses various dimensions of this problem.

Cartographic Dilemmas: The Sir Creek Dispute

India itself has a long coastline of 7,417 kilometres. Among the eight maritime states Gujarat, situated on the western coast, has the longest coastline, i.e., 1,663 kilometres, which is one-third of the entire coastline of the country. It is a principal maritime state endowed with favourable strategic port locations and is the nearest maritime outlet to the Middle East, Africa and Europe.[5] Two major gulfs—the Gulf of Kutch and the Gulf of Cambay—are characteristic of the Gujarat coast. Gujarat has abundant marine and fish resources due to its extensive continental shelf, long river months and a rich fishing ground in close proximity. Some of the richest fishing grounds in India are located off Saurashtra and Kutch. Part of Pakistan's coastline is adjacent to that of the Gujarat coast. However, so far there are no bilateral agreements defining the maritime boundaries between the two countries. Not only are these boundaries unsettled, there is an absence of any other clear-cut fishing laws. Further, the Maritime Zones of India Act 1976 and 1981, under which the fishermen are detained and punished, do not correspond with the United Nations Convention on the Law of the Sea (UNCLOS), of which India is a signatory. The same is true with the Maritime Zones of Pakistan Act, which is virtually identical to that of India.

At the heart of this lie the 'rival geographies'[6] and contested cartographies between the two countries. As has been pointed out, almost all nations are imagined or constructed, in connection with a specific area of the globe, a homeland in which that nation is naturally rooted by means of a 'divine cartography'.[7] In the nationalist imagination this homeland is seen as uninterrupted, homogenous and bounded. For both India and Pakistan, struggle over maps, specifically sea borders, is critical for representing their pure spaces and political identities. The dispute between India and Pakistan over Sir Creek[8] is central to this endeavour. Sir Creek is a 100 kilometres long estuary in the marshes of the Rann of Kutch, which lies on the border between the Indian state of Gujarat and the Pakistani province of Sindh. The Sir Creek is a fluctuating tidal channel, not truly a flowing 'creek', along which the boundary between India and Pakistan has not been demarcated. Till 1954, the borders around Sir Creek were virtually open, with free move-ment on both sides. However after 1954, the stances on both sides became rigid and a controversy evolved around Sir Creek.[9] The dispute is intricately tied to the cause of the fisherfolk since the area around it can be regarded as the biggest Asian fishing ground.

There are two issues involved in the dispute—the delimitation of the boundary along the Creek and the demarcation of the mari-time boundary in the Arabian Sea. As a result of the continuing Sir Creek boundary dispute, neither India nor Pakistan can submit their claims under the UNCLOS on the limits of their respective continental shelves, the deadline of which ends in 2009, nor define the limits of their EEZ.[10] Without the maritime boundary demarcation between them, neither country can exploit the resources in its EEZ (up to 200 nautical miles) or its continental shelf (up to 350 nautical miles); and this in an area that could have sub-sea oil and gas deposits. The problem is also intrinsically linked with the fishing rights of the two countries. The area around the

Gulf of Kutch and Sir Creek and the mouth of Indus delta is the richest in fish. It is where a large number of fisherfolk of both countries congregate to earn their livelihoods, and also from where the largest number are arrested.[11] The repeated apprehending and detention of fishworkers on grounds of boundary violations, particularly around Sir Creek gives this dispute acute humanitarian overtones.

One side of the Creek is under Pakistan's control, whereas there are Indian naval installations on the other side. Pakistan lays claim to all the 17 creeks on the Sindh coast. India maintains that almost half of the area of Sir Creek, the 17th one, is under its control. What has made the boundary dispute along the Creek further complicated is that its position keeps shifting over time. How then is the exact position of Sir Creek or the boundary along it to be defined on a map? Both India and Pakistan refer to a map, which was actually finalised in 1925, but which is attached to a 1914 agreement of the Government of Bombay signed between the then Government of Sindh and Rao Maharaj of Kutch (see Map 3.1). This resolution defined the boundary between Kutch and Sindh as the 'green line' from the mouth of Sir Creek to the top of it, at the point where it joins Sir Creek due east until it joins Sindh on the map. Pakistan states that the entire Sir Creek with its eastern bank defined by the 'green line' belongs to it. India repudiates this claim, stating that the green line is an indicative line and feels that the boundary should be defined by the 'mid-channel' of the Creek, as shown in the map of 1925. Actually, accepting Pakistan's premise on the green line would mean a loss of about 250 square miles of EEZ for India. Pakistan rejects India's proposal for a mid-channel demarcation because it claims that this notion is applicable only to navigable channels, whereas Sir Creek is not a navigable one.

Veteran Indian lawyer and analyst A. G. Noorani, who has done substantial work on this, tends to side with the Indian view, stating that Pakistan itself had admitted in 1958 that 'this map was intended to be no more than an annexure to the Bombay Government resolution', and from this he concludes that 'Pakistan was right. It is the resolution, not the attached map, that is decisive'. The significance of this, Noorani points out, lies in a letter from the Bombay Government referred to in the resolution, which in turn refers to the Commissioner of Sindh writing 'that the

Map 3.1: Sir Creek Dispute

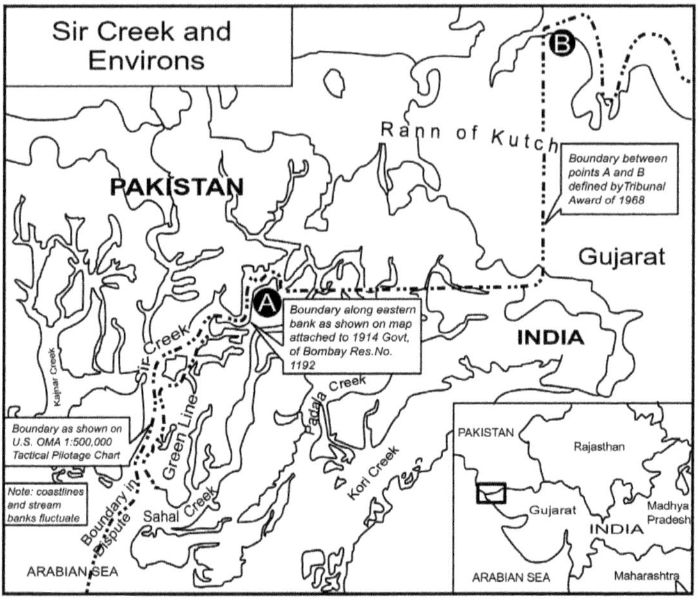

Sir Creek changes its course from time to time and the western boundaries of the area, which it is proposed to surrender to the Rao (of Kutch), should, therefore, be described as the centre of the navigable channel of the Sir Creek'.[12] This according to Noorani, supports the principle of demarcation that India has proposed. This would also be in consonance with the international principle of *thalweg* (*thal*—valley, *weg*—way)—the line connecting the deepest points along a river channel or the lowest points along a valley floor.

Today Sir Creek does not flow as shown in the old map. It has shifted westwards. However, the head of the creek as it existed then is marked by a boundary pillar called the Western Terminal— it was from this point that some 38 pillars marked the boundary going eastwards.[13] Pakistan does not recognise the existence of the Western Terminal. Since Pakistan wants to demarcate the Sir Creek boundary on a historical basis, India is ready to go by the 1925 map and demarcate the boundary following the middle of the channel as it existed then. By extending this line further to the last point on land, a base-line point could be defined to determine the maritime boundary. Pakistan, meanwhile, has defined a base-line point by extending the boundary along the eastern edge of the Creek on the map. This point, notified by Pakistan in 1996, lies eastward of the Creek on an Indian low tide elevation (landmasses that keep appearing and disappearing depending on the tidal conditions). This is not acceptable to India.

The Sir Creek dispute between India and Pakistan is also a carry-over problem of the boundary demarcation in the Rann of Kutch—an exercise that was carried out in 1968 by the India-Pakistan Western Boundary Case Tribunal. This tribunal only helped demarcate the boundary to the east and north-east of Sir Creek over which armed clashes had taken place between the two countries in 1965. The central point of the tribunal's award was that it rejected Pakistan's claim that the border between Gujarat and Sindh should run roughly along the 24th parallel beginning at the head of Sir Creek and moving eastward from there. This would have involved dividing the Rann in the middle and consequently transferring about 3,500 square miles of territory from India to Pakistan. The tribunal upheld India's claim that the line from the head of Sir Creek went a short distance eastward and then turned sharply northwards at a right angle and finally the border ran along the northern edge of the Rann. This northern edge had also formed the boundary between the British Indian state of Sindh and Kutch state before 1947. The tribunal broadly upheld India's contention and only about 300 square miles of territory was awarded to Pakistan. Both countries accepted the award of the tribunal. This left the boundary from the head of Sir Creek to its mouth in the Arabian Sea and the maritime boundary between India and Pakistan un-demarcated.

India and Pakistan have held nine rounds of discussions so far, starting in 1969, the last being in December 2006, but to no avail.[14] In the November 1998 talks, Pakistan had wanted India to agree to take the dispute to an international tribunal. Pakistan believes that the boundary along Sir Creek must lie along the eastern edge of the Creek. India believes the boundary should be fixed along the middle of the Creek. India's prime concern is the maritime boundary. In demarcating the maritime boundary, Pakistan wants to follow the principle of 'equity' (i.e., it must get as much maritime zone as India along this border). This involves the determination of the median line on the basis of equal distance from the shore. India does not accept this principle. The method India has proposed for determining the maritime boundary uses a seaward approach (equidistant line method) without any reliance on a base-line point on land. This means adjustments of the median line, taking into account the physical characteristics of the coastline. Using the Indian approach, the land boundary along Sir Creek can be left to be negotiated later while in the short run agreeing, to the extent possible, on maritime boundary. However, Pakistan wants the boundary of Sir Creek to be demarcated first and only then to delimit the maritime boundary. It maintains that the demarcation of land and maritime boundary at Sir Creek need to be addressed as one package. The problem remains unresolved, with both sides unwilling to change their respective positions even slightly till date.

The Sir Creek boundary dispute has been totally caught up in methodology and maps. Involved here are also substantive connections between mapping and national identity. In fact, there is a long and globally varied history connecting mapping and nation building.[15] The connections here go beyond the practical business of charting the length and breadth of national territories. They extend to the complex power relations underpinning the two nations involved here. The Sir Creek dispute goes against nation-alistic desires to produce a complete and secure cartography; instead, it points to the diversity in the very process of mapping, since the Creek is a shifting terrain. At the same time, it is not an intractable problem provided both countries approach it in a spirit of negotiation and compromise, and recognise the possibilities of in-betweenness, which refuse fixed framings and provide spaces for creative ambivalences. On the one hand is this boundary dispute and on the other hand is the declining fish catch in this entire region, to which we now turn.

Depleting Fish Catch

For the coastal fishermen of India and Pakistan, fishing has been their sole occupation for generations. They also play a large part in the prosperity of the two countries by earning a substantial foreign exchange. However, it is not just disputes over boundaries which have created problems for the coastal fisherfolk of the two countries; there are actually a broad range of threats to their livelihoods. Critical here has been the excessive damage to marine resources in the coastal areas. Environmental concerns naturally tend to cross national boundaries: there is declining fish catch on both sides; pollution has affected both nations (see Box 3.1).

Box 3.1: Ecological Problems of Coastal Fisherfolk in Pakistan

- One of the major problems is the constant reduction in the fish catch, which has badly affected the incomes of the fisherfolk communities and has consequently driven them towards worst-ever poverty. The catch of many fish species, including Sindh's special fish Palla, as well as big-sized shrimp locally known as Jaira, has drastically reduced.
- Influential jagirdars, previously related to the agricultural sector in the coastal region, have forcefully occupied coastal creeks after losing their lands in the progressive seawater intrusion and salinity. They are depriving indigenous fishermen from their livelihoods and are exploiting the fish resources in unsustainable methods through non-fishermen labour.
- The coastal waters are being polluted by drainage schemes like Left Bank Outfall Drain (LBOD), which disposes off thousands of cusecs of agricultural effluent containing pesticides, chemicals etc., threatening the survival of fish species, specially juvenile fish. Despite such damages, the government planners have decided to dispose off the effluents of Right Bank Outfall Drain (RBOD), as well as the agricultural effluents of the whole country, with the completion of mega drainage project National Drainage Programme (NDP).
- The fisherfolk population of the Indus delta is faced with the problem of marketing of the fish catch. Due to poverty as well as lack of institutional credit systems, they are in the grip of middlemen, who provide them loans on high interest rates and bind them to sell their fish catch to them at reduced prices. Resultantly, the fishermen of the area are under debt burdens since generations, despite working day and night.
- Due to the overall lack in fish catch, many fishermen have resorted to unsustainable methods of fishing, which result in genocide of the juvenile fish species, further aggravating the problem of livelihood resource depletion in the deltaic region.

(Contd.)

(Contd.)

- The deltaic communities are facing the worst ever socio-economic problems—lack of basic human facilities of clean water, health facilities as well as schools for their children—which have badly hampered the social development of the area.
- Overall mismanagement and lack of sustainable fisheries policies and management at the governmental level has further aggravated the sorrows of the fisherfolk communities. They are being exploited by various agencies, from ranger officials to coast guards. Their fish catch is usually snatched and they are beaten up and humiliated by the agencies operating in the areas. Interestingly, some natural fish lakes in the coastal areas are directly being managed and auctioned off by Pakistani rangers, despite the land being a provincial subject.

Source: 'Seminar on Indus Delta', organised by the PFF on 16 February 2002 at Keti Bandar, Sindh, Pakistan.

Let us first take the case of Pakistan's marine coast.[16] Fishing is the only source of livelihood for about 3 million people living along the 1,050 kilometre coast. Pakistan's coastline is divided into two parts: the Sindh province, with a 350 kilometre area and the Balochistan province of 700 kilometres.[17] Spread over 1,000 kilometres between Sir Creek and Jiwani (adjacent to Iran), the largest concentration of marine fish harvesters and workers here are within the Karachi division. Almost all the commercial fishing (including shrimp trawling) is clustered around the seaport of Karachi. The Indus is the largest river of Pakistan, which discharges into the Arabian Sea. The Indus delta is a typical fan-shaped delta, built by the discharge of large quantities of silt, washed down the Indus river from the Karakoram and Himalayan mountain ranges. Presently the delta covers an area of about 600,000 hectares. This deltaic environment is characterised by the presence of extensive mangrove forests that grow on the edges of the interwoven creek system.[18]

However, there has been a steady decline of fishery stocks in the region due to the degradation of natural resources through large-scale pollution of coastal waters and through a sizeable reduction of fresh water flows to the Indus delta. Thus the Indus deltaic region, particularly the coastal areas of Kette Bandar, Kharo Chhan and Jatti are very vulnerable, facing both reduction of fresh water and increase of polluted water. The threat of degradation is so serious that experts usually refer to it as the 'gradual death of delta'. This has adversely affected mangrove forests, which in turn decrease breeding of fish. The increasing salinity of creeks is also detrimental to fish stocks. The decline of fresh water flows has degraded croplands along the coast, directly as well as through sea water intrusion.

Mangroves are nature's coast guards. Mangrove forests occur in coastal areas in the tropics where waters are shallow and river deltas receive suspended sediment. Mangrove roots trap sediment from ebb and flood tidal currents, gradually extending land seaward. Mangroves are an integral part of the coastal ecosystem in Pakistan as they are considered highly productive marine and estuarine ecosystems, crucial to the livelihoods of coastal fisherfolk of the region.[19] They provide nurseries for fish, and generally afford protection to and supply food for various species, and varieties of shrimp and fish. Around 90 per cent of tropical marine fish species pass at least one stage of their life cycle in mangrove estuaries. Creeks around healthy mangroves become fishing grounds easily accessible to small fishermen. Coastal communities depend upon mangroves as a cheap source of fodder and fuel as well as for other timber needs. By acting as a barrier, healthy mangrove forests check intrusion and erosion by the sea, thereby protecting both coastal cropland and homes. Being a dynamic living resource, mangroves are self-sustaining and renewable, but only if the ecological processes governing the system are maintained. Before the deterioration of the mangrove forests of Pakistan began, it was one of the largest mangrove countries in the world.[20] However, there has been heavy destruction of mangroves over the years, primarily due to decreasing fresh water supply as well as overharvesting. Mangroves occupied 345,000 hectares along the entire Sindh coast. Recent estimates show their area to be only 160,000 to 205,000 hectares.[21] Remarks Muhammad Ali Shah, Chairman, Pakistan Fisherfolk Forum (PFF): 'There were thick jungles of mangroves, herds of buffaloes, cows and camels and bumper crops of red rice. Fish-catch of palo, shrimp and other fishes was in abundance. Today, palo is extinct, red rice is no more and the mangroves are depleting.'[22]

Additional threats have come from high levels of pollution. The main source of pollution continues to be the urbanisation and industrialisation of Karachi. Very large volumes of untreated domestic sewage and industrial effluents flow through nullahs and rivers into the sea. Of the nearly 300 million gallons per day of fresh water consumed by Karachi, nearly as many gallons of urban and domestic sewerage, and about 37,000 tonnes of industrial waste and effluents are dumped untreated into the sea daily. The effects of pollution extend from degradation of breeding areas to poisoned stocks of adult fish. Fisherfolk bear the burden of this pollution directly—they have to venture further offshore to harvest fish. Shah comments: 'Although I am not an expert on the subject, I can say with authenticity that if the flow of fresh sweet water of Indus stops to the sea once and for all, both ports of Karachi can be damaged by the sea erosion, posing serious threat to the city of Karachi.'[23]

Oil refineries, terminals, the large ship breaking industry at Gadani and coal and oil-fired power plants are other sources of marine degradation. The construction of dams and barrages and increased irrigation has also affected the flow of fresh water in the Indus estuary.[24] The estimated fresh water flow down the Indus river was about 150 million-acre feet (MAF) per year in the past. The Indus also carried around 400 million tonnes of silt. However, over the past 60 years, with the construction of dams, barrages and reservoirs, the fresh water flow has reduced to less than average 35.2 MAF, while silt discharge is now estimated to be 100 million tonnes per year. Remark scholars:

> The decreased influxes of nutrient rich waters and sediments have affected the offshore fisheries. Yearly catches of fish off the Sindh coast fell progressively after the construction of the Kotri barrage in 1956. The annual catch per boat before construction of the barrage was about 20 tons per boat and remained the same for about two years after the construction of the barrage. From 1958 to 1962 the catch per boat fell down considerably and remained at an average of 75 tons per boat. Before Kotri barrage the average catch of shrimp was about 300 tons per unit effort. In the 60s the catch fell down to about 120 tons as a result of the Kotri barrage. There is also some indication of subsequent drop in the 70s and also in the 80s, which appears to have reasonable connection with the construction of Mangla and Tarbela dams.[25]

Excessive and indiscriminate harvesting and mangrove deforestation due to growing needs of timber and fodder by an expanding population has further affected fish production. Overfishing, both economically and ecologically, has meant a substantial depletion of marine resource; it has entered a vicious cycle, where attempts to protect current real incomes through increased catch effort have led to subsequently lower stocks and lower incomes for fisher-folk. Overfishing and degrading marine breeding grounds are recognised by many fisherfolk as very serious obstacles to sustainable livelihoods. There are both internal and external factors responsible for depletion of stocks. There are numerous indicators of overfishing in the Sindh coastal waters. One concern reported by fisherfolk is the decrease in catch per craft in offshore waters despite an increase in the time spent and the distance covered on an average fishing trip. Increasing indebtedness of fisherfolk suggests excess capacity in marine fisheries. Data on harbour landings shows decreasing total catch for many species. Given that official data are usually underestimates—excluding landings at private jetties, and ignoring poaching and waste by catch from foreign vessels—overfishing is more acute than is evident in such data. Information on the number, gear and size of fishing crafts also indicates a rapid increase in exploitation of a threatened resource. Use of destructive nets, including *boolo* and *gujjo*, has played havoc with natural resources.[26] Oysters have disappeared from the Manora Channel. In recent years the level of fish catch in Sindh was about a one-fourth of what it was a decade earlier. Fishermen complain of the reduced catch of small pelagics.

In Pakistan, as elsewhere, exports affect marine fisheries. For example, the average rupee price rose by the late 90s to 20 times its level in the early 70s. There are no reliable estimates of currently precautionary sustainable yields for either Balochistan or Sindh. But it is obvious that fisheries are highly depleted in the coastal areas directly accessible to the fisherfolk. Otherwise, numerous fisherfolk would not take the regular risk of heavy fines imposed on poachers in the Balochistan waters. Neither would hundreds take the risk of being imprisoned for many years when caught by the Indian security agencies. Mechanisation of sailboats, introduction of larger crafts, massive increase in trawling operations, expanding use of fine mesh nets, virtual disappearance of traditions of seasonal bans on fishing, and entry of foreign vessels have compounded the problems of Pakistani fisherfolk. Muhammad Shah states that with commercialisation, the sustainable tradition of fishing has declined. In addition, thousands of fisherfolk have been displaced from their livelihood through the destruction of the Indus delta. Many fishing communities have been left with no option but to migrate to the nearest city.

According to Sikander Brohi, a Karachi-based researcher, 70 per cent of Pakistan's fish production is affected by globalisation. Specifically, it is the advent of industrial fishing that has adversely affected and marginalised artisanal and traditional fisherfolk. The quantity of their catch has steadily depleted because of the kind of nets and techniques used by the industrial trawlers. These changes have also had a direct impact on the role of women in the fish business. In the past, women were involved in both fishing and processing. Although some of them continue to play an active role, particularly along the Balochistan coast—in Sindh, largely as a result of increasing commercialisation, women do not go out in boats any more.

The situation on the other side of the border, i.e., on the coast of Gujarat in India is the same.[27] Gujarat has a rich heritage of live corals and coral islands in the Gulf of Kutch. Coral reefs offer an enormous variety of habitats to marine life. However, they are being dredged out and systematically destroyed. Saurashtra and Kutch particularly have about 20,000 hectares of mangroves. Mangrove forests are locally known here as 'cher forests'. Again, over the last two decades or more, there has been large-scale destruction of these life-giving mangroves all along the coastline from Umbergaon in the south to Koteswar and above in the north. Remote sensing techniques used by the Space Applications Centre (SAC), Indian Space Research Organisation (ISRO) in Ahmedabad have shown beyond doubt that the mangroves are depleting at a very fast rate and in cumulative proportions. There has also been indiscriminate exploitation of seaweeds. Sand dunes and mud flats are being removed. As a result, the natural defences to tidal waves and cyclones are diminishing, resulting in enormous coastal damage and destruction together with loss of lives. Protected areas and reserved areas are being denotified in the name of 'development'. Coastal Regulation Zone (CRZ) laws are constantly flouted.

The pollution along Gujarat's coast is in fact more than that of Pakistan, and thus the decline of marine ecology here has been greater. Gujarat now ranks second in India in terms of industrialisation and aims to be in the leading position. The state is investing heavily in chemical industries: fertilisers, textiles, chemical dyes and paints, insecticides, refineries, pharmaceuticals, soda ash, cement, salt and much more. The liberalisation policy is expected to bring in more industrial investment worth about Rs. 600 billion. Various factories on the Gujarat coastline like the Birla factory in Porbandar, GHL in Sutrapara, LNT and cement factory in Bhavnagar and Jafrabad and several others on the Saurashtra–Kutch coastline have been dumping millions of litres of industrial effluents and toxic wastes into the coastal waters, as they have no treatment plants. For example, there are four soda ash industries in Saurashtra producing more than 60 per cent of the country's total production. One factory or another at any one time releases effluents with more ammonia than maximum permissible limits.

A large number of the salt-works are located all along the Gujarat coastline, accounting for more than two-thirds of the country's current salt production. This has caused increasing salinity, leading to further destruction of mangroves. Industrialisation in the Baroda-Broach–Ankleshwar, Hajira–Surat and Bulsar–Vapi belts in Gujarat has reached a saturation point, leading to an alarming increase in air and water pollution levels, coupled with an ever-increasing industrial waste. A huge quantity of municipal sewage is dumped in the sea from Surat to Vapi, adversely affecting marine ecology.[28] Radioactive wastes from the Tarapore atomic power plant go into the coastal waters. Pollutants are never removed from water, they are only added. The government of Gujarat declared a specific area in the Gulf of Kutch from Okha port to Jodiya in Jamnagar district with the Gulf as a Marine National Park and Sanctuary, or *Abhyaranya*, a place where flora and fauna can thrive without fear of exploitation or desecration. And yet, paradoxically, there are two major oil terminals, Kandla and Vadinar, in the Gulf of Kutch. Oil spills and oil leakages, which are a frequent occurrence, are grave threats to the aquatic ecosystems.

In Gujarat too, despite a ban on fishing in certain months, some fishermen continue to fish. The fishing gear and nets used in Gujarat are also harmful. Mesh sizes of cod ends are very small and juvenile fish and prawn get caught by the millions without ever getting a chance to breed. Processors are also responsible as they accept any and all sizes of fish and prawn. Further, the number of mechanised boats and trawlers used for fishing in Pakistan are much fewer as compared to those used in Gujarat. There has also been a substantial increase in the number of fishing vessels. Veraval, the largest fishing harbour in Gujarat, has seen a steady rise in mechanisation of boats. In Gujarat, the number of trawlers has grown by leaps and bounds. While in 1984–85, there were about 1,030 trawlers of 32–48 feet length, by 1995–96 there were 4,191, which made up 58 per cent of the trawler fleet of Gujarat.[29] The undue explosion in boat construction has adversely affected the catch per boat. According to Ramesh Divandanriya, a boat-owner based in Porbandar: 'There has been a massive decline in fish catch in the last four years especially, and their prices have also declined. Fishermen just cannot help going further deep into the sea. Bagga, scuttle fish and prawns are just not available on the Gujarat coast.'[30]

An important reason for the decline in fish catch and marine ecological malaise in Gujarat has perhaps been the lack of a Gujarat Fisheries Act for a long time. The state finally enacted a Marine Fisheries Regulation Act in 2004. Before that, the Fisheries Department had no legal clout and was like a toothless tiger, with no power to control many aspects, and could not take any punitive action. The fishermen feared the Port and Customs Department more than the Fisheries Department. In an interview in 2002, I. C. Jadeja, Superindent of Fisheries at the Fisheries Department in Porbandar had stated his inability to do much in this regard.[31] Before the Act came into being, R. K. Nair of the Fisheries Survey of India, Porbandar had remarked:

> Fisheries is a state subject, and the centre cannot do much in it. The Marine Fishes Regulating Act was not enacted in Gujarat, because a Jain woman sitting in the Ministry of Law did not want to touch it. She considered it 'polluting' and also believed that by implementing this Act, she would be sanctioning the 'killing' of fish, which went against her religious beliefs. She could not even conceive that the Act was essentially meant for the preservation of fish.[32]

In Pakistan, there are numerous municipal, provincial and federal laws and agencies to deal with pollution. None have been used to effectively protect the coast from recognisable and substantial private and public damage. Marine pollution is not minimised because no penalties are levied. Failure to seriously contain marine degradation reflects both implicit and explicit policies to develop industry and agriculture at the cost of fisheries. Fisherfolk receive no compensation, even from public projects, for a variety of reasons. There is little comprehension of ecological relationships, and hence of larger environmental costs. Most importantly, fisherfolk have a weak lobby to advocate and pursue their claims to compensation for diminished and destroyed livelihoods. There are various laws like the Sindh Fisheries Ordinance 1980, Karachi Fisheries Harbour Authority Ordinance 1984, Exclusive Fishery Zone Act 1975 and Territorial Waters and Maritime Zones Act 1976. However, the provincial and federal governments have not invoked and enforced these laws for promoting conservation of marine resources. The Deep Sea Fishing Policy is very detrimental to the interests of the fisherfolk.

Activists, fisherfolk groups and NGOs on both sides of the border have been continuously suggesting concrete measures to reduce the decline in fish catch (see Box 3.2). In Pakistan, for example, it has been suggested that there should be no additional pollution of the sea arising from the sewage of Karachi; fair compensation be given to fisherfolk by private and public polluters; there should be no additional diversion of water from the Indus river for agriculture or urban use; no further increase in local fish harvesting capacity; implementation of existing closed seasons; ban on destructive nets; a strict limit on the number of deep sea fishing vessels; enforcement of the ban on fishing or trawling under 35 miles by large crafts; and participation of fisherfolk communities in a more careful and restrained harvesting of mangroves.

Box 3.2: Demands of Pakistan Fisherfolk Forum (PFF)

- No more mega irrigation projects, especially big dams, be constructed on the Indus river.
- The coastal population of the Indus delta should be considered as the real affectees of all the previously completed irrigation projects, including dams and reservoirs, and special programmes be launched for the economic rehabilitation of the coastal population, providing them compensation for their economic losses, along with ensuring alternative livelihoods.
- The coastal population of the Indus delta and their representatives should be consulted before launching any future project on the Indus river.

(Contd.)

(*Contd.*)

- Since many years the Indus water has not flown towards delta downstream Kotri barrage. This has further degraded agricultural lands, livestock and fishery resources on which millions of people of the Indus delta depend for their livelihoods. Similarly, mangrove forests, which are the breeding grounds for fisheries, are facing threats of extinction. Therefore, the participants of this seminar demand of the federal as well as the provincial government of Sindh that at least 10 million acre feet of fresh Indus water should be ensured downstream Kotri barrage as envisaged in water accord of 1991.
- The federal and provincial governments must stop draining out agricultural, industrial and urban effluents into the Indus delta. Treatment plants must be established for the treatment of urban as well as industrial effluents of Karachi. Similarly, in place of draining out the drainage effluents of all the provinces of the country into the Indus delta, the respective provinces should make arrangements for the treatment and re-use of their drainage water at their provincial levels.
- Many influential non-fisherfolk people have occupied a number of Indus delta creeks, which are nurseries for fish species. They have posted their armed persons at the mouth of these creeks, from Korangi creek near Karachi to Sir Creek near the Indian border to stop the local fishermen from fishing in those areas. These sea lords, in their bid to exploit fishery resources use harmful nets widely. They take hold of the boats and nets of fishermen who mistakenly enter their 'occupied areas' for fishing. This seminar demands that government authorities take severe action against these sea lords, and ensure that the indigenous fishermen can fish freely in these coastal creeks.
- The fishermen of the Indus delta are being widely exploited due to the inefficient marketing system, under which they are forced to receive loans from middlemen. It has created a situation of bonded labour in the Indus deltaic region. This seminar demands of the government to improve and modernise the marketing system in fisheries, which should include latest marketing facilities, including infrastructure development, as well as soft loans to the fishermen from the public sector banks.
- The fishing rights of the indigenous fisherfolk communities of Pakistan on coastal as well as inland waters be acknowledged in the legal framework of Pakistan.
- Sustainable fisheries policy as well as sustainable coastal fisheries management plan should be prepared and properly implemented.

(*Contd.*)

(*Contd.*)

- Overfishing, resorted to by the industrial fishing fleets as well as the local fishermen should be stopped by properly implementing the existing laws and introducting of new laws and rules.
- Deep-sea fishing by the foreign deep-sea trawlers should be banned due to overfishing, violation of rules and coastal pollution.
- The use of harmful nets in the coastal as well as inland fisheries should be stopped by strengthening the existing legal provisions, as well as by government monitoring.
- A fresh survey of the fish stocks in the coastal region should be conducted to bring forth the actual status of fish stocks and for preparing policy plans for the sustainability of remaining stocks as well as recovery plans for the depleted fish species.
- Increasing community participation and ownership should be encouraged in various projects and plans launched in the fisheries sector.
- Alternative livelihoods for the fisherfolk communities should be ensured so as to minimise the burden on coastal fishermen.
- Proper and sustainable representation of the fisherfolk communities and their representatives should be ensured in all the federal as well as provincial policy-making forums, institutions and departments related to the fisheries sector.
- Licence system for fishing in the inland waters should be restored in place of contract system.
- The federal as well as provincial governments with complete consultation and participation of the fishing community representatives should formulate a sustainable fishing policy. This policy should also follow the FAO Code of Conduct for sustainable fishing.
- Complete ban of harmful fishng nets should be properly enforced not only in the mangroves and creeks but also within three miles of the coast, for ensuring the breeding of various species of fish.
- Courses on Marine Biology including the Indus delta should be included in the primary textbooks to create awareness among our new generation about the natural resources of the coasts. Short courses should be launched on the national level about coastal resources management.
- The government authorities of Pakistan as well as India should make clear lines of demarcation at their boundaries with 'signals' or 'light houses' so as to minimise the possibilities of crossing the sea waters of both the countries by the fishermen, which results in their arrests.

(*Contd.*)

(*Contd.*)

- There should be a sustainable policy for the release of the arrested fishermen of both the countries. The strained political relationships between Pakistan and India should not be reflected in the arrest and release of fishermen, and the arrested fishermen should not be considered as 'prisoners of war'.

Source: 'Seminar on Indus Delta', organised by the PFF, on 16 February 2002 at Keti Bandar, Sindh, Pakistan.

On the Indian side, many official suggestions have come up: state should officially declare a specific sustainable number of boats and discontinue boat building for a specific period; it should decommission old and obsolete boats and cancel their licences; and processors must stop buying small-sized prawn and fish and force fishermen to increase the mesh size of trawlnets. The NFF branch in Gujarat has been continuously demanding that fisheries should be given an industrial status; aquaculture should immediately stop; that subsidy for diesel should be increased and the government should stop giving permission to foreign trawlers to fish in the Indian waters.

The decline in fish catch actually lies at the root of various hardships faced by thousands of fisherfolk on both sides of the borders. Preservation of marine ecology and increase in fish catch on the coast is the basic long-term solution to the problem of arrests of fisherfolk.

Structures of Fishing

There has also been a Blue Revolution in the state of Gujarat, particularly since the 1990s. It has resulted in a social and economic transformation in the fishing structure with intimate connections between the marine policy of the state and the social economy of the fishing community. There has also been a penetration of capitalism in this industry, alongside its internationalisation and expansion. The geopolitical influence of the fisheries sector has expanded considerably with fisheries playing a large role in the prosperity of this state. As per the data available for

2004, Gujarat ranks first in terms of quantitative marine production in India. Marine production has reached 585,000 metric
tonnes. Fishing fleet has increased to 30,153 (18,369 mechanised
and 11,784 non-mechanised). Export has gone up to 120,000
metric tonnes worth Rs. 7,636 billion, bringing in foreign
exchange of about 5 billion for the Gujarat government. The state
contributes 26 per cent to the national marine export in quantity
and 10.60 per cent in terms of value.[33] Some of the important
species of fish available here are shrimp, ribbonfish, promfret,
Indian salmon, hilsa, prawn, perch and bombay duck.

Even though fishing has been traditionally regarded as polluting
and those engaged in it were treated as outcastes, it has been the
ancestral profession of many in the coastal areas of Gujarat.
According to Census of 2003, there are 493,225 fishermen in the
state, of which more than half are on the marine side. There are
88,358 fishermen households and 970 fishing villages.[34] Many
people belonging to castes like Wagher, Mugaina, Machhiara,
Koli, Kharwa, Machhi, Mangola and Kahar are fishermen, for whom
fishing and fish trade are the main source of livelihood. For example,
Machhiara are Muslim fishermen living in villages along the coastline of Saurashtra. They migrated originally from Sindh and Kutch
long time ago. The Kharwa[35] community of Saurashtra, also
referred to as *Sagar Putra* (son of the sea), forms about 70 per cent
of the total fishing community and has a 2,000-year-old history
of maritime activity. They are reported to be traditionally a
seafaring community who were mainly navigators, engaged as
sailors in the commercial vessels, carrying cargo to distant places
like Malaya, Singapore, Hong Kong and even the African coast.[36]
The Kharwas have invested heavily into fisheries and their main
occupation is marine fishing. Many have become boat-owners
though some of them are still engaged in cargo vessels. In the
mid-1970s, the Gujarat government granted them various
concessions like credit facilities and diesel pumps to promote
exports. There was a major boom in fishing, especially in the
1990s, and this resulted in their upward mobility, which found
many expressions. First, they themselves stopped fishing and
employed other backward castes for it, especially skippers and
crew from Valsad and Andhra Pradesh.[37] Second, in the process
of seeking upward social mobility they became involved in a subtle
Hinduisation process with the Svadhyaya movement, launched

by Pandurang Athavale, and started identifying themselves as Rajputs. Most fishermen communities have a very rigid caste panchayat system formed on a regional basis. The head of the caste panchayat called *nyat patel* or *mota patel* is elected annually by the representatives of the community. The whole community is divided into a number of groups called *dayra* or *baithak*, each with a head called *patel*.

Although some of the fishermen have become boat-owners, there is a difference in the economic and the social milieu of these two groups. In Porbandar for example, there are mostly boat-owners, about 2,000 in number, while the fisherfolk come from Diu, Kodinar, Valsad, Una, Vallar, Vapi, Umargaon and other areas. In Veraval, the largest fishing harbour of Gujarat, there are more than 20,000 fishermen during the season, but they have no space of their own in the town.

The boat-owners have a large stake in coastal fishing. There are around 1,500 trawlers in Porbandar itself and about 700 canoes (smaller boats). According to Vinod Bhai, a boat-owner in Porbandar, a boat can cost between Rs. 12,00,000 and 15,00,000. A medium boat has 8 to 10 tonnes of fish carrying capacity. The maintenance cost of these fishing vessels is very high. For example, maintenance cost per year on each boat is Rs. 150,000, which includes engine parts, anchors, ropes and nets. Another 800,000 is spent on diesel consumption and on each trip it works out to about Rs. 3,000. A further 600,000 to 800,000 rupees is spent on crew payment, insurance and customs. The ice room or the cold room where the fish catch is kept has to be changed every three years and the cost of rebuilding it is Rs. 100,000. The owner of the boat usually acts as the leader.[38]

The fishworkers are usually in the age group of 14 to 60 years. They come largely from the southernmost parts of Gujarat and many come from the fishing villages of Andhra Pradesh. Often, hundreds come from a single fishing village. Some of them are experienced fishermen but a lot of them have learnt on the job. The traditional fishermen from Valsad area are called *mota bhais* (big brothers) and they are probably the best paid. The head fisherman or the person in charge of the boat at the time of an operation is called *tandel*. He remains at the stern end to operate the helm *(sukhand)* and guides the movement of the boat. He earns around Rs. 8,000 a month during the fishing season, which is from 15

August to 15 May. All the other fishermen work under him as dock-hands and are known as *khalasi*. They earn around Rs. 3,000 to Rs. 5,000 a month. The *tandel* usually recruits the *khalasis* from his own village. The *tandels* and *khalasis* often bring their teenage sons along, together with their brothers and other relatives. Once they take charge of a boat, it remains their home for the next eight months. Earlier a fishing trip used to take 4 to 5 days, but now due to the declining fish catch it often takes at least 9 to 10 days as the fisherfolk have to go further into the ocean. These fisherfolk carry food with them. The fish catch is kept in ice. After a trip, they get exactly 24 hours to offload and reload in the harbour and relax a little. While on the boat, they are not allowed to drink alcohol. The boat-owner handles all accounts and he also sends money to the families of the workers on their request. But settlements are made only at the end of the season during which they are at his mercy. Much of the business runs on trust and is built on the sweat and toil of these fishworkers.[39]

Due to the arrests of fishermen and capture of boats, boat-owners and fishermen suffer huge financial and mental losses. Once a boat is caught, it is a very tedious and long process to get it released, often resulting in the boat-owner going bankrupt. They have to first submit their case to at least four departments, with all details, including the Fisheries Department at Porbandar and Gandhi Nagar, coast guards and the central government. And thereafter too, they are uncertain when, if ever, their boat will be released. The arrested boat is kept in anchor in the other country under the security department. Its water needs to be taken out and its machine run regularly. However, even the minimal maintenance is usually not carried out. Once the fishing season is over, it becomes even more difficult to recover the boat since the sea becomes extremely violent. Moreover, boat-owners have to go to Pakistan to get their boat released, a very difficult and expensive exercise for which they often have to take bank loans. Once the boat is released, it is usually in such a bad condition that a huge sum is again needed to make it usable.

Manish M. Lodhari, a prosperous boat-owner from Porbandar was unfortunate enough to have five of his boats arrested by the Pakistan Marine Force in January 2000. The total cost of these boats was estimated to be Rs. 10 million and he had to run from pillar to post to recover them. He repeatedly wrote several letters to the prime minister, external affairs minister, chief minister of Gujarat, district magistrate of Porbandar and many others, requesting them to expedite the process of getting his boats released. Ramesh Divandanriya, whose boat had been captured in early 2002, complained:

> Since my boat has been arrested, I am running from pillar to post. I have written several letters to the concerned ministries, but to no avail. I feel completely helpless. My mind has stopped working. I feel like crying. I do not know anything besides catching and selling fish. I have never ventured out of Porbandar and do not know what will happen to me. My only hope is the NFF and the fishworkers bodies of Pakistan.[40]

While the financial loss suffered by the boat-owners cannot be under-estimated, it is the arrested fisherfolk, who suffer the most.

Omnipotent State and Marginalised Populations

A large number of Indian and Pakistani fishermen, most of them poor, have been intermittently lodged in the jails of each other's country for years together,[41] deprived of basic legal and human rights. Latest reports between 2004–06 from newspapers and fisher-folk organisations reveal a grim picture, where the cycle of arrests persists. For example, very recently it was claimed by the spokes-person of the External Affairs Ministry of India that between September 2005 and February 2006, 400 Indian fishermen were arrested by Pakistan.[42] These fisherfolk are caught for crossing the ocean borders. They represent the economically and socially marginalised subjects that have been left behind in the con-struction of an omnipotent nation-state. They are the victims of a world obsessed with national pride and rampant with boundary wars. Both India and Pakistan take as given state power configur-ations and bordered state sovereignties, where anyone seeming to challenge it—even covertly—is treated as a threat. There is also a fear of insecurity, which gives no space to marginal voices or interests. Thus both the countries continue to physically and discursively trivialise or destroy various aspects of centrifugal otherness. The crossing of sea borders by the fisherfolk in a way proclaims the tenuous hold of the two countries over territories, boundaries and fixed identities; hence the repression.

These fisherfolk have consistently been objects of state policies; never their subjects. More important, they are treated as people with fixed and homogenous identities, where citizenship becomes critical, however fictive it may be. They are recognised first and foremost as citizens, and other affiliations and identities are allowed no recognition and affectivity. When arrested, it is their citizenship that makes them the victim. Ironically, in their own country they are often on the outskirts and are treated as merely 'populations'. They complete their term of punishment as per the court orders, but even then they are not released. Often they are never tried and are just locked away in prison. They have to wait years for a formal process of exchange of prisoners to take place. They are usually released only through an 'exchange protocol', almost similar to the procedure followed for the release of prisoners of war.[43] Their release is mainly dependent on the state of relations between their governments. They are often exchanged in equal numbers, an exercise whose logic forces Indian and Pakistani authorities to continually catch straying fishermen in each other's territorial waters.

An Anthropology of Pain: The Fettered Fisherfolk

The stories of these fisherfolk are immeasurably tragic and on several levels. They are tragic, of course, because their livelihood is converted into a crime. They are harassed by coast guards and jail authorities, weakened economically and excluded from their only source of livelihood. But it is also tragic in other subtle ways. It takes a heavy toll on their families left behind, who live in a state of constant uncertainity and anxiety. There is gross violation of basic human rights. There is the tragedy of loss of self. Further, their families get no compensation and even the boat-owners rarely send them money.

The intense trauma, pain and personal suffering that the fisher-folk and their families go through are intrinsically linked to political power and rivalries of states and governments. The personal here is very much political. These people are desperate, poor and powerless. Their suffering is individual and collective, local and global.[44] More often than not, the arrested fisherfolk have remained merely statistical numbers in the government records.[45] But suffering and innumerable stories of pain, anguish and anxieties, not only of those arrested but also of those left behind, their families, boat-owners and other fisherfolk, can never be conveyed by mere statistics and numbers. The victims on both sides of the border may not share religions or countries; rather, what they share is the experience of being treated as criminals for their livelihood, of gross human rights violations and of occupying an insignificant position in the social ladder in inegalitarian societies. Many have suffered and their suffering should be taken seriously. To say more is to simplify, but to fathom the statement is also to make the fact bearable. This is just a small effort to record their suffering. However, in the process also emerges their continuous effort to live, to survive and to cope.

During fieldwork in Gujarat, in 1996, 1997 and again in 2002, what greeted us were repeated outpourings of reports of arrests and sufferings and of separation and poverty. We do not know how to write these accounts. No words are adequate to describe them. The experiences of pain and human violations are not just events; they are tied here with complex issues of nation-states, boundaries, state rivalries, ecological malaise and political conflicts.

Pakistani Fishermen in Indian Jails

According to the records of the Porbandar police station,172 Pakistani fishermen had been arrested in Porbandar between 1997 and 2001.[46] We met a number of jailed fishermen during our fieldwork in 1996. However, when we went in 2002, there was not a single fisherman from Pakistan in the Porbandar jail. We came to know that at the time just two boats were in police custody and the fisherfolk were in the Jamnagar jail. However, the chronology of arrests has seen various ups and downs, depending on the political situation prevalent in the two countries. Also, detailed information on the arrested fisherfolk is hard to come by. Some of the arrested fishermen were interviewed in 1996–97 and much of it recorded.[47] Here we recount some of their stories.

Table 3.1: Selective Official Data on Arrested Pakistani Fisherfolk

Year	Number of Pakistani Boats Captured	Number of Cases Registered	Number of Pakistani Arrested
1997	05	05	68
1998	05	03	60
1999	Nil	Nil	Nil
2000	06	03	44
2001	Nil	Nil	Nil

Source: DCP, Porbandar, Official Data.

Thirty-one-year-old Ghani Rehman had been imprisoned in Porbandar jail for two-and-a-half years. He was the captain of the *Al Jashan* boat, which had on board 14 fishermen. All were caught and penalised. They were punished for 2 years and 2 months and after having completed their sentence, they were moved to the police headquarters on 1 January 1997. Residing in the Sarhad state, Ghani Rehman's father, Sayid Rehman, was a fisherman, as were his three brothers. They used to fish in the ocean for 10–15 days and then return home. Ghani's wife and children were completely dependent on him. Hoping for a better income, Ghani came to Karachi and started working on the boat of a businessman. He narrated:

> This time we were on the ocean for more than a month. We were throwing our net to catch fish and it was impossible to make out where the wind and water were driving the boat. If there were some signposts on the ocean, it would make it easier to discern boundaries. Suddenly the navy came. We did not even know whose navy it was. And then we were all captured in the Indian checkpost.[48]

After being arrested, Ghani wrote a letter to the boat-owner but got no reply. He wrote to his family to try and intervene but they were helpless. While in jail, Ghani was worried about his wife and children. They struggled to survive by asking for help and loans. Ghani's wife wrote to him and never talked of her difficulties, but her helplessness was clearly visible.

Muhammad Alam is an 18-year-old crew member of the *Al Kabutar* boat. He lives on Madipur Road in Karachi with his parents, wife and two children, and recounts a similar experience. On 8 January 1996 he along with five other crew members—

Muhammad Hussain, Abdul Sakur, Nurul Islam, Abdul Kalaam and Nur Alam—left on a boat to fish. The next day at dawn the coast guards caught them and kept their boat at Porbandar. They were sent to the police station and then to the Porbandar jail.[49] On 8 October 1989, Naushad Ali, Muhammad Iqbal, Abu Usmaan, Ali Abu Samariya, Babal Gulmuhammad, Gaunar Khan Bahadur, Nisar Ahmed Usmaan, Ibrahim Adam and Khasina Ramzaan, were all on the *Al Ameera* boat when they were apprehended on Indian waters. After undergoing a torturous process of captivity, police custody and court cases, in September 1991, they were sent to Kutch where they remained in police custody. Naushad Ali contemplated suicide as he ached for his family. Hiding his trauma he asked: 'Why should we bear this pain because of tensions between two powers? Our heart is dead. Our hopes have been constantly belied.' Muhammad Iqbal observed: 'Sometimes I feel that as a fisherman, if I am caught between a pirate and a coast guard, I would prefer to give myself to the pirate. I think I will be safer.'[50] In early 1998, Naushad Ali and the other crew members were finally released.[51]

We also met six people from one family of Sindh. In 1994, three brothers—Sikander, Nizamuddin and Nissar, their cousins Didaar, Ashiq Ali and Muhammad Azhar—and their uncle Muhammad Yakub were all caught while fishing. They never knew when they had trespassed the Indian border in the ocean. Even after completing their jail term, they kept asking what their crime was. Didaar did not want to say much: 'What is left to say? Every brother has three, four children. All of them are now begging on the streets. They are dying of hunger.' His uncle was very bitter, 'Here and there, workers are languishing. No one gives a damn.'[52] After this experience, many young fishermen decided to give up fishing and work as daily wagers instead, as the trauma proved to be too much.[53]

Mai Khatoo, wife of a Pakistani fisherman who has recently been released after serving several years in an Indian prison laments: 'You cannot imagine the pain and agony I went through when my husband was imprisoned in India. Besides worrying about his safety, I had to work day and night to feed five children as he was the only bread earner.'[54]

Majeed Golani, a fisherman from Ibrahim Hyderi, a village on the Karachi coast, was one of a dozen fishermen arrested by Indian forces a few years back. He gives the following account of his experience: 'They did not give us food for two days until we were finally put in jail. We were mentally and physically tortured. They treated us like prisoners of war. We go for livelihood and they arrest us; it is injustice.'[55]

The pain and torture of the fishermen can sometimes take extreme forms. On 17 May 2004, three Pakistani fishermen were killed, one seriously injured and five others arrested after two Indian navy vessels opened fire at their boat. They had entered the Indian waters in the Arabian Sea and their boat was intercepted around 10 nautical miles off the Gujarat coast in the Rann of Kutch. Pakistan authorities termed these killings as 'callous and unwarranted'. They pointed out that fishermen straying into territorial waters of the other country was routine which at worst called for their arrest. Pakistan claimed that despite frequent trespassing by the Indian fishermen, it had never harmed them.[56] As recently as April 2006, Pakistan alleged that on 18 March, an Indian coast guard had killed one of its fishermen in 'unprovoked' firing.[57]

Indian Fishermen in Pakistani Jails

Jail is our destiny... They caught us by force in the ocean. For five days we were kept in the boat itself. Then they took us to the jail. We get one cup of pulses and two slices of bread to eat. The bread is baked only on one side. We do not wish this punishment even on our enemies. There is one Pakistani prisoner who helps us sometimes and gives us cigarettes and soap.
—Dhanji Harji Rathod of Vanakvada village, Diu, India, arrested in 1995, writing to his family from Barrack No. 11, Karachi East 34, Landi Jail, Pakistan, in 1997.

Kismet mein likha hua pardes, vatan ko kya yaad karoon.
Yahan apna nahin hai koi, fariyaad kisko kaise karoon.
(Foreign land seems to be a part of my fate, so how do I remember my own country. In this land I know no one; to whom should I appeal.)
—Nathu Bhai of Vanakvada village, arrested in 2001, wrote this quote in a letter to his family, dated 24 March 2002.

To live without a husband is to exist like a container without a cover. Everyone in the village considers you *bhabhi* of the village and looks

at you with strange motives. Being a widow is better. At least you
have a fixed identity.
—Savibahen Sosa, Dalit, 22 years old and mother of two daughters.
Her husband was in a Pakistani jail during 1995–96.

Within two months of my marriage, my husband was arrested by
Pakistani authorities. Our home was like a *jannat* when he was around.
—Bilkishbanu Shaik, Muslim Sunni, 20 years old. Her husband was
arrested from Kutch border on 26 December 1998.

My husband and I got along like a house on fire. The kids love their
father so much and say that their mother has been arrested in Pakistan.
I really miss him. I have been reduced to a rag picker. Let him come
back home this time; I will go hungry, but never let him go fishing
again.
—Savita, Kori, 28 years old, mother of four daughters and one son.
Her husband Ramesh Bhai was arrested in January 2002.

These narratives of the arrested fisherfolk and their families
hide innumerable stories of pain and agony. None of them are
unique; they are representative of many experiences of similar
kinds. The second quote by an arrested Indian fisherman captures
his pain and his dilemma; he craves for his nation—a nation that
cannot even ensure his livelihood. The arrested fisherfolk face
the trauma of exile, being uprooted and displaced for a long time,
losing all contact with their lifeworlds. Their family members left
behind suffer no less.

All these people quoted here belong to the two villages of
Vanakvada and Saudvara in the Union Territory of Diu. Fishing is
their sole source of livelihood. These villages are a catchment area
for fisherfolk living here and also for those of the nearby areas.
There are more than 2,000 fisherfolk in these villages and almost
the same number have come here from outside. Both villages are
replete with narratives of anguish and pain of fishermen caught by
the Pakistani coast guards or navy on the charge of crossing ocean
borders. According to Lakhan Bhai Puja, chief of the Boat
Association Vari Vistaar at Vanakvada, in the past 20 years more
than 500 fishermen of this area have been arrested by the Pakistani
coast guards and more than 150 boats seized. Between January
and May 2002, 32 Indian boats had been arrested.

During fieldwork in 1997 and 2002, we met various family
members of the arrested fisherfolk and even some of those who

had returned from Pakistani jails after many years. While letters from those jailed are few, some of them reveal much, even when the fisherfolk try to hide their pain. One fisherman, Uga Raja, arrested in January 2002, wrote from Barrack no. 3 at the Landi Jail in Karachi: 'From sunrise to sunset, I remember you.... Have your written any letters to me? I have received none. Please write to me every fifteen days, as I feel that will be my only link with India for the coming many months. I don't know when I will see all of you again.... Do not worry about me. Whatever is in my fate will happen. Keep my kids happy.'[58]

On 2 July 2000, letters written by prison inmates—Kader Taiyab Thaim and Ram Nathu—and on 16 May letters written by the convicts—Pujabhai Maya, Kanabhai Bava, Hirabhai Kaga and Babhubhai Ramji—revealed that many of them suffered from different types of diseases as they did not have access to clean potable water and two square meals a day. The letter written by the prison inmate Kaderbhai to Jayaben Vadher of the Samudra Shramik Suraksha Sangh, a Kodinar-based fishworkers' grass-roots organisation, talked extensively on how they got 'four half-baked chapatis with very little dal and half-a-cup tea' a day; how they were made to sleep on 'rack-type beds, one above the other'; they were forced to drink water of the toilet; they were given 'water to take bath only once a month'. He further complained, 'Obviously, we fall ill. Instead of treating us, the doctors scold us and say that they aren't bothered whether we live or die.' Kedarbhai also regretted that the boat-owners for whom they were fishing had turned a blind eye to their families at home in Gujarat. He said, 'We have been told that they have not paid anything for the last nine months. How would our families live?'[59] The letters also revealed that they were usually monitored and thus most fisherfolk could not express their true sufferings.

On 23 January 2002, the boat called *Radha Kishna*, owned by Ramesh Divandanriya of Porbandar, was captured by the Pakistani authorities and all seven fishermen on board were arrested. They were kept in the Landi jail in Pakistan. When the boat did not return, the NFF used its contacts in the Fishermen's Cooperative Society, Karachi, which informed them about the arrest. The *tandel* of the boat, Uga Raja, wrote from the jail, appealing for release.

During fieldwork in 1996–97, we heard many such stories. One fisherman of Nawa Bandar died in a Pakistani jail. Three

aged fathers—Lakshman, Kanji Veera and Devji Nathu—lost their
sons, Velji Lakshman, Kanji and Devji, respectively—who never
returned from their fishing trip. These fishermen and their boats
were   caught by the coast guards and their families suffered
extreme hardship back home.[60] Mulji Lakhman had been in a
Pakistani jail for three years, leaving behind his wife Ramila Mulji,
and four young children. The family had a small piece of land,
which was filled with saline water and thus unfit for cultivation.
Ramila did some casual labour under the 'Jawahar Rozgar Yojana'.
She got work for 10–15 days in a month. She was thus able to
earn between Rs. 350 and 400 per month; for the rest, she was
assisted by her brother and father. She made both ends meet
with difficulty. Ramila met the collector, commissioner and others
for the release of her husband; she also requested them for some
financial help. But in those three long years, she only got empty
promises. A fisherman, who returned to his village after spending
six years in a Pakistani jail remarked, 'We go to do our job. We fish
for our livelihood. How can we be involved in anything illegal? Do
we look like criminals?' However, the arrests continue unabated.[61]
And worse, as recently as February 2006 it was alleged that an
Indian fisherman, Shantilal Mangal, was killed in firing by the
Pakistan maritime security agency while he was fishing west of
the Gujarat coast.[62]

The families often lacked information about the arrested
fishworkers. Survival became one of the main issues, as most of
them had no income with the loss of the breadwinner. We also
witnessed increasing tensions within the family, with the wife
having to suffer the most. The education of the children was
adversely affected. The families had no social security. There was
no proper coordinating body to provide assistance to them, and
authorities and politicians rarely cooperated with them.

Narratives by women—mothers, wives and daughters of the
arrested fisherfolk—disclosed the manner in which they were
forced into vulnerable positions and experiences of sudden loss.
Their voices expressed agonising doubts about lost connections
and memories which could not be erased and wounds which could
not heal. Often it was difficult to get the women to speak openly
about their anguish. Perhaps talking made their grief deeper;
silence made it bearable. However, we witnessed emotional break-

Plate 3.1: Wives of Captured Indian Fisherfolk
in Saudvara Village, Diu, India

downs, a deep nostalgia for the days gone by and a craving for the return to 'normal' circumstances. These women often constructed their past, when they had their husbands, sons and fathers around them, as a glorious one. They expressed their bitterness towards the state, authorities on both sides and the boat-owners. Kamta Devi observed: 'I cannot feel the change in seasons any longer. Spring and autumn merge into each other but I have lost the count of time. My memories are all that I have. My grief is deep. But I have to survive and live on for my children and in the hope that some day my husband will be released.'[63]

Children of a Lesser God

In course, over 200 Indian children, mostly from Gujarat, have been caught for 'unintentionally crossing the international borders'.[64] There were 50 children in these villages who went with their fathers on the boat and were caught and jailed in Pakistan. For years they languished either in jails or the Edhi Welfare Centre at Karachi. These children had lost the innocence and laughter of childhood; their lives had changed and they remembered this experience.

Recently, the Pakistan government released 38 such children as a goodwill gesture.[65] Manji Dayar, an 18-year-old from Vanakvada village in Diu, was fearful as he remembered that day in 1994 when he was caught in the ocean, 'It was early morning when suddenly there was firing in the air. The Pakistani navy stopped the boat and cut the net.' All the five people on board were caught and taken to Karachi. Initially, they were in police custody for three days, then jailed, and finally sent to the Edhi Centre.

Manji had old parents and two younger brothers. After returning home, he became a wage labourer; he did not venture to the ocean nor had plans to do so in the future. Manji recalled the Edhi Centre where they did not have too many problems. But his family was distressed and no one helped them. Three years of their lives were wasted for nothing. Manji did not want to remember his days of captivity, but he was also very bitter of the present. When he and the others returned, there was a meeting at Diu attented by the collector, commissioner and others. They promised help, but it came to nothing. He argued that if son of a collector or commissioner was imprisoned, they would have realised his pain. Manji was anxious for his future. He was worried for his family; he did not want his brother to face the same fate; he wanted him to get an education.[66]

Although 12-year-old Nanji Murji was released, his father remained in the Karachi jail. Nanji had a mother, two younger sisters and one younger brother. In 1994, when he was captured, he was studying in VII class. School was closed for a month and he had gone with his father to enjoy the ocean for the first time. Nanji stayed in jail for five months and then went to the Edhi Centre. The centre had good eating and living facilities, but there was no freedom and no friends. Nanji felt very sad, as he missed his family. He wrote letters to his father who was lodged in the other jail. Nanji's studies were discontinued and now he has no desire to resume his education.[67]

Life goes on even amidst these numerous chronicles of suffering and human rights violations. Cross-border arrests have become a part of the everyday existence of coastal fisherfolk.

Plate 3.2: 12-year-old Nanji Murji of Vanakvada Village of Diu, India

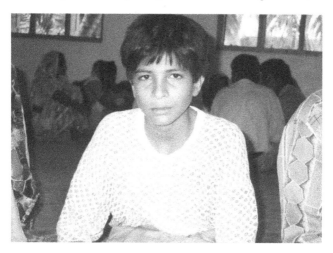

Hidden Transcripts: Challenging Borders

I am not the Wall that Divides
I am a Crack in that Wall

—Kamla Bhasin[68]

We do not wish to end this section by just chronicling the suffering of the fisherfolk. There are often two polar views regarding these fisherfolk—the state usually sees fisherfolk who cross the borders as potential threats to national security; the fisherfolk and their organisations portray them primarily as victims. It is a fact that there are no clear demarcation lines defining sea borders, which makes it difficult to realise when one is trespassing; hence, some of the violations are unintentional and accidental. Some of the fisherfolk even stated that they were probably arrested from their own waters. Further, tidal factors, oceanic currents and storms also lead to these crossings. At the same time, there is often a 'feigned ignorance' on the part of fishworkers about such crossings. It has been remarked in a different context by Amitava Kumar: 'Before professors in business schools were talking about global economics, illegals knew all about it.... The illegal immigrant is the bravest among us. The most modern among us. The prophet.... The peasant knows the reality of our world decades before the Californian suburbanite will ever get the point.'[69]

We thus hear muted, hidden voices among the fisherfolk which reveal that they are often aware that they are crossing the borders. These are actually hidden strategies of everyday survival within available resources; of abilities to secure their daily living. It is their way of coping with declining fish catch, and increasing their fish stock. Perhaps these can be partially seen as their 'agentive moments'.[70] Simultaneously, increase in prices of fishing crafts and gear may also force them to cross the borders to cover their expenses. The boat-owners may also compel the crew members to do so.

Most important perhaps, fisher people exercise their customary fishing rights as they practiced them in the past.[71] For them fishing is a way of life; where they have been fishing in these waters for ages. The borders of these fisherfolk communities are only partly related to the nation-state boundaries; there are different spaces of belonging created here. They challenge the border by playing with it; it is a necessity not only to cross the border, but also to deconstruct it. The fishermen feel that their activities position them on one or the other side of the border just as they like. It is even possible to position oneself on both sides of the border at the same time. The border here loses its conventional dividing function and opens up alternatives other than the 'either-or', which are normally associated with borders. This can perhaps also be regarded as a 'hybridity' of identity, a hyphenated identity. Thus Shamji, a fisherman from Vanakvada village in Diu remarks: 'I am a fisherman and only a fisherman. I love my occupation. I have no other identity besides that. I do not know what borders and boundaries mean. I will go and fish wherever I can. It has been my customary right. How can I now allow the state to determine and change a right that I have always had?'[72]

Perhaps it would be a little far-fetched and also romanticisation to see in these acts of 'conscious crossing of borders' hidden transcripts of 'everyday resistance'.[73] At the same time, these acts do signify ordinary weapons of subordinate and marginalised coastal fisherfolk, what has been termed as the 'weapons of the weak'. This daily crossing is less dramatic or headline-worthy, but it signifies a routine way of survival and in its own way challenges notions of borders and boundaries. After all, behind a few hundred arrested there are thousands who fish in other's waters and escape.

Despite increasing policing of the seas, these fishermen have found clandestine ways of surfing the seas. Daya Govind, a fisherman of Vanakvada village declares: 'Even though I have been arrested once, I will continue to take the risk of crossing the border. I know it is treated as a crime, but do I have a choice? I have to survive. I cannot afford not to cross.'[74]

Or, states another fisherman: 'Like all other fishermen, I too am afraid to cross. I am nervous, but I will do it, as it is a part of me. It is what I have to do if I have to survive. I will do so again and again. I may make it, and that is a risk I am willing to take. I will go wherever I can get fish.'[75]

Thus the risks of apprehension and arrest have not deterred the fishermen from crossing the seas. Haji Shafi Mohammad Jamawar, chairman of the Pakistan Fishermen's Cooperative Society, admits: 'We sometimes go across deliberately. Most fishermen worth their salt know where they are from the position of stars, from the creeks. But we go in search of fish.'[76]

These fisherfolk defy the waves of the boundless sea and at the same time find moments of subversive fulfilment in its flow. Here boundaries and nations dissolve; there is instead an indifference towards them. Through their actions, these fisherfolk provide a space and create a discursive frame that can enunciate alternatives. Their actions subvert the grammar of nationhood. The addresses of these alternative voices have not appeared in the directories provided by overwhelming nationalist and border concerns.

The fisherfolk and their families learn to endure and also transcend their suffering.[77] The women of these fisherfolk families particularly reveal their extraordinary capacity of continuing relationships and providing nurturance. According to Kalavanti of Vanakvada village, whose husband is in jail: 'Everyone in our family fishes. We do not know any other work. We will continue to do it. However long it takes, I will wait for my husband. Meanwhile I have to look after my children, and also work towards my husband's release. I am doing any work I can get. I will, I have to, survive.'[78]

Along with the stories of despair, there are also stories of hope (see Box 3.3). There are healing processes that take place, especially when after an excruciatingly long wait these fisherfolk are released. In June 2001, 157 fishermen were released after 18 months. Many reports were published at that time. Sindhhu Suresh states in one such report:

For 18 months they had waited patiently. Now, as 25 mechanised boats bring back 157 fishermen arrested by Pakistan for straying into its territorial waters, their families wait, restraining their joy and praying for the 202 others yet to be released.... Gangaben has come from Dhagasi village near Diu to receive her 22-year-old son Hitesh Varzan, the breadwinner of her family.... She sadly confesses, 'I cannot ask him to quit fishing since that is our means of living'.[79]

On the fishermen's return, he further states:

> After an excruciatingly long wait, when the first four boats appeared like specks on the horizon at 11.30 a.m. on Saturday, overwhelmed relatives of the 157 fishermen released from Pakistani jails crowded the shore for a glimpse.... When the first lot of 21 fishermen came ashore, they rushed forward, each eager to see if their loved one was among the group. After the first fisherman, Ramji Karsan, cleared customs and came out, his sister and daughter hugged him, garlanded him and applied tilak on his forehead.... However, another 202 Indians are still languishing in Pakistani jails.[80]

Box 3.3: An Indian Fisherman is Home After 21 Years

Narayan, a boat mechanic from Shimoga in Karnataka, was released by Pakistani authorities in July 2003 after having spent 21 years in jail for no crime. The 48-year-old, is back home in Moovalli village of Tirthahalli taluk of Shimoga district. Narasamma, his mother, could not believe that her long-lost son, whom she had presumed to be dead, had returned after so many years. To Narasamma, the gaunt pale-looking man at her doorstep was a 'stranger' till he took her down memory lane, and she finally believed him.

For Narayan freedom is proving to be strange, blinding and yet exhilarating. He narrates, 'We were like sheep running out of their pond. We ran with joy and a sense of freedom. But soon we realised we were not strong enough to even walk a short distance. We couldn't keep our eyes open in daylight. We were always in a state of trance.'

Narayan along with 13 others of the fishing vessel *Jeevandani* was arrested by the Pakistani navy in 1982 for straying into Pakistan's territorial waters. He like others voices, 'We didn't know that we had entered Pakistani waters. We were just on a fishing trip.' However, he along with others, was tortured initially. Once innocence was proven, the torture stopped, but they were kept in a dark room. Since

(Contd.)

(Contd.)

Narayan was not allowed to communicate with anyone, they all thought he was dead.

The days of darkness were endless. Twenty-one years is a long period to have suffered for a minor transgression, even if intentional. Narayan is still not used to the sunlight. He just wishes to erase the whole experience from his memory.

Source: Hindustan Times, 7 July 2003, New Delhi, p. 11; *The Indian Express*, 4 July 2003, New Delhi, p. 6.

An Exchange Protocol: A Chronicle of Arrests and Releases

There has been no clear-cut policy regarding the release of arrested fisherfolk on both sides of the border. The measures on behalf of the government have been governed largely by ad-hocism and political considerations, where the fisherfolk are used as mere pawns, either to intensify the tension or to reveal a face of compromise and humaneness. Recently, in September 2005, India stated that it would release 101 Pakistani fishermen, and Pakistan was to release 371. This was announced just ahead of the talks between the Pakistan President Pervez Musharraf and the Indian Prime Minister Manmohan Singh.[81] Earlier in April 2005, while Manmohan Singh welcomed Musharraf to New Delhi, 156 fishermen were released on humanitarian grounds in Ahmedabad.[82] Again at the end of official talks in June and August 2004, joint statements were issued by the two countries stating that all apprehended fishermen in each other's custody would be released and mechanisms put in place for the return of fishermen who have transgressed unintentionally from the high seas, without being apprehended.[83] On 4 September 2003, the Pakistan government freed 269 Indian fishermen, all from Gujarat, out of 343 lodged in different jails in Karachi.[84] It was publicised as a follow-up to the confidence building measures (CBMs) announced by the Pakistan Prime Minister, Mir Zafarullah Khan Jamail, in response to the peace initiative by the then Indian Prime Minister, Atal Bihari Vajpayee.[85] India reciprocated by releasing 74 Pakistani fishermen, lodged in the Jamnagar prison of Gujarat.

During the course of this study—beginning from 1990 till date—we have heard, read, cut and collected innumerable chronicles and short clippings of arrests and releases of the fisherfolk. However, after more than 16 years of gathering information on arrests and releases, we conclude that while every effort to free the fisherfolk needs to be appreciated—since we are talking of actual lives, livelihoods and families—this problem will persist till there is a political will to search for long-term solutions. We have witnessed that when political tensions between the two countries escalate, or relations between them sour, the arrests of fisherfolk increase and they become one of the first groups to get caught in the crossfire. And then in negotiations of peace, they become tools to express regional cooperation and peace measures. For example, just prior to the Agra Summit in July 2001 a proposal was presented for settlement of issues related to such fishermen at the local level, without involving the foreign ministries of respective countries. Unfortunately the proposition was never implemented due to tensions arising out of diplomatic expulsions.[86] This kind of ad-hocism will not work. The bottom line is that most of the time political considerations, lack of a strong will to search for permanent solutions, and rivalry have prevented officials from taking definitive action.

The Indian government and its several departments (jail, police, coast guards, etc.) are aware of the problem and have also expressed their desire to solve it, but their practical responses towards the suffering fishworkers and also towards any initiatives in this regard seem to be lukewarm. They often have a callous and non-committal attitude. In January 2002, the Prime Minister of India declared that no Pakistani fishermen will be captured due to the goodwill this country shares with Pakistan, and as a result the number of arrested fisherfolk decreased. However this lasted only for a short while, and very soon the chronicle of arrests and releases resumed.

The territorial waters are policed by coast guards, BSF, customs and army inland units. Patrolling of seas by these bodies is seen by the state as the 'bedrock of sovereignty'. They adopt means of coercion under the legitimacy of the state, fulfilling a prime function of the state, which is to police territory and people.[87] Thus in many cases, agencies arrest fishermen for spying, suspecting them to be terrorists. Indian fishermen are often interrogated about their relations with Research and Analysis Wing (RAW), while Pakistanis are investigated for their association with Inter-Services Intelligence (ISI). If terrorism is defined as a transnational crime, then by seeking illegal movement and entry into EEZs, either intentionally or unintentionally, these fisherfolk could be called terrorists. Or else, they are seen as criminals who have sought to cross the sea border illegally.

However, according to K. C. Pande, Commandant at District Headquarters of coast guards in Porbandar, there are no signals on the sea which demarcate the sea border. Moreover, there is no agreed boundary on the Arabian Sea between India and Pakistan. For their mutual convenience, the patrolling agencies have worked out an imaginary line along the Sir Creek region, off the coast of Kutch. He admitted that the fishing boats could unwillingly and unknowingly cross into the other's territory because of tidal currents, wind force, cyclone and engine failures. The captured Pakistani fishing boats lack navigational aids. Also, Pakistani fishing boats have never been found with arms and ammunitions on board.[88] We also need to acknowledge that declining fish catch on both sides and contemporary realities of transnational movements make these fisherfolk cross sea borders temporarily as acts of survival and livelihood.

But this does not stop the coast guards from continuing the blatant practice of arresting the innocent fishworkers, as it is seen as a part of efforts to control prohibited cross sea border flows. Mr. Pande said that when they spot boats trespassing, they arrest them, lodge an FIR and hand them over to the police. Their responsibility ends there; normally, they do not go to the courts and they have nothing to do with the exchange. According to him they have better things to do than this. The coast guard officials also candidly admit to the practice of 'tit for tat' among the enforcement agencies patrolling the territorial waters, where 'they capture so many of our boats and we capture that many in retaliation.'

At times, in moments of goodwill, the attitude of authorities also changes. Thus when in June 2001 both sides released fishermen, A. K. Mahajan, Director (Personnel) of the coast guards, said: 'We would now like to err on the side of caution and try and send the intruding fishing boats back to Pakistan instead of

Plate 3.3: Released Pakistani Fisherfolk Waiting in Police Camps at Porbandar for the Exchange to Take Place

sending the fishermen to jail.'[89] Mr. Jadeja and Mr. H. M. Shah, jailers in the Porbandar Jail, clarify that they do not inform the Pakistani High Commission on their own. The consular access for the Pakistani prisoners was available only in the Central Jail of Jodhpur, Rajasthan. But they were sent there only on the orders from the Union Home Ministry, routed through the Gujarat government. There are a large number of fishworkers who completed their period of conviction, but even then they waited in police camps at Porbandar for the exchange to take place (Plate 3.3). The so-called Police Headquarters at Porbandar became a new jail for them. Atul Karwal, DSP, Porbandar, in-charge of these particular cases of 'freed but fettered' fishworkers, accepted that these people should have been deported immediately on completion of conviction.[90]

Arbitrary orders are often passed by the state authorities. Box 3.4 shows one such order.

> Box 3.4: Order of the Central Excise and
> Customs Commissionerate, Ahmedabad
>
> 1. I order for absolute confiscation of the boat 'Al Madad' of Pakistani origin v/a Rs. 10,00,000 and the fish catch weighing 722 kgs. v/a Rs. 11,646 and other items found in the boat u/s 111(d) of the Customs Act 1962.
> 2. I also order for absolute confiscation of Foreign Currency of Pakistan Rs. 1,745 u/s 111(d) of the Customs Act 1962 read with section 30 of FERA.
> 3. I order for imposition of penalty of Rs. 1,000 each on each of the seven notices u/s 112(a) of the Customs Act 1962.
>
> K.K. Agarwal
> Commissioner of Customs
> Gujarat: Headquarters Ahmedabad
> Date: 30.3.2000

The official delegation, which usually goes to have a batch of fishermen released, is not without lacunae. The Government of Gujarat and the Ministry of Surface Transport sends delegates to get the fisherfolk released. However, middlemen often get involved, and demand 50–70 thousand rupees, usually from the boat-owners, to get their boat and the fishermen released.

The government officials also had some suggestions based on their specific experiences. For example, the DCP suggested that there should be a permanent structure to house the detained fishworkers, who have completed their conviction. The coast guard commandant proposed that there should be visible demarcation lines on the sea. In case of violations, the boats should be seized, but the crew and fishermen fined and released. Further, there must be separate and speedy courts for these types of offences.

Some other positive suggestions have also come from the authorities, but they have often remained on paper. It has repeatedly been proposed that a hotline be set up between coast guards of both countries to prevent the detention of fishermen who may have strayed into each other's waters and to tackle emergencies at sea. A hotline will mitigate the sufferings of fishermen.[91] Sureesh Mehta director general coast guard observes: 'The boundary is notional and no markers are possible on high seas. Unable to afford costly direction-finding equipment, fishermen stray into the maritime zone of the other country where they are arrested. At the time of arrest, they cannot understand the gravity of the crime.' It has also been stated that there should be a 'common fishing zone', a buffer zone, extending five nautical miles into each other's national maritime boundary, where no arrests will be made by either side. [92] We sincerely hope that something comes out of these talks, though till date nothing has been concretised.

The Pakistan marine security agencies believe that they should close the border as their maritime security is in grave danger from the Indian fisherfolk. Most of the officers justify the arrests of the fisherfolk by stating that they are 'just doing their jobs'. As an officer said, 'I do what I am hired to do, and that it is a matter of sacred duty to me'. However, this statement suggests that the discourse of work is often used as an instrument of state control, an instrument whereby certain sections of society are deprived of essential aspects of their humanity through the work of others.[93]

Efforts by Labour and Fisherfolk Groups

Since many years, the Fishworkers' Unions, Boatowners' Associations and trade unions of both countries have been asking from their respective governments to work out a long-term solution. In fact, the fishermen's organisations from both sides have often met to discuss this problem and offer solutions. Since 1988, Shree Akhil Gujarat Machhimar Mahamandal, Fishermen Boat Association at Diu, Porbandar Machhimar Boat Association, Gujarat Marine Products Exporters Association, NFF and others have sent several petitions and representations to the Indian government. Similar efforts from Pakistan's side have made a limited exchange of fishermen possible in recent years. It is only through the efforts of these associations that the respective governments are aware of the number of arrested fishermen of their respective country.

On 4 December 1996, labour leaders from India, Pakistan and Sri Lanka, representing the South Asian Labour Forum (SALF), met the Foreign Minister, I. K. Gujral and the Home Minister, Indrajit Gupta and drew their attention to this problem, and both of them assured immediate and long-term action. I. K. Gujral confirmed that no charges were levelled against any of the detained fishermen except on their violation of territorial waters of the respective countries. On 15 July 1997, 194 fishermen were freed due to the sustained efforts of SALF. Since then, SALF has been instrumental in the release of fishworkers in 1998 and also in 1999.[94]

The SALF has continuously demanded the unconditional release of all the detained persons and an end to the mid-sea arrest and imprisonment of fishermen. The SALF's Indian Chapter, which consists of central trade unions, like All India Trade Union Congress (AITUC), The Centre of Indian Trade Unions (CITU), Hind Mazdoor Sabha (HMS), Hind Mazdoor Kisan Panchayat (HMKP) and labour support groups like Centre for Education and Communication (CEC) have criticised the absence of a clear policy of action to prevent the arrest and detention of innocent fishermen. H. Mahadevan of AITUC said that the act of exchange currently was devoid of any clearly worked out policy. This did not give any guarantee that arbitrary arrests and illegal detentions would not happen again. The Forum demanded a bilateral agreement between India and Pakistan that clearly defined the maritime boundaries; the establishment of effective steps to make the boundary visible to the fishermen in the sea; and a regional agreement at the SAARC level, whereby the fishermen of South Asian countries could fearlessly and peacefully fish in the Arabian Sea, the Indian Ocean and the Bay of Bengal. Late Premjee Vhai Khokhari, then Secretary, NFF and Shri Porbandar Machhimar Boat Association—who was one of the consistent campaigners on this issue—showed us a number of petitions addressed to the Prime Minister, and Home and External Affairs Ministers. He told us that fear of arrests forced a number of fishermen to discontinue fishing. Despite such frequent happenings and their protests, no effective measures have been taken so far.

These organisations have also been making certain immediate and interim demands: they have requested the Gujarat government to provide interim relief of Rs. 2,000 per month for every fisherman detained in Pakistan, and demanded that the Prime Minister's Fund release money for the same. Premjee Vhai Khokhari further stated that recognised and registered bodies should go in a delegation to get the fisherfolk and the boats released, and should include delegates from boat-owners and fishermen's bodies.

In Pakistan, like efforts continue. The Fishermen's Cooperative Society Ltd., Karachi; the Fishermen's Union, Karachi; Pakistan

Institute of Labour Education and Research; Pakistan Chapter of SALF had taken up similar issue with the Pakistan government. Karamat Ali, Convenor of Pakistan Chapter of SALF, and Director of Pakistan Institute of Labour Education and Research (PILER) in one of his letters to Mohammad Nawaz Sharif, the then Prime Minister of Pakistan, commented that as long as the two governments could not take decisive action even in a matter that did not have anything to do with issues of national security of either country, but was surely a question of continued violation of the fundamental human rights of these fishermen, they felt there was no point in claiming that the two governments were sincerely working for the improvement of relations between the two countries. A team went to all the jails in Sindh where Indian fishermen were detained, and collected information on them. They also met 242 imprisoned Indian fishermen and delivered to each of them blankets, coats, towels, chappals, medicines and other basic things for daily use.

The PFF stated, 'It is important that legislation to deal with the arrest and detention of fishermen in other coastal states' waters should not violate the spirit of Article 73 of the 1982 Fisheries Convention, the 1976 International Covenant on Civil and Political Rights, and the 1976 International Covenant on Economic, Social and Cultural Rights'. It has further pointed out that if illegal operations were conducted within state territorial waters rather than EEZ, fishermen should not be more severely punished than they would for a similar violation within the EEZ.[95]

Muhammad Ali Shah says: 'Fishermen should not be made the victims of enmities and boundary disputes between the two countries. Nowhere in the world is such a practice in place. This is the tragedy of this region where fishermen are treated like prisoners of war.' Karamat Ali points out that even in cases of crossing of borders, fishermen are not guilty because there is no proper demarcation of sea borders between the two countries. He remarks: 'It is a criminal negligence on the part of both the countries. There should be a demarcation according to the UN Sea Conventions. Further, according to international sea laws, the maximum punishment for fishermen on violation is seizing their fish-catch. But in this case, they end up serving ten years in prison.'

Nationalist Jingoism?

During our fieldwork, while being extremely moved by many of the narratives of fisherfolk and activists, we also felt that it was equally important to be careful while chronicling these stories. They should not become another means to arouse anti-Pakistan sentiments, or to exacerbate the already existing rivalries, since often attempts were made to show that Indian authorities were more humane, while those on the other side of the border were decidedly more cruel and vice versa. This revealed a xenophobic dark side of nationalism. The coast guards, local intelligence bureau, central customs, naval intelligence unit and the district police in Gujarat for example at one point tried to show that the Pakistani navy was not only instigating its fishermen to sail into Indian waters, but also that it was projecting some of the small ports on the Gujarat coast as being a part of Pakistan's territory. It was even stated that some Pakistani fishermen had confessed to being sea pirates who looted Indian fishermen at sea.[96] Our study, however, revealed that more Indian fishermen tended to stray towards Pakistan borders than vice versa, as the sea on the Pakistani side has more marine life.

There was a flip side to many of the narratives in India, particularly when rumours of grave torture of Indian fisherfolk in Pakistani jails gained currency, with some vernacular magazines even attempting to arouse a nationalist frenzy out of this.[97] Similarly while the case of boat-owners is also very genuine, often their letters written to the authorities are problematically worded. Thus states Manish Lodhari: 'Pakistan Marine Forces had forcibly captured our five fishing boats from Indian water territory approx. before 2 months (on 30 January 2000) and our crews on those boats have also been taken away to Pakistan…. Pakistan is already on the map of cruelty, due to which, I along with the aggrieved family of crews, am worried for the life of the crews.'[98]

Even fisherfolk organisations at times arouse feelings of nationalist jingoism by claiming that the condition of Indian fisherfolks in Pakistani jails is much worse than the other way round. They also show that the Pakistani coast guards and authorities are crueler. Thus, Balubhai Socha, President of Saurashtra Paryavaran Suraksha Parishad, while expressing his concern for the arrested Indian fisherfolk, also repeatedly stressed: 'Pakistani marine guards have been victimising Indian fishermen, and arresting them even at a small pretext. It is they who have been violating human rights and it is their security guards who have been breaking the law. We are much more humane on the Indian side.'[99]

In other words, the problem is stated as not 'us' but 'them'. 'We' are good, while 'they' are bad. Even sensitive activists like Premjee Vhai Khokhari succumbed to this and stated that the problem was much more acute from the Pakistani side.

Our feeling is that while it may be true that often there are more Indians in Pakistani jails than vice versa, one important reason for this can be that the catchment around Pakistan coast is much more than that around the Indian coast. With rapid depletion of catch off the Saurashtra coast, many fisherfolk from Gujarat are venturing into the waters off the Rann of Kutch and the Indus delta, which is close to Pakistan. Further, the number of Indian fisherfolk and boats far exceed those in Pakistan. A third reason can also be that the Kutch sea tidal wave current tends to take the Indian boats more to that side. Thus rather than blaming each other or trying to prove that the other side is more cruel, a more fruitful approach is to realise that ordinary fisherfolk on both sides are victims, and need solutions worked in harmony and not in retaliation.

Conclusion

Fisherfolk continue to be detained on the high seas. Both India and Pakistan inhabit a political system that elevates borders, boundaries and abstract security concerns as engines of an imagined nation—a nation that cannot feel the misery and suffering of the poor fisherfolk. They see these fisherfolk as standing outside the definitions of nation-state and its boundaries, who need to be taught a lesson. While the authorities of the two countries invariably cite the issue of national interests, they appear to have ignored two major questions—the fisherfolk's right to resources and livelihood and the incompatibility of their national laws with regard to the seas and international laws and conventions. Shouldn't questions of livelihood, of human dignity and the right to live feature in any discussion of national security and the drawing of borders? The daily life practices of coastal fisherfolk cannot be treated as criminal activities. Criminalising or victimising the cross-border movements of fisherfolk will only force them to continue to move through more illicit channels, and remain vulnerable, stigmatised and illegitimate. As remarks Thomas Kocherry, a leading light of the NFF, 'People are more important than territory and all the borders in the world.'[100]

At an abstract level, the need of the times is to have a region of productive ambiguity, in which there is a decentralisation of settled conventions. We need to move away from unnecessary anxieties of national security and border threats; they are one of an endless series of efforts to corral the future and subject various people to yet another arbitrary discipline.

The history, actions and voices of the coastal fisherfolk of India and Pakistan reveal similar concerns and problems. Theirs is a space where one can seek and discern the strains in nationhood, as they posit a radical and subversive potential. Their journeys pose a challenge both to the nation-state and the fictional sea boundaries buttressed by it. Institutionalisation of the rights of these coastal fisherfolk is not only needed to protect their interests; it can perhaps lead to a reduction in cross-border tensions and be a step towards peace and democracy.

4

The Killing Waters:
India and Sri Lanka

The consul banged on the table and said:
'If you've got no passport you're officially dead'.
But we are still alive, my dear, but we are still alive.
W.H. Auden[1], Collected shorter poems 1930–1944

Date	9 February 2001
Court	Judicial First Class Magistrate, Kochi, Kerala
Complainant	State Represented by the S.I. of Police
Accused	Sisira Fernando, Vieyna Mahadev, Sri Lanka
	Stanly Reginol Fernando, Varuthanpolothoduwavu, Sri Lanka
	Upply Hedson, Hilset Magono, Sri Lanka
	Kjan Fernando, Thirukolombu, Sri Lanka
	John Pauli Karp, Jayasuryavath Pahhle Ettanerya, Sri Lanka
Offence	Violation of Maritime Zone of India Act 1981
Plea	Not Guilty
Finding	Guilty
Sentence or Order	Sentenced to pay fine of Rs. 1 lakh each and in default, to undergo sentence for six months each. The fishing vessels, fishing gear, equipments, cargo and sale proceeds of the fish found in the vessels is confiscated by the Government of India.

It was in early 2001, when Sisira and four others were interrogated by the magistrate in court. They were furnished with copies of prosecution records; particulars of the offence were read out and simultaneously explained to them with the help of an interpreter: On 12 February 2000 five fishing vessels with 29 crew members transgressed into the Indian Ocean and poached fish from the EEZ of India. The Indian coast guards detected and apprehended them, found frozen and fresh fish in the vessel and took them to a police station in Kochi. The police registered cases against them, and the magistrate's court in Kochi—designated under the MZI Act—proceeded with the case. Prosecution witnesses and exhibits like inspection reports, navigation chart, list of inventory and extract of log register were presented. Defence witnesses and their exhibits and material objects were nil. After the court proceedings, the accused were taken to different jails in Kerala. On that day, the magistrate was eager to hear the accused speak because until then the language and the lengthy proceedings had not given any opportunity to the accused to speak for themselves.

The exchange between the government lawyer and Sisira was as follows:

> Lawyer: Which country are you from?
> Sisira: I belong to the Tamil fishermen community.
> Lawyer: Yes. But where do you belong to—Sri Lanka or India?
> Sisira: To the Tamil land.
> Lawyer: Oh! Which country, which place?
> Sisira: I live in Sri Lanka. My forefathers lived in India. Relatives are here and there. I go off and on to meet them. I work and live in the sea. India or Sri Lanka does not come to me.
> Lawyer: What is your citizenship? What passport do you hold?
> Sisira: What is citizenship? Passport? I have none.
> Lawyer: But you came from the Sri Lankan side. Your vessel is licensed there. Thus, you are a Sri Lankan, trespassing into India.

The magistrate saw that the public prosecutor was getting nowhere. He said, 'You know there are many kinds of citizens and non-citizens under the state laws. You came from the Sri Lankan shores; you are not offering any mitigating proof to disapprove that.' Thereafter he wrote, 'Sri Lankan, trespassing into India—a fit case to invoke the benevolent provisions of the MZI Act.'[2]

The few words of Sisira, subsumed completely in the magistrate's ruling, reveal the sheer domination of the state's claim to the seas, borders and citizenship. Whenever coastal fisherfolk of India and Sri Lanka give a voice to break the trappings of rigid boundaries, there is an agreement between the rival states for a clear classification of coastal borders, in order to locate and fix identities, and lives and livelihoods of the subjects there. While Sisira was comfortable and could deal with ambiguities of identities, the anxieties that both the state and its forms of social management face when confronted with blurred communities and cultures, places and practices, were also revealed.[3] Such ambiguities on the one hand and anxieties on the other are endless.

The Manifold (Ab)uses of Law

Consider the hundreds of ways in which the law and the legal processes can be used against the fisherfolk with regard to coastal borders between India and Sri Lanka. Here the law and its discourse is quite clearly a discourse of power, where the fishworker is denied any recognition as a subject of concern in his own right, even over a space that has been his own. The Indian and Sri Lankan states become the natural governors and custodians of the seas, and this eventually becomes the dominant, indeed the only mode of reference on this subject.

India and Sri Lanka share a maritime border of more than 400 kilometres, which cuts across three different seas: the Bay of Bengal in the north, the Palk Bay in the centre and the Gulf of Mannar (which opens to the Indian Ocean) in the south. The geographical aspect is worth mentioning here. The maritime boundary (also know as the International Boundary Line or IBL) is quite close to the shores of both countries in the Palk Bay region, where the maximum distance between two countries is only around 45 kilometres, and the minimum is just 16 kilometres—between Dhanushkodi on the Indian coast and Thalaimannar on the Sri Lankan coast (see Map 4.1). Crossing the IBL would imply entry into the territorial waters (12 nautical miles or 22 kilometres) rather than the EEZ. The distances between the Indian coast and the Sri Lankan coast are longer in the Bay of Bengal and the Gulf of Mannar. As far as the Gulf of Mannar is concerned, except for a few centres like Mandapam, south of Rameswaram, the distances are substantial. With regard to the Bay of Bengal, except for centres close to Pt. Calimere (Kodikarai), the distances to Sri Lanka are considerable.[4]

Even before the Law of the Sea was negotiated at the United Nations and India declared its 200 nautical miles of EEZ, there existed maritime agreements of 1974 and 1976 between India and Sri Lanka. The 1974 Agreement demarcated the maritime

Map 4.1: India and Sri Lanka

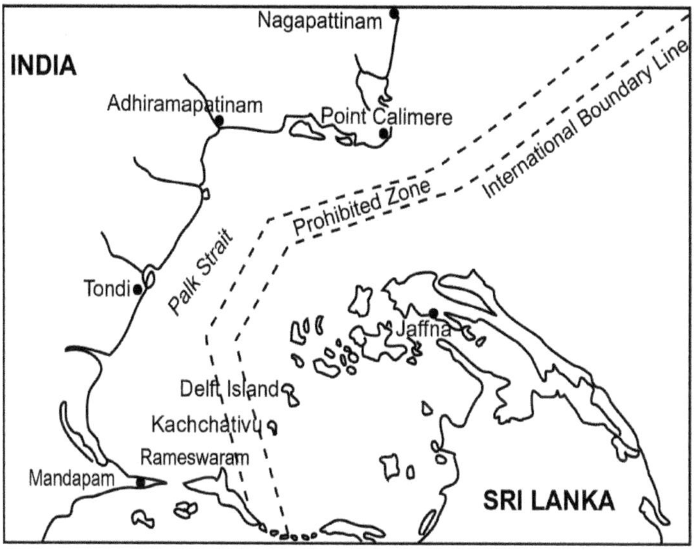

boundary between India and Sri Lanka in the Palk Strait and ceded Kachchativu to Sri Lanka. The 1976 Agreement demarcated the boundary in the Gulf of Mannar and the Bay of Bengal and barred each country's fishermen from fishing in the other's waters.

The 1974 Agreement ceded Kachchativu to Sri Lanka. It is a small, uninhabited island, and is situated in the Palk Strait at a distance of 8 and 10 miles from the nearest points of Sri Lanka and India, respectively. With cession, Article 5 of the agreement said, 'Subject to the foregoing, Indian fishermen and pilgrims will enjoy access to visit Kachchativu as hitherto, and will not be required by Sri Lanka to obtain travel documents or visas for these purposes.' And Article 6 said, 'The vessels of India and Sri Lanka will enjoy in each other's waters such rights as they have traditionally enjoyed therein.' Moreover, the Lok Sabha was informed on 23 July 1974 by the External Affairs Minister, Swaran Singh (citing a 1921 Agreement):

The Western side of the fishery line was the exclusive fishery right of the Indian citizens and to the east of that was the right of Sri Lankan fishermen. But in spite of that division, the fishermen generally were free to fish round about Kachchativu and they also used the Kachchativu island for drying their nets.... About the traditional rights... he will get the answer... that although Sri Lanka's claim to sovereignty over Kachchativu has been recognised, the traditional rights of Indian fishermen and pilgrims to visit the island remain unaffected.[5]

On the basis of this, V. Suryanarayan, a well-known Indian academic on this subject, argued, 'Article 5, read in conjunction with Swaran Singh's statement, clearly provided for the continuation of the rights of Indian fishermen to fish even round about Kachchativu.'[6]

But the Government of Sri Lanka rejected this standpoint and claimed that Article 5 did not confer any fishing rights, but only the right to dry the fishing nets and the right of the pilgrims to visit Kachchativu for religious purposes. The Indian side argued that there is a fallacy in this line of reasoning. It contended that the drying of nets pre-supposes that the nets had become wet and this could happen only if they had been used for fishing in and around Kachchativu.[7]

The 1976 Agreement was entitled 'Agreement between India and Sri Lanka on the Maritime Boundary Between the Two Countries in the Gulf of Mannar and the Bay of Bengal and Related Matters'. There was an exchange of letters on the same day between India's Foreign Secretary and Sri Lanka's Secretary to the Ministry of Defence and Foreign Affairs. These letters also constituted an agreement between two countries. Significantly, this agreement was done when India was under Emergency and no discussion or dissent was given any space. Paragraph I of the Exchange of Letters read:

With the establishment of the EEZs by the two countries, India and Sri Lanka will exercise sovereign rights over the living and non-living resources of their respective zone. The fishing vessels and fishermen of India shall not engage in fishing in the historic waters, the territorial sea and the EEZ of Sri Lanka, nor shall the fishing vessels and fishermen of Sri Lanka engage in fishing in the historic waters, the territorial sea and the EEZ of India, without the express permission of Sri Lanka or India, as the case may be.[8]

It was the different interpretations of this portion of the Exchange of Letters and of Article 5 in the 1974 Agreement that led to the controversy over whether or not Indian fishermen had the right to fish in and around Kachchativu.[9] The Sri Lankan government argued that the relevant portion of the Exchange of Letters superseded Articles 5 and 6 of the 1974 Agreement. However, V. Suryanarayan argues:

> If these two statements, categorical in nature, are applicable to all sectors of India's maritime boundaries with Sri Lanka, including the Palk Straits, what happens to the fishermen's rights guaranteed in Article 5 of the 1974 Agreement? Were the rights secured in 1974 bartered away in 1976? Or, to be more specific, did the fishermen in 1974 have only the right of 'access to Kachchativu' (for drying the nets) and not any fishing rights?[10]

On the other hand, Sri Lankans also have a sense of loss regarding 1974 and 1976 agreements. According to Soosai Anandan, Reader in Geography, University of Jaffna, the very productive Wadge Bank, south of Kanyakumari, went entirely to India. Even though India allowed fishing by Sri Lankan fishermen in the Wadge Bank for some years, the benefit was only for the Western Province; the Northern Province fishermen had no real chance to fish in the Wadge Bank. As far as the Pedro Bank on the northern side is concerned, two-thirds of it went to India after the boundary was demarcated. Thus, the fishermen of the Northern Province have limited fishing areas.

The agreement or any of its provisions were not discussed with the state governments, fisherfolk organisations or political parties. It was also not debated in the Indian Parliament before its commencement. There were said to be other dominant considerations among the head of the states.[11] The aftermath of the 1971 insurrection of the Janatha Vimukthi Peramuna (JVP) witnessed a sharp fall in the credibility of Bandaranaike's government in Sri Lanka. The country went through a severe economic and political crisis. Thus, the Kachchativu settlement contributed to a large extent in lifting the morale of the Bandaranaike regime. The Maritime Boundary Settlement between the two countries also helped in curbing the anti-India hysteria in Sri Lanka. In fact, the agreement strengthened the relations between the governments of Indira Gandhi and Sirimavo Bandaranaike.

Sri Lanka also extended its support to India on some vital issues. While several countries condemned India's 'peaceful' nuclear explosion in May 1974, Sri Lanka accepted India's stance on using its newly acquired nuclear capability only for peaceful uses. Besides, when Pakistan tried to use the 15-member ad-hoc UN Committee as a forum to condemn India over the nuclear explosion, Sri Lanka in its capacity as Chairman of the Committee prevented the forum from doing so. The decision to concede Kachchativu to Sri Lanka has also been justified in the larger interest of India's diplomatic initiatives to mend fences with its neighbours, which received an impetus after the liberation of Bangladesh.[12]

Although the issue of rights and representations of the fisherfolk has been commented upon, the fact remains that the state dictates the domain and the character of fisherfolk problems. In the process, it assimilates the fishworker as merely an element in the march of the nation-state. Even a critic of the agreements, who is under no obligation to think like a bureaucrat–diplomat, is conditioned to write on the issue of fisherfolk as if it is some other issue—that of peace and security, or bilateral relations, and agreements. Both Sri Lanka and India want to claim their sovereign territories in the seas and the maritime laws become critical tools for this purpose. The legal processes and their implementation, especially with regard to fisherfolk make the needs of the nation-state more forthright. They enforce the need to adhere to defined territories and refuse to allow their subjects to operate anywhere beyond their domain. The legal processes open up ways, implicating state laws in the suppression and the suffering of the fisherfolk. It also reveals the complex, cruel, cunning and subtle forms in which the state rein-forces deeply drawn zones, relations and roles. The implementation of laws and agreements is an act which regularly contributes to the suffering of fisherfolk, through the very construction of its role and responsibilities.

We hear a case story from H. Mahadevan, deputy general secretary of the All India Trade Union Congress (AITUC): On 25 May 1998, 15 Sri Lankan fishermen were freed from the Madurai Jail in Mandapam. They had been charged under the Customs Act for 'smuggling' sharkskins. Nothing incriminating was found in the vessels and the only material available was fish. A 'confession' was obtained to the effect that sharkskins were being brought for sale in India to obtain a better price. Sri Lanka has a much better price for marine fish than India and sharkskins is an internationally traded item for which no significant price differences are likely. In fact, merchant exploitation ensures that our beach prices are often lower than they should be. Customs at Tuticorin levied a penalty of 47,000 rupees. In addition, they also went for a prosecution in the court. The owner of one of the boats arrived in India and he arranged for the boats and the fishermen to be released. What followed was a miscarriage of justice and innocent fishermen were convicted as common smugglers.[13] In September 2001, the *Sea Queen* boat with four Sri Lankan fishermen on board was arrested in the Andaman and Nicobar Islands. The skipper was charged under the Maritime Zones of India Act 1981, while the crew-members were charged under the Andaman and Nicobar Fisheries Regulations 1938.[14]

Plate 4.1: John, Sebastian and Arulanandan

On 14 July 1997, five Indian fishermen—John, Sebastian, Arulanandan, Austin and George—from Ramanathapuram district, Tamil Nadu were in a mechanised fishing boat when they were suddenly attacked and fired by the Sri Lankan navy (see Plate 4.1). Their boat got damaged and it drowned. Sebastian showed the deep

cuts of a wound on his right hand as he narrated the course of events. Austin and George died on the spot. The rest swam to the Nedundhevve Island in Sri Lanka. There some Sri Lankan fishermen rescued them and a local organisation took them to Jaffna for medical treatment. After hospitalisation for five days, they were jailed in Jaffna and produced before a court. There were no cases against them, but after every 14 days they were shuttled between the court and the jail. They were in the jail for five and a half months. The families of the dead fishermen are not adequately compensated; they also haven't received the death certificates. Sebastian's right hand is permanently crippled and he is unable to fish any more. He is anxious about his future, as he is married with three children and they are now dependent on his father. The owner of the destroyed boat, K. Raj, now works as a helper on somebody else's boat.

The process from arrest to release of the Indian fisherfolk are as follows: After being apprehended, they are usually charged for trespassing into the Sri Lankan territory. Quite often, the charges may be under the Prevention of Terrorism Act. In the initial few weeks, they are shunted from location to location and kept in more than one jail. The actual court case and the entire process vary and remain uncertain. Only the pressure from the Indian side leads to a compromise or a withdrawal of the case. After the withdrawal or settlement of the case, the fishermen are taken to the Mirihana camp in Colombo. Once in the camp, they wait for the Indian government and the Indian High Commission in Colombo to work out the details of repatriation. Quite often, the fishermen would return to India after having spent anywhere between three months to a year in Sri Lanka, only to be confronted with the problem of getting their boats back. There are innumerable cases where retrieving the boats has been extremely difficult and many of them have been damaged beyond salvage. Some fishermen complain of bitter experiences, of third degree methods, by Sri Lankan policemen.

The situation is worse for the Sri Lankan fishermen. The Indian coast guards try to strictly implement the MZI Act and capture Sri Lankan boats promptly, which have strayed in the Indian EEZ. On shore, the fishermen and boats are handed over to the civilian authorities; police stations take charge of the fishermen. Usually, the fishermen are charged for violating the MZI Act, the Passport

Act and the Foreigners' Act. They are produced before the designated court for MZI offences and are then remanded until a final decision is taken. It takes a long time for the authorities to take a decision on the fate of the jailed fishermen. Both state and central governments have to coordinate between themselves. It is the Home Department that takes up the matter on behalf of the state government and at the central level, the Ministries of Home, External Affairs and Agriculture are involved in deciding the course of action. The state government makes the necessary inquiries about the bona fides of the arrested fishermen and then sends a report to the Central Government. If all the three ministries give their 'no objection', the cases are withdrawn and the fishermen are sent home. The withdrawal of cases is a long, cumbersome process involving a great deal of red tape. It is rare for the arrested Sri Lankan fishermen to return home within few months. Often the whole process can take up to a year. 'It is extremely unfortunate that fishermen are held up to a year in prison on remand for offences, which are not punishable with imprisonment, or for offences that the Government of India is not ready to prosecute', comments V. Vivekanandan, Convener, Alliance for Release of Innocent Fishermen (ARIF).

Tormented Bodies: Fisherfolk and their Families

Pathinathan, S. P. Royappan, Susha Raj, John, Sebastian, M. Sahayam and Pandi were among those thousands of marine fishers of Palk Bay, who fished in the seas bordering India and Sri Lanka. They got arrested, injured, harassed and even killed in the sea. Their boats were drowned or captured, never to be returned. Sri Lankan fishermen—K. S. Nicholas, W. Wilbert, K. S. Joseph Washingtoo, Sirinimal Fernando, Wijendra Waduge Chandra and many more—met the same fate in the seas in the hands of the Indian navy and coast guards.[15] The fishermen of both countries were being charged for illegal entries into the sea territory of each other's countries for fishing. They all suffer continuously and it is an everyday problem. Paradoxically, their living and working is not concerned with how to avoid suffering, but how to suffer. That is, how to make the physical pain, the personal loss, the physical defeat or the helpless contemplation of other's agony bearable. Their pain and suffering arise from the sheer compulsions of their daily life and disrupt their whole known world. They go through the brutal experiences actively created by the sea order. On their bodies, they bear the stamp of authority of the organs of the nation-states.

Tamil Nadu has a fisherman population of about 0.69 million, of which 0.262 million fishermen from 591 marine fishing villages located along the east coast are actively engaged in fishing. As per the government records, 10,278 mechanised fishing boats and 49,000 traditional crafts (including 20,000 crafts motorised with outboard motors) are active in marine fishing.[16] Fisherfolk live on the fringes of society with comparatively poor development indicators. The density of population in the affected fishing villages is almost three times higher than the average density of population in the state. In terms of literacy levels, sex ratio and life expectancy, fisherfolk compare very poorly with the rest of society in all the affected districts (see Tables 4.1–4.4).

Table 4.1: Fisherfolk Population in the Main Affected Districts in Tamil Nadu

District	Number of Fishing Villages	Marine Fisherfolk Population
Chennai	44	77,067
Cuddalore	49	44,014
Nagapattinam	51	86,516
Kanyakumari	42	149,607
State (Total)	591	737,203

Table 4.2: Population Density in Fishing Villages along the Tamil Nadu Coast

District	Population Density in District	Population Density in Fishing Villages	Fisherfolk Per sq. km of Coastline	Active Fishermen Per sq. km of Inshore Waters (0–50 metres depth)
Cuddalore	626	1,412	706	17
Nagapattinam	548	849	425	9
Kanyakumari	992	3,858	1,929	26
State (Average)	478	1,338	669	

Table 4.3: Literacy Rates in Affected Fishing Villages in Tamil Nadu

District	Entire District	Fishing Villages	Percentage Gap between District and Fishing Villages
Chennai	80	68	12
Cuddalore	72	59	13
Nagapattinam	77	57	20
Kanyakumari	88	78	10

Table 4.4: Sex Ratio in Affected Fishing Villages in Tamil Nadu
(Number of women per thousand population)

District	Entire District	Fishing Villages	Gap in the Number of 'Missing Women' in Fishing Villages When Compared to the Rest of the District
Chennai	951	944	7
Cuddalore	985	946	39
Nagapattinam	1,014	955	59
Kanyakumari	1,013	942	71
State (Average)	985	957	28

Source: All tables, Frontline, 11 February 2005, pp. 15–18.

In the Palk Bay region, in which the island of Kachchativu is located and which divides the coastal regions of Nagapattinam, Quaid-e-Millath, Thanjavur, Pudukkottai and Ramanathapuram districts from Sri Lanka—firing, detention and jailing of fishermen is a regular event. On 22 February 1998, an Indian fisherman, Krishnan, of Menandai near Rameswaram, was killed by the Sri Lankan navy. On 4 March, Indian coast guards arrested three Sri Lankan trawlers and their 15-member crew in the Gulf of Mannar on charges of violating the Maritime Zones Act. On 11 May, an Indian fishing boat was fired upon off Talaimannar and out of the five-member crew, three were arrested. The arrests have continued; for example, in June 2004, 15 Sri Lankan fishermen were arrested off Nagapattinam.[17]

On 3 June 1997, five Sri Lankan fishermen were arrested in the Indian waters. On 10 June, Ganesan and three other Indian fishermen went for fishing and were fired upon by a Sri Lankan patrol boat. Ganesan was injured on his legs and shoulders and the others escaped. On 12 June, four fishermen from Rameswaram went for fishing in the night, when a Sri Lankan naval vessel fired on the boat. A fisherman, Lourduraj, fell inside the boat with bullet wounds and the other three jumped into the sea and swam to safety. On 18 July, two Sri Lankan naval helicopters allegedly sprayed bullets on a motorised country boat off Nagapattinam coast, killing two fishermen on the spot. In 1996, the External Affairs Minister, I. K. Gujral informed the Indian Parliament that 11 Indian fishermen were killed in 20 incidents of shooting at the Indian fishing vessels. The Sri Lankan navy had acknowledged its involvement in three incidents, but denied responsibility in other reported cases.[18]

These individual incidents over the years have been taking a heavy toll. The Tamil Nadu government presented the situation till 1991, 'Since 1983, till the end of August 1991, there have been 236 incidents of attacks by the Sri Lankan navy on the Tamil Nadu fishermen. Three hundred and three boats have been attacked and 486 fishermen have been affected. Fifty-one boats have been destroyed. One hundred and thirty-five fishermen have been attacked and injured. Over 50 fishermen have been killed. Fifty-seven fishermen have been injured in firing incidents. The Sri Lankan navy has seized 65 motorboats and arrested 205 fishermen. There has been an increase in these incidents, particularly this year [1991].' Further, in November 1993, the Tamil Nadu government noted that in the last three years, the Sri Lankan navy had killed 25 Tamil Nadu fishermen in firing. Besides, 109 were injured. A total of 136 attacks had taken place on fishing boats; 15 of these had sunk. Thus, these incidents occur more frequently and dangerously.[19] On 9 May 2007, the Indian Defence Minister stated in Parliament that the Sri Lankan navy had killed 77 Indian fisherfolk from 1991 to mid-April 2007.

Rameswaram, an island in the Ramanathapuram district, is situated in the south-central Bay of Bengal coast of Tamil Nadu. Its coastline is of 80 kilometres approximately, a land area of 15 square miles, and a fishing community of around 35,000, of which 8,000 are active sea-going fishermen. In the island's south is the Gulf of Mannar and on the north, Palk Bay. On the eastern tip of the island is Dhanushkodi from where it is only about 16 kilo-metres to Talaimannar of Sri Lanka. In Pamban village near Rameswaram, Saghai Nagar is a settlement of 1,000 fishermen where a large number of sea-going fishermen witnessed firing, injuries, detention of fishermen and damage to boats in the seas by the Sri Lankan navy (see Plate 4.2). Here, 45-year-old Pathinathan lived with his wife and six children. He recounted the time when he had a country boat. On 5 November 1996, he and three others went for fishing. It was a very windy and stormy night and their boat crossed to the Sri Lankan side near Talaimannar. When they realised this, they started to return. Suddenly, they were confronted and surrounded by a Sri Lankan navy boat. They begged for mercy, but the navy kept on firing and shouting at them. It captured them, took off their shirts, tied them around their eyes and beat them up. Thereafter, they were taken to the Manar jail in Sri Lanka. Next day they were produced in a court in Kothi Manar. They were in Manar jail for two more days and from there they were taken to Marihana police station for a week. The fishermen went on a hunger strike for one and a half days, as they were getting very less food and that too at odd hours.[20]

Plate 4.2: The Family of a Dead Fisherman in Pamban Village

Pathinathan added that after 10 torturous days in captivity, an official from the Indian Embassy met them and assured them that they will get justice. But they had to spend 100 days in several police stations and jails before they were taken to Jaffna and handed over to an Indian naval ship mid-sea. His life and work have changed after this incident. They did not get their boat back. They had to go to Talaimannar in Sri Lanka on five occasions to get it back and when after four months of their release, they got the boat—it was badly damaged and without the engine. They never received any compensation for loss of work, employment, boat or engine. Their families survived only on loans. Now Pathinathan was no longer a boat-owner but only a boat worker with huge financial debts.

Susha Raj of the same settlement was the owner of the boat *RMS-30*. He took a bank loan to purchase the boat worth Rs. 500,000. On 5 January 1995, the sole bread-earner of his six-member family along with six others went fishing. At night around 11 o'clock, near Kachchativu, the Sri Lankan navy opened fire at them. Susha Raj narrated:

> Everybody except me was missing. We went to the sea next day to search for others. We found the body of a co-fisherman, Arulanandan. On the second day of our search operation we found the dead body of Vinanzis, another co-fisherman. On the third and fifth day of our search into the sea, we found the dead bodies of Michal, Panja Fllice and Anthony near Irumeni and Sashmanakodhi seashore, all co-fishermen. The last dead body of Moscow was found near Danushkodi after the seventeenth day of the incident.[21]

Susha Raj is a coolie with heavy debt. He was fortunate to be saved, but the situation of the remaining families of the other six haunts him everyday.

Ganpati from the same village, had one hand amputed after a bullet injury by the Sri Lankan navy. Satya Sellan lost his one leg due to the merciless beating by the navy in the seas. Xavier, another fisherman of the same village, bitterly stated that the government figures of deaths and injuries were quite partial. They had estimated that in the last seven years, around 600 Indian fishermen were shot dead and an equal number had been injured. If this continues, they would have to leave fishing and take to begging.

In another village Vercode, 22-year-old Antony Doss worked as a coolie in a fishing boat. In the first week of May 1998, he went in Anananth's boats to fish near Talaimannar. He had a very troublesome experience for days together. There were eight boats in their group, which went fishing together in the sea. The Sri Lankan navy captured all the boats, but they released four boats instantly. The captive four boats were kept in the sea in Talaimannar under the constant vigil of the navy. They were forced to do fishing for four days and the catch was taken away. No food was given, except one bread in the morning and evening.[22] On December 1997, fisherman Sahayraj along with four other fishermen of the same village, left for fishing in his boat *RMS 1829* but never returned. All the four other fishermen disappeared. The parents keep asking about their sons, but Sahayraj had no answers. He had spent around Rs. 40,000 to search for them. He suspected that the Sri Lankan navy must have hit their boat and all of them must have drowned in the sea. Sahayraj was arrested in March 1998, when he along with three other crew members went for fishing near Nedundhevve Island. The Sri Lankan navy captured all of them. Their belongings comprising fish catch, compass, radio, tape recorder etc., were confiscated. They were badly beaten up and were released after 24 hours. He asked, 'Is this the 50th year of independence for us? Our very lives and livelihood are in danger and no government does anything.'[23] Thirty-one-year-old fisherman M. Sahayam was detained, arrested and harassed 13 times in the last eight years. He recounts an incident in 1994, when in one go, the Sri Lankan navy captured 18 boats and all 70–80 fishermen were taken to the Talaimannar naval camp. For 24 hours, he was forced to do menial work without food. 'What can you do when you cannot see the border? But in this situation, we cannot continue fishing. There is however no other way out', he lamented.[24]

Various incidents came to light, which were not officially being counted: On 19 November 1997, two boats (Nos. *RMS-1986* and *R-350*) left from Rameswaram for fishing. Both sunk in the sea due to firing by a Sri Lankan naval ship—killing eight fishermen. An FIR was lodged, death certificates were procured and claims were made, but no compensation is given till date. A fisher woman Irulayi from Rameswaram said that her husband went for fishing on 20 November 1989, but did not return. She has neither a death certificate, nor has received any compensation.

Felix Gomez, assistant director, Fisheries, of Rameswaram gave the following figure of casualties of Indian fishermen: From 1983 to 1997, 74 fishermen were shot dead and 251 injured in the sea.[25] It was not only limited to Rameswaram region; fishermen of Pudukkottai and Nagapattinam districts were also suffering heavily. On 29 January 1990, James, Chellathurai, Karuppan and Raja went to fish in their mechanised boat, *ARS-32 Arulmurugar*, from Kottaipattinam in Pudukkottai district. The Sri Lankan navy fired at them; the boat caught fire and sunk and Raja died in the firing. On 20 May 1991, the fishing boat *BDK-609 MP* started from Jegathapattinam along with four fishermen. It capsized in the sea due to heavy firing by the Sri Lankan navy and the four fishermen have still not been found. Muthuvel, Rajendra, Samsu, Justin, Kumar Ravi and many more like them from this district had suffered or been injured in firings. Chinnathambi, Murugan, Veerappan, Govindarasu and many more were missing for many years, after various incidents of firing. In Nagapattinam district, many fishermen live with injuries on their limbs or chests after several instances of firings in the sea. Since April 1990, Palyaniyandi, Subramanian, Kuttiyandi, Rajakannu and Anandavel were traceless from the border areas of the sea. Losses of fishnets, confiscations of fish catch or damage to catamarans were immense.

Sri Lanka has a coastline of 1,800 kilometres and a continental shelf of 31,250 square kilometres. Nearly 54.3 per cent of its population lives in coastal districts. The south-western coastal districts stretching from just north of Colombo to Galle has 15 per cent of the total land area, but more than 40 per cent of the population live here. A majority of this population is dependent on fisheries. Sri Lankan women have been engaged in various fisheries-related activities, such as harvesting and post-harvesting activities, since a long time. A close collaboration between women and men in day-to-day activities is evident in the chain of activities from production, to when fish or fish products reach the consumer. The role of women in fisheries varies with ethnicity and religion. In the Catholic communities along the western coast, women play an active role in fish handling and marketing at the beach. Participation of women in active fishing and net mending activities is also noted in these communities. In the predominantly Buddhist southern coastal fishing communities, the presence of women at the beach is not socially accepted and they hardly get involved directly in fisheries activities. Overall, fisher women's contribution to earning supplementary incomes remains quite high and far exceeds that of their men. Many women prepare food for sale, for which they are forced to get up early in the morning and take the cooked food to the nearby boutique or hotel for sale. In the southern fishing communities, women are involved in various other activities like rope making (from Dondra to Rekawa), brick making (Kirinda, Thissmaharama, Medilla and Marakolliya), agriculture (Kahamodera, Rekawa, Kirinda and Hambantota) and animal husbandry (Kirinda and Hambantota), which bring in supplementary income. Instances of fisher women getting engaged in ornamental fish farming, pond fish farming to raise fingerlings from fry (to be subsequently released in tanks or reservoirs), making packets of powdered condiments for sale and working in fish processing sector have also been reported, although the exact numbers are not known.[26] However, it is the men who largely go for fishing in the seas and get arrested, leaving behind their intensely suffering womenfolk.

Like their Indian counterparts, Sri Lankan fishermen are also caught regularly in the seas by the Indian coast guards and the navy. There have been different estimations of their numbers at different times. According to one Sri Lankan newspaper report, in 1998 around 80 Sri Lankan fishermen were under detention in India and their 25 vessels had been confiscated.[27] In the same year, S. Gautama Dasa, deputy high commissioner of Sri Lanka stated that according to their information, there were more than 100 Sri Lankan fishermen in Indian jails.[28] According to National Fisheries Solidarity, a network of Sri Lankan fisheries organisation, 224 Sri Lankan fishermen were arrested and imprisoned between 1995 and 1997 and an average of 69 boats per year were arrested in the same period (see also Table 4.5).[29]

Sebastian Appuhamy, a boat-owner from Mankuliya village near Negombo in Sri Lanka is shattered. A fisherman by caste and occupation, he bought a multi-day fishing boat in early 2002 and took a bank loan of Rs. 300,000 by mortgaging his house. Unfortunately after a month, on 2 February, the Indian coast guards captured his boat along with five fishermen. Four of them were released after nine months, but the skipper remained in jail till January 2003. Sebastian's boat never returned, even though he went to Kochi, Chennai and Delhi to seek its release. He narrates, 'I have a family of six people, dependent on me. I had to

Table 4.5: Arrested Boats and Fishermen of Sri Lanka between 1998 and 2000

Year	Number of Boats Captured	Number of Fishermen Arrested (5 per boat)	Number of Family Members Affected (5 per family)	Monthly Allowance Rs. 600/person/month (Inflation@10% pa)	Total Cost
1998	70	350	1,750	3,000	5,250,000
1999	80	400	2,000	3,300	6,600,000
2000	90	450	2,250	3,630	8,167,500

Source: National Fisheries Solidarity, Sri Lanka.

sell my house to repay the bank loan and am now working on somebody's boat to earn my living'. According to him, in a day, 15 Sri Lankan boats had been captured. Powerful boat-owners with many boats and money managed to retrieve their captured boats and his was the only boat that did not return.

In north-western provinces, there are many fisherfolk villages in Puttam district (Plate 4.3). After 2000, a large number of

Plate 4.3: A Fisherfolk Colony at Thalwilawella,
Puttam District, Sri Lanka

fisherfolk have been arrested by the Indian navy in Barudalpola, Thalwilawella, Kudamaduwella, Thoduwawa and some other nearby villages. Loyal Peiris, a local activist of National Fisheries Solidarity, presents a list of 78 such fisherfolk. In Barudalpola village lived Prasad Denzil and W. Sunil Antony Fernando, two fishermen who were apprehended in February 2000 and released in December. Both lament, 'We were arrested in the mid-sea. We were so far from Kochi that it took three and a half days in the sea to reach over there. Our skipper was released after one and a half year. Life in jail was not so difficult, except the food. However, life after the jail became miserable as the family had a heavy loan. We had no source of income and we were very scared to venture into the seas again.'

In Munnakkara village of Gampaha district, we met Nirmala Fernando, wife of an arrested fisherman Benildus Peris. In February 2001, Benildus who was the skipper of a boat was arrested. Three arrested fisherfolk from the same boat returned with minor injuries, but the skipper had been taken to Kochi. Says Nirmala: 'I was receiving letters from my husband. He asked me to send some money through a messenger. As I was left here with two children with nothing to fall back upon, I started selling chickens, eggs, etc. The boat-owner was generous and also gave us some money to survive.'[30] K. S. Dilani, Dorine Jaeinla Mellow and Mourine Fernando are wives of arrested Sri Lankan fisherfolk in Mankuliya village. K. S. Dilani had to bear with the teasing of neighbours and villagers. She and her child felt quite lonely and depressed at times. Her husband returned after seven months. Dilani feels guilty, as her husband has to go back to the seas again for his livelihood. 'He suffered and is going to suffer again because of us', says she.[31] Mourine Fernando had to work in a garment factory for a year. Besides a daily wage of Rs.100, there was nothing for her, her two daughters and son.

In May 1998, W. Antony Vincent, a Sri Lankan boat-owner from Munnakara, Negombo, was desperately waiting outside the Madurai Central Jail in Tamil Nadu. He had come to India to get his confiscated boat *Philip Sahana* and secure the release of five fishermen. Vincent had already spent more than Rs. 10,000 in reaching Trivandrum, Madurai and in meeting several people. His five-year-old boat had cost him Rs. 900,000, out of which Rs. 300,000 was bank loan. He had to repay Rs. 15,000 every month to the bank. He was a very sad and desperate person. He recounted the events:

> I was not on the boat. So I do not know how the capture had taken place. The captive fishermen—K.S. Nicholas, W. Wilbert, K. S. Joseph, Sirinimal Fernando and Wijendra Wadugu Chandra—wrote to me that they were fishing on their side of the Gulf of Mannar, when the Indian navy came and captured their boat and them. The boat is kept in Keelakarai, South of Mandapan. I want my boat to be back soon, and then only can I survive. I am also trying for the release of the fishermen. Maybe after some time, I will get rid of all this and shift to some other profession. One day is one country, tomorrow is another country—how can one survive in this way![32]

In Madurai Central Jail, we met W. Wilbert. On 3 April 1998 when he along with other crew members was returning after fishing, the Indian navy/coast guards followed them. They asked them to surrender, but they tried to flee. The navy stated that they were caught because Sri Lankan navy was killing Indian fishermen. Wilbert and others were first taken to Mandapan. They remained there for two days, without being produced before any magistrate. Thereafter, they were kept in the custody of customs for two days in Rameswaram. After four days of arrest, they were produced before a magistrate. Wilbert informed that the magistrate did not ask them anything; neither did they tell anything. There was nobody to give them any advice regarding what to do. They were produced before the magistrate several times. Till date they do not know what their fault was and what were the cases imposed against them.[33]

The everyday life of the arrested Sri Lankan fisherfolk and their families is confronted with many problems. The boat-owners come to know about the arrest of the boats and the crew, but many-a-times the families of the crew members remain unaware. They continue to live in dark and have to run from pillar to post to gather information about their missing ones. The survival of these families becomes a crucial issue. Most of the time, the boat-owners do not provide any assistance to the families. The government provides some support to the families, but there are frequent complaints of delay, partial coverage and irregularities in the payment. Education becomes a secondary issue for the children in the affected families. The women have a very difficult time and the wives of the arrested fisherfolk are often harassed. These broken families have many other consequences to face. The arrested Sri Lankan fisherfolk also suffer because of the severe communication gap, as most of them can speak or understand only the Sinhala language and only a few can speak the Tamil language, which is spoken in India. This communication gap also becomes a handicap in dealing with the local lawyers. The food provided in the Indian jails is also unfamiliar and some of them fall ill after having it. Some of the jailed fisherfolk shared their pathetic situation of no clothes (they have only one sarong and a shirt), no medicine, no money to send a letter to their families, and no basic facilities like soap, toothpaste and brush.[34]

The affected fisherfolk and their families in both countries live through their suffering in two distinct but related experiences. The sheer hardships and uncertainties in their life, in which their sufferings, arrests and firing take place, become overwhelmingly dominant. In the next course, the suffering becomes an accusation against their own life, being and working. This mode of thinking, emphasised also through the discourse of law and legal processes, accentuates that the responsibility for suffering must be borne by the sufferers themselves. They many-a-times mask the real reason and the manner in which the crossing of borders, arrest and punishment have taken place, accentuated and distributed by an unjust sea order. Cosmologies of the fisherfolk hold the capriciousness of gods, fortune, luck and the sheer intensity of the events responsible for what has befallen on them. When a freed fisherman of Munnakkara village, Ironious Fernando, says— 'Keep good faith in God. God helped us in all these difficult days and will do so in the future'[35]—he is virtually closing the possibilities of fisherfolk to exorcise their suffering. When W. Antony Vincent, Sebastian Appuhamy and other Sri Lankans, and M. Sahayam, Xavier and many more Indians plead their innocence and ignorance of the everyday happenings in the sea, other than their painful experiences, they close up the potential of freeing themselves from the real sources of their oppression. Their pain and suffering is indeed unbearable, closing resembling a severe punishment. As injustices of life and work go on, testified by their sufferings, they can only be atoned further by more suffering in the given situation.

A Fluid and Dispersed Community

There is a widespread, clearly demarcated community of the pained and suffering fisherfolk on the sea borders of India and Sri Lanka. Several villages and many areas inhabited by fisherfolk consist of innumerable suffering individuals. In the very process of living, this suffering located in individual and family lives becomes transformed into community lives. However, till the beginning of the 20th century, fisherfolk communities and their life experiences were fluid, in the sense that first, the conflict and the competition over fishing, and the pain and the suffering involved in this did not claim to represent all layers of living and working of its members. Second, the communities, though identifiable by their fishing practices and their social interaction, did not force their members to live only in a single world of working. This fuzziness and dispersal of the community gave many possibilities to co-exist and at times, work together with different types of fisherfolk and fishing practices.[36]

Take the case of the history and origin of fishing in Rameswaram island. The island does not have a long history of fishing by settled fishers. Till the middle of the 20th century, traditional fishers from few southern villages in the Gulf of Mannar frequented the island with their catamarans during certain seasons, which could last for two to three months. They built temporary thatched huts here as their women also accompanied them, for helping with salting, drying and marketing of their catch. These fishers came here during the off season of the Gulf of Mannar coast and they fished at Palk Bay, where the season would be good. Some of the migrant fishers also went to Kachchativu island, which is situated in the north-eastern side of Rameswaram island and fished in the seas there. It was in the early 1940s that the fishers started building permanent houses in the island. At that time, these fishers were using only *thattumadi* (boat seine) in large catamarans. The migrant fishers used to catch large quantities of *karal* (silver bellies), *parava* (butter fish) and *kathala* from the sea off the upper side of the island. As the fishers started settling in the island, some merchants also settled here and started marketing the produce.

At Kachchativu island, traditional fishers from Ceylon also used to migrate for a week-long fishing during season time. As they were also mostly Tamils, there was closeness at various levels. There was a church in this island and a priest used to come from Ceylon during the annual feast and many people from both countries used to gather at that time. Although fishers of two countries used to fish in the same waters, their fishing practices differed and they were targeting different species of fish, hence there were no clashes or conflicts. The large catamarans coincided with the *vallams* (canoes). This also continued with the introduction of mechanised boats in Rameswaram. The traditional fishing crafts included large *vallam* (mechanised canoe), small *vallam* (mechanised small canoe), *vatha* (small non-mechanised canoe) and small catamarans.

There has been a special reference to the St. Antony's feast, connected with Kachchativu, which was never complete without Indians. Even the Maritime Boundary Agreement acknowledged this and wrote so in a specific clause, permitting Indian fishermen to attend the feast. Until the time it was discontinued in 1982, the Kachchativu feast was not just a religious meeting point for people of the region from both countries, it was also an occasion for informal trade. The Palk seas had always lent themselves to a thriving contraband business, but on the day of the Kachchativu festival it was like a *laissez faire*. During the festival, the island would be transformed into an open-air market, with Indians peddling much sought after lungis for coconut oil, spices and cakes of foreign brand shop. 'Currency was not accepted. It was purely by barter. I used to go every year for the business opportunity', said 59-year-old K. Thambirash, a resident of Delft in Sri Lanka.[37]

Fishers who migrated to the island and settled here during the past 50 years mainly belonged to four major castes: Parava, Kadayar, Valayar and Karayar. There were a few Muslim fishing families also. Paravas, who formed the major group, migrated from the Gulf of Mannar coast south of the island and most of the others were originally from the Palk Bay coast. There were other communities also living here as it was a major port for commercial as well as passenger transport during the British period and an important pilgrimage centre. One community named Servar was mainly involved in petty business, providing passenger amenities and acting as tourist guides in the island at that time.[38] V. Vivekanandan terms this as 'historic contacts' and further describes:

The fishermen communities on either side of the Palk bay are Tamil-speaking and have common origins. Further, the Bay is a common fishing ground for fishermen of both countries. It is therefore not surprising that there has been close contact between the fishermen of both countries for centuries. There has also been a free movement of goods across the bay before independence, which did not completely stop after independence. The coming of independence and the creation of two modern nation states did not alter the picture substantially as far as the coastal fishermen were concerned.[39]

However, an important change affected the fisherfolk community since the early 1970s: there has been a slow and gradual disappearance of the earlier fluid and diverse identities, and a clear appearance of conflicting communities increasingly driven by capital and technology. The new technology and the capital, once acquiring their place in the life and work of the fisherfolk in both countries, started to fashion the community precisely by monopolising the development of the fisheries sector in the sea borders in such a manner that often made peaceful co-existence a difficult and a near impossible proposition. Capital, technology, growth and development got established both theoretically and instrumentally as the key to describe the fisheries of Indian and Sri Lankan sea borders. If capital and technology rather than the community and its practices were what characterised this sector, those fluid and plural communities of both countries had to be singular entities in themselves, with fixed and protected boundaries, so trapped in their differences with one another as to be incapable of being worked together into larger, common, working and living identities.

The Universalising Impact of Capital

One of the features, which could be a basis for understanding the changes in the community, relates to the universalising impact of capital and technology in the marine fisheries sector of India and Sri Lanka. This growth derives from the gradual expansion of capital in this sector. Its role has been to create a profitable market for the capital and its owners, subjugate all other modes of production, and replace all jural and institutional concomitants of such modes, and particularly the entire edifice of fisherfolk practices, by maritime borders and laws, institutions, structures and other elements of a system appropriate to market rule. The drive to change the structure of fisheries is involved in the nature of capital itself. And the more expanded the capital and the new technology is, the more extensive and competitive is the market that it creates, which becomes its prime orbit. In this course of development, the capital strives simultaneously for expansion and further annihilation of ecological and social spaces. In the coastal borders of India and Sri Lanka, capital and technology have created a new community in the last two decades, with a universal appropriation of nature as well as of the community and social bond itself. Significantly, this is not only a local development of fisheries in the border areas; it is happening alongside the same course of development in this sector all over the country. With this development, the capital and its owners drive beyond any barriers and borders as much as beyond ecological concern, as well as all traditional, communitarian, social, fluid, diverse, complacent ways of living and working and reproductions of old ways. We see the destruction of all this, and constantly breaking down of boundaries here and there that hinder them in their pursuit of the catch, the expansion of trawlers, multi-day fishing vessels, big mechanised boats and of their needs, the one-sided, fast development of fisheries production, and the exploitation and destruction of natural and social forces.

The overview of the marine fisheries and fishers in and around Rameswaram, which is the most affected place in India, shows how the expansion of capital and technology has the capacity to transform the whole sector and also, that this expansion coincides inevitably with certain limitations that capital and technology can never overcome; it is not simply a trend governed by the possibility of unstopped growth, but a trend predicated on the certainty of its failure to continue. According to A. J. Vijayan, editor of *Waves,* a fortnightly on fisherfolk, there are roughly 1,000 trawling boats operating from the island. In the traditional sector, there are about 1,500 crafts of four types—large mechanised canoes, small mechanised canoes, small non-mechanised canoes and small non-motorised catamarans—operating from here. Most of the mechanised boats are engaged in all forms of trawling viz., bottom, mid-water, pelagic and pair trawling during different seasons with different types of nets. A mechanised trawling boat with many gears requires a capital investment of 1 million Indian rupees. People from the traditional fishing community do not own more than half of the trawling boats operating at Rameswaram. Even amongst those owned by members of the community, many are no more active fishers. Many merchant capitalists from non-fishing castes and other social backgrounds have entered this sector and own a good number of boats.[40]

According to the CMFRI (Central Marine Fisheries Research Institute), Government of India, Rameswaram topped the state in mechanised boats landing out of its 70 landing centres from 1980 to 1984. During this period, Rameswaram accounted for an annual average of 22,607 tonnes (18.68%) of landings, followed by Tuticorin fishing harbour with only 11,763 tonnes (9.96%). Ramanathapuram district ranks first in total marine fish landing in Tamil Nadu, contributing 23.57 per cent during 1993–96. The three-year average marine fish landing growth rate figures of the district as well as that of the state from 1984 to 1996 are quite revealing. The growth rate for the state was 9.9 per cent in 1987–90, 8.3 per cent in 1990–93 and 9.2 per cent in 1993–96. Whereas the growth rate for Ramanathapuram in the same period was 44.9 per cent, 10.6 per cent and 20.7 per cent, respectively. This shows that the growth rate of the marine fish landing of the district is higher than that of the state and this further increased during 1987–90 period. Although the growth rate of marine fish landing of the state is almost stagnant, the district shows wide fluctuations with an upward trend.

Tamil Nadu has a coastline of 1,000 kilometres and it has four specific coasts: Coromandel (350 kilometres), Palk Bay (270 kilometres), Gulf of Mannar (320 kilometres) and the West Coast–Arabian Sea (60 kilometres). However Palk Bay, with a shorter coastline in comparison with other coasts, has a larger contribution in the marine fish production of the state since the last two decades. According to the Department of Fisheries, Government of Tamil Nadu, during the 1980s (1980–84, 1984–88), all four coasts had an almost equal share in the marine fish landing: During 1980–84, Coromandel, Gulf of Mannar, West Coast and Palk Bay contributed 24.3 per cent, 27.9 per cent, 22.6 per cent and 25.2 per cent fish production, respectively. During 1984–88, it was 20.5 per cent,

27.8 per cent, 25.0 per cent and 26.7 per cent. However, the situation changed in the 1990s and the contribution of Palk Bay continued to grow and the other coasts witnessed either stagnation or decline in their fish production. During 1988–92, Coromandal, Gulf of Mannar and West Coast had a four-year annual average contribution of 23.3 per cent, 30.3 per cent and 11.5 per cent, respectively; whereas Palk Bay increased its share to 34.9 per cent. This trend continued during 1992–96 where the contribution of Coromandal increased (28.6%), but it declined in the case of Gulf of Mannar (25.9%) and West Coast (8.8%). However, the growth of Palk Bay continued steadily (36.7%). This high growth of fish production in the Palk Bay amidst the general decline or stagnation in other coasts seems highly unnatural. V. Vivekanandan cites 'fisheries compulsions' as the reason; as every alternate day, around 500 Rameswaram trawlers cross the IBL and go into Sri Lankan waters to fish. They are compelled to do this because of limited trawling ground on the Indian side, but the trawlers are unlimited. Also, the growth of the trawler fleet in Rameswaram has exhausted the Indian grounds and its survival depends on fishing in the Sri Lankan waters (see Table 4.6). In the area between Rameswaram and Nagapattinam, the total trawl fleet is 4,000, representing an investment of around 1.2 billion Indian rupees (approximately 2.5 billion Sri Lankan rupees). The total debt of trawl fishermen would be at least 600 million Indian rupees. The total number of fishermen manning this fleet is around 20,000. If shore-based workers and dependent families are also counted, the number would be in the range of 200,000–300,000 in this area.

What forces fishermen from Rameswaram to the Sri Lankan waters beyond Kachchativu, up to the Delft island off the Jaffna coast, even at the risk of being killed? What compels the Assistant Director of Fisheries for Rameswaram region to say: 'If fishermen do not cross the border today, tomorrow there will be no fishing in the region!' The answer lies in the massive capitalist growth of fishing activity in the region. Together with this growth comes the income sharing in the sector in which fisherfolk are like wage earners, deprived of any other rights and stakes in the seas. Most of the trawling boats operating here, of 38 to 42 feet size, require normally six members as crew, one driver, one second hand and four deck hands. The second hand assists the driver and should also have some basic knowledge about fishing grounds and

Table 4.6: Details of Trawlers Engaged in Transboundary Fishing

District and Trawl Bases	No. of Trawlers	No. of Trawlers that Cross over to Sri Lanka	Areas in Sri Lanka Where Fishing is Done	Dependence on Sri Lankan Resources
Ramnad district (Rameswaram, Mandapam)	1,700	900	Arc between Thalai Mannar and Delft island	Very High
Pudukottai (Kottaipatinam, Jagadapatinam)	1,000	1,000	Delft Island to Jaffna within the Bay	High
Nagapattinam (Kodikarai and further north on Bay of Bengal coast)	1,200	600	Palk Straits and beyond; Jaffna, Vadamarachi area	Medium to low; mostly seasonal incursion into Sri Lankan waters
Total	3,900	2,500		

Source: V. Vivekanandan, 'Historic Goodwill', *Samudra*, No. 38, July 2004, p. 28.

operation of nets. The deck hands do manual jobs like pulling in nets and sorting fishes. Although most of the crew in these boats are from the traditional fishing community, a large number of people mainly landless agricultural labourers are entering this sector as boat workers. Unlike other places in the state, where the net income is shared between the boat-owner and the crew in the ratio 60:40, in Rameswaram the boat-owners pay daily wages. There are special wages for overnight trips and incentives based on the catch in bottom trawling. For every one kg of shrimp, the driver gets Rs. 20, the second hand Rs. 15 and the deck hands Rs. 10 each. Thus the crew intensify fishing in dangerous waters.

The situation along the shoreline of the Gulf of Mannar is alarming. The Gulf, which supports the livelihood systems of over 180,000 fishing families in the 96 hamlets between Rameswaram and Thoothukudi, accounts for an annual fish catch (which includes prawn, crab and lobster) of over 100,000 tonnes. But in the last few years, the catch has declined sharply due to the exploitation and degradation of critical ecosystems. As a result, the fishing families have been caught in a vicious circle: a degraded ecosystem, decreasing fish catch and hence income levels, exploit-ation of resources, and further degradation of the ecosystem.[41] The destruction of physical and biological resources of the ecosystem by bottom trawling, which affects Gulf of Mannar, coral mining in the southern part of the Gulf and pollution by the industries, also largely on the southern parts, are the main threats to the ecosystems. According to the 1993 Marine Fishing Regulation Act, trawlers can only fish beyond a distance of three nautical miles from the shore. The traditional fishing sector alleges that trawlers routinely violate this rule, as the best fish catch is found within that range.

'Corals and sea grasses are within the three nautical mile range', said A. Baluchami, president of the Meenpidi Thozhilalar Sangam (Fishworkers Trade Union) in Mandapam, Ramanathapuram. He added, 'When trawlers scrape the seabed, the breeding grounds of a variety of animals—sea cucumber, *chank* [conch], crab, squid, coloured fish, turtle—are all gone. Twelve to 15 years ago, shoals of dugongs used to come out of the water and breathe. Today they too have disappeared. Our struggles have been of no avail.' He continues, 'The variety and size of the fish catch have declined over the years. Twelve years ago, I used to catch four baskets of fish or prawn using 10 nets. Now I need 150 nets to get the same amount.' However, the Mannar coast has some of the poorest villages in Tamil Nadu. For example, Mundalmunai, just off the national highway to Rameswaram, has no electricity and its 75 families live in huts with no *pattas* to the land their homes stand on. It does not have a primary school, a health centre or a ration shop. The traditional fisherfolk here get work once in 20 days or so. The women of the village sometimes make shell necklaces. For an intricate three-stringed necklace, a woman is paid Rs. 3. 'We have to borrow just to exist', said S. Suryakala. She further lamented, 'Our small children have to go by bus to school and must study by candlelight. The food we get in the ration shop is inedible. Only we women eat the rice, our men won't touch it.' There are many villages like Mundalmunai on the coast. According to one study, the literacy rate of fisherfolk in the Mannar region is 31 per cent, far less than the state average; women's literacy is even lower. As many as 54 per cent of the fisherfolk live in huts. Even a cursory investigation reveals very high levels of indebtedness amongst traditional fishing families.[42] 'If you do not decongest Rameswaram and other affected areas, there will be no solution to the problem of fishermen from India crossing into the territorial waters of other's country', comments K. R. Suresh, commandant of coast guards in Mandapam.[43]

The situation is similar in Sri Lanka, which has a 1,760 kilometre coastline, of which 1,150 kilometres are sand beaches. In 1977, trade liberalisation policies were implemented here. Since then, the fisheries sector has been fully integrated into the global economy. The capital is striving constantly to go beyond the spatial and temporal limits in its expanding process. The development of the Sri Lankan fisheries sector indicates that capital, technology and market are breaking spatial barriers to intercourse i.e., to expand and conquer the surrounding environment for its profit and market. It reaches in motion from one place to another. The more overwhelming the capital in one sea border therefore, the more extensive the other sea border over which it starts circulating over time, which forms the spatial orbit of its circulation. The more there is a striving for the expansion of the capital and the market, the more is the annihilation of coastal space by time.

The marine resources in Sri Lanka are divided into two subsectors: coastal and offshore fisheries, and deep-sea fisheries. Fishing activities in the sea extending up to 40 kilometres from the coast are considered as coastal fishery. The offshore fishery consists of fishing activities concentrated between 40 kilometres and 96 kilometres from the coast while the deep-sea fishery is in the area beyond 96 kilometres from the coast. The Ministry of Fisheries and Aquatic Resources Development (MFAR), has estimated that the fish production of marine fisheries in coastal areas increased from 140,270 tonnes in 1985 to 154,470 tonnes in 2004. In 2004, the total marine fisheries catch including offshore fisheries was 253,190 tonnes.[44] Studies by National Aquatic Resources Research and Development Agency (NARA)[45] recommended against granting of subsidies for the construction of offshore gillnet vessels because this fishery had already achieved maximum economic profit. Sri Lankan fish export consist of ornamental fish, fresh and chilled fish (like tuna), crustaceans (lobster, shrimp and crab), etc. In 2000 the export value of fish products amounted to Rs.10,327 million, accounting for 2.46 per cent of the total export earnings of the country.

The marine sector accounts for 85 per cent of the employment in the fisheries sector. There are thousands indirectly employed in this sector, especially in marketing and other ancillary services. About 87,808 households live in 1,050 marine fishing villages. Around 98,444 people are actively engaged in the marine fishing sector.[46] A rough estimate indicates that the fishworkers' population consists of 10 per cent craft owners, 30 per cent crew workers, 5 per cent fish merchants, 1 per cent fish processors (fish drying and curing), 5 per cent gear suppliers and 49 per cent women and children. In 1994, the total number of people dependent on fisheries as their major source of income was around 520,238, consisting of 461,738 in the marine sector and 58,500 in the inland sector.[47] However, the MFARD has estimated the total population associated with fishery to be around one million.[48]

Deep-sea fishery is of fairly recent origin in Sri Lanka; it commenced in the late 1980s. The multi-day boats, 45–50 feet in length and powered by 50 hp engine, are mainly engaged in the exploitation of deep-sea resources. Their number has increased from a mere 72 in 1984 to 1,591 in 2000.[49] Large-meshed gill netting, long-lining and trolling are some of the common techniques employed by these crafts. In the early 1990s, these boats began to venture outside Sri Lanka's EEZ, first to fish in the neighbouring Indian, Maldivian and British Indian Ocean territorial waters and then in international waters to the north-east (Bay of Bengal) and north-west (Arabian Sea). The continuing pressure to stay at sea for longer periods and to travel further in search of fish is reflected in the increase in the length of multi-day boats. According to the skippers of the above 40 feet category in Beruwala and Dondra villages, in the southern and western provinces of Sri Lanka respectively, territorial waters of Andaman and Nicobar Islands, Maldive Islands, Lakshadweep Islands and occasionally, Bangladesh, Thailand, Madagascar and Australian Islands are the areas of operation of most of their crafts from October to April, when the sea is calm. Long-lining for shark (for shark fins) and tuna is the major technique employed. Incidences of these crafts fishing in the Red Sea have also been reported. During the monsoon period (from May to September), these crafts from the southern and western provinces of Sri Lanka usually fish in the EEZ and in the international waters and the fishing trips are shorter.

Oscar Amarasinghe of the University of Ruhuna, Sri Lanka, in his study on the 'Economic and Social Implications of Multi-Day Fishing in Sri Lanka'[50] observes that about 75 per cent of the owners of multi-day fishing craft are non-fishing owners, of whom a sizeable number represent a class of businessmen who have no history of fishing. The shift of craft-owners from the traditional to the modern sector is quite low. With the entry of 'outsiders' into fishing communities to undertake multi-day fishing, the traditional pattern of labour recruitment, employer-employee relations and work conditions of labour have undergone tremendous change. A labour market has emerged in which anonymous relations tend to prevail, the forces of supply and demand are at work and labour mobility is unaffected by customary practices of personal attachment. Recently, some large multi-day boats for deep-sea fishing have adopted a method of paying wages to crew workers.

The social and economic relations between a deep-sea boat-owner and a deep-sea fishworker have become polarised by the steady capitalisation of the sector; it is also being researched that the deep-sea fishworkers are exploited. Simultaneously, fishworkers continue to be vulnerable to the dangers associated with deep-sea fishing, an inherently high-risk profession, because of lack of legal provisions defining acceptable working conditions in this sector. The United Fishermen's and Fishworkers' Congress of Sri Lanka in its report suggested the introduction of written contracts of employment between boat-owners and fishworkers. They also recommended onboard safety facilities, first-aid, and statutory requirements for all deep-sea fishing boats over a specified length to be equipped with single-side band radios and satellite navigation equipment. The other proposals were to introduce the provision to permit independent monitoring of boat design and safety, the insurance of deep-sea fishing boats and that boat-owners be responsible for the welfare of their crew-members when they are engaged in fishing.[51]

A fisherman in Moondramchatram near Rameswaram says, 'Politicians only make noises about Sri Lankan navy personnel attacking Indian fishermen but, more often than not, the truth is that we are forced to go into their territorial waters by our employers.' He added, 'They insist that we go well past Kachchativu and near Talai Mannar since that is where the big game is found aplenty. If we refuse and return without a catch from within India's waters, we are not paid our full wages.' He further lamented, 'With little chance of being gainfully employed otherwise in the island, we cannot afford to stay away from the sea for long. Only a few lucky ones have escaped this slavery.' Of course, the women help by picking firewood in the casuarinas groves lining the shores but that is not enough for the families to make ends meet. 'And when some of us are killed, our employers pay our kin between Rs. 2,000 and Rs. 5,000 each as compensation. This is the value of human life here', he said. So why don't they take it up with the administration? 'Who will believe us? Every time we stray close to Talai Mannar and there is a shooting incident, our employers forbid us from speaking the truth to avoid being hauled up themselves', he insisted.[52]

While analysing the processes of globalisation and Sri Lanka's fisheries, Oscar Amarasinghe and Herman Kumara concluded: The process of globalisation that started after 1977 has led to a considerable expansion of Sri Lanka's modern mechanised fishing fleet, within a short period of time. During 1985–2000 there has been a 6-fold increase in the volume (from 3,240.60 MT to 19,566.80 MT) and 22-fold increase in the value (Rs. 453.11 million to 10,328.00 million) of fishery export. They remark:

> The introduction of mechanised crafts and the construction of fishery harbours brought craft owners from various villages to one anchorage

location: the harbour. The new arrangements threatened the
functioning of the local rules 'entry', because the 'outsiders' had no
obligation to abide by the local community's customary laws.... Due
to the capital-bias nature of the new mechanised fishing technology,
fishermen needed credit to have access to new technology. Of all
categories of craft owners, those engaged in traditional fishing activities
have the least access to credit facilities extended by state-owned banks.
In general, formal lending schemes appear to have a high bias towards
asset-rich individuals probably due to the latter's ability to provide the
required collateral at ease on the one hand, and their ability to use
political influence on the other. Granted that access to new technology
is directly related to fishworkers' access to credit, the asset poor
fishworkers in fishing societies are put at a serious disadvantage in
adopting new technology due to their inability to offer collateral
demanded by lenders. About 75 per cent of the owners of multi-day
crafts today are non-fishing owners, of whom a sizeable number
represent a class of businessmen who have no history of fishing.[53]

Steve Creech, a researcher on Sri Lankan fisheries, poses the
question of the arrest and killing of Sri Lankan fisherfolk more
pointedly:

Sri Lanka is the only South Asian nation, thanks to international
development agencies and huge government subsidies, to have
developed a multi-day deep sea fishery, which currently boasts a fleet
of around 1800 vessels, the most modern of which are up to 60 feet
long and are equipped with satellite navigation equipment. The entire
fleet uses non-discriminating gill nets to catch tuna and shark. In
1996 it was estimated that the fishing fleet used 11,130,00 gill net
pieces, each piece 83 metres long, equivalent to a total of 9,24,000
kilometres of net, set to catch fish. On an average, each boat employs
four to five crew-members. This is by no means small scale, as many
people would perceive it. In contrast to Maldivian and Indian day
boats, which land their catch fresh on the beach every day, Sri Lankan
multi-day fishing boats return to port after spending 30 to 45 days at
sea, with fish at least 10 to 15 days old in their un-refrigerated, ice
packed holds.... Sri Lanka is now exporting its overcapacity, exactly
like the EU does to Africa and South America.... One of the key
problems perpetuating the arrest of Sri Lankan fisherfolk is that the
people engaged in the debate are refusing to face up to a number of
simple, though unpalatable truths. Really addressing the issue would
require tackling Sri Lanka's over-capacity and developed dependency
on gill nets. It would require the withdrawal of government subsidies

for more multi-day boats and fixing terms and conditions for employment of fisherfolk in the multi-day fishing sector, therefore reducing owner's profits.[54]

With this growth of capital and technology in the sea borders of India and Sri Lanka, there is a beginning of a new ownership and a new working order. The universalistic reach of capital and commerce on both sides of the divide demonstrates the power of the capital, striving towards extensive exploitation and profit. At the same time, however, the multilayered deep tensions making dents over it also show the reality of the weaknesses of this capital.

Caught in a Conflict Warp

It is not by their pain and suffering alone that the fisherfolk of the sea borders come to know of themselves. It is not only the crushing capital that fundamentally reorders the fishing sector in this region. Alongside in the sea borders, a new sense of identity is now being created among the fisherfolk, by virtue of their nation, borders and official standing. They are becoming aware of their living and working as 'different' and 'distant' from others—a difference expressed not in terms of differentials of caste, class, wealth and status, but in terms of national rights, sovereignty and exclusivity. The border fisherfolk are articulating themselves not in a language of commonality of the past and present of the region, but by a negation of these. They are caught in a conflict warp, which is taking many new forms. The fisherfolk from both sides are getting increasingly sensitive to the border, which separates them from one another. The border and its adherence are being regarded by them as almost a natural condition of their living. Actually, the authority of the nation-state has created the very same border to dispossess the fisherfolk and has always forced them to reconcile to it. However, paradoxically and ironically enough, many times the cries and conflicts of the fisherfolk in their respective countries, derive much of their strength from the very same awareness and language.

In recent times, the coastal conflicts between Indian and Sri Lankan fisherfolk are also manifesting themselves explicitly in the form of violence directed by the fisherfolk of one country against the other, in different times and under different pretexts. The regularity with which this happens shows a particular mindset and a wilful commission on the part of the fisherfolk as well. The way it happens and the way it is being articulated by the fisherfolk are also indicative of a 'rationale' of defined and conscious hostility. The objects of the fisherfolk attacks are exclusively fisherfolk, along with their whole work systems. These attacks also point to another characteristic, where the fishermen are attempting to appropriate for themselves the same methods of suppression by which the state has been suppressing them. In this way, older grievances revolving around the loss of resources, increasing ecological malaise, and a corresponding hardship for the fisherfolk has been submerged in a strongly manipulated sense of outrage against fisherfolk of the other country, who are depicted as the main reason for declining fish catch.

The fishermen of the main Sri Lankan fishing village Pesalai in the Mannar Island say, 'Continued poaching by Indian trawlers has not only hit our livelihood, but also destroyed the continental shelf, which we have protected for all these years.' According to official figures, Mannar has 4,175 families that depend on fishing as a livelihood (see Plate 4.4). A total of 4,593 people, spread across 34 villages, are engaged in this occupation and they have 1,673 boats. Only 75 are mechanised boats, which operate from Pesalai village. The ethnic conflicts in Sri Lanka resulted in the seas being closed to them, while their Indian counterparts continue to poach in these waters. The four northern districts of Sri Lanka—Jaffna, Mannar, Kilinochchi and Mullaithivu—had a dismal contribution of an average annual marine production of 6,300 tonnes between 1994 and 2000, to the national average of 230,000 tonnes. With the peace process under way in Sri Lanka, these areas have once again been opened to the Sri Lankan fishermen, who perceive the transgressing Indian fishermen as their main enemies.[55] S. Madhuvalan, an unemployed graduate who has fallen back on his family occupation, says, 'We can see the Indian fishermen with our own eyes from the shore. This encroachment is what hits us badly.'

Mataraja Kadiravelpillai, president of the Citizens' Committee of Nainathivu, a small island off Jaffna peninsula says, 'The Indians come close to the coast in their mechanised boats and cut and

Plate 4.4: Family of Affected Fisherfolk at Pesalai, Manner Island

destroy our nets. Our fishermen suffer great financial losses due to this.' According to him poaching begins usually after dark, 'Poachers come in large numbers, with their petromax lamps shining. From here it looks as if the entire village is about to descend on the tiny island. They all sometimes come as close as 300 mts. to the Nainativu coastline.' An official comments, 'It is a situation of despair. It is turning out to be a battle between fishermen of two countries, who depend on the seas for their livelihood.'[56]

Thus we witnessed many of fishermen in the northern districts of Sri Lanka participating in protest marches against Sri Lankan government's lack of action to stop the encroachment by Indian fishermen on the island's waters. Angry marchers were raising slogans and carrying banners urging the government to protect Mannar's marine wealth. 'Save our resources', read one banner. 'Sri Lanka is our land, its seas our home', said another.[57] 'The Sri Lankan navy must protect our waters from Indian fishermen. Already we live and work under so many restrictions. The Indian fishermen have only been adding to our problems', said S. Vimalanandan, a fisherman from Delft.

Caught in conflict warps, the violence shows signs of spreading from its initial attacks on a few 'enemy' fisherfolk, into a general attack on all or most of them; thus, violence permeates an entire domain, population and area. The logic of this extension can be traced to the prevailing situation, as much as to the fisherfolk. This is blindly hitting out against all and this pattern occurs repeatedly in the course of major activities in the sea borders. Thus, on 3 and 5 March 2003, Sri Lankan Tamil fishermen from Pesalai and Neduntheevu attacked 154 fishermen from Rameswaram and Mandapam and seized 21 boats because they were fishing beyond Kachchativu. Two fishermen from Rameswaram fractured their hands.[58]

According to fishermen in Rameswaram, on 3 March 2003 at dawn, when 112 fishermen from Rameswaram in 21 mechanised boats were trawling their 'double nets' off Kachchativu for lucrative tiger prawn, they were surrounded by a few hundred fishermen from Pesalai in Mannar and Neduntheevu, in the Jaffna peninsula. One Sri Lankan fisherman shouted, 'Why do you come into our sea and churn it up?' They then boarded the mechanised trawlers, damaged them, and assaulted the fishermen with iron rods, wooden logs and a 'mugandu', a weapon shaped like the alphabet 'C'. Arul (26) and Rajan (35) fractured their hands. 'We begged them not to hit us, but they would not relent', said Sakthivel, an injured fisherman. He continues, 'They came in 24 boats and surrounded us. There were seven or eight persons per boat. After they seized control of our vessel, they used it to encircle the other trawlers. We have made a mistake, but why should they beat us up?' The Sri Lankan fishermen commandeered the boats to Mannar, where the Tamil fishermen were produced before a magistrate.

Two days later, on 5 March, 42 fishermen from Mandapam who sailed into the seas in nine mechanised trawlers were 'abducted' by fishermen from Mannar. One Sri Lankan fisherman reportedly said, 'Some of you cross the border and fish, and also damage our nets. Since you trouble us often despite our warnings, we have to behave rudely with you.' Even after a week of these incidents, emotions continued to run high at Rameswaram, Pamban, Thankachi Madam and Mandapam in Ramanathapuram. About 1,200 mechanised trawlers and around 100,000 fishermen and workers went on strike. N. Devadass, secretary, Rameswaram Port Mechanised Boat-owners' Association asserted that the strike would continue till the government guaranteed their traditional right to fish in the waters around Kachchativu.[59]

From the other side of the border, there was a similar kind of echo. J. A. Santhiogu Cross, president of a fishermen's cooperative society of Pesalai fishermen, reasoned: 'If someone comes to our house and takes our property, what do we do?' When asked to comment on the district-wide protest plans by Pesalai fishermen, after they attacked them, he viewed it as their show of strength: 'Once the Tamil Nadu fishermen said that they were protesting, those held under custody here were released. We on this side can show our strength as well.' This reveals a new and very ominous politics.

All the forces of the ruling establishment especially the government, also imbued their fisherfolk with a sense of protection, and assertion over the issue of borders, and pandered to their 'nationalism' by extolling the virtues of their continued loyalty and devotion to it. The political and social atmosphere could be thus induced to look upon 'their' fisherfolk as the fighter and the others as the aggressor. Between India and Sri Lanka, there are sea border cults like Kachchativu, created and nurtured by the states to keep people charged and to direct their dedication to the doings of the state, on the sea as well as on the land, as a matter of national commitment. Thus, we could see as to how Sri Lankan navy opened fire on fishing boats from Tamil Nadu a number of times in 1993 and 1994 and many Rameswaram fishermen were killed. This prompted Chief Minister Jayalalitha to write a series of letters in September/October 1993 and February 1994 to the Prime Minister P. V. Narasimha Rao to demand that India must issue 'a notice of retaliation' to Colombo. Even before that incident, in August 1991, during her first tenure as Chief Minister, Jayalalitha had announced that she was prepared to 'fight' the Centre to get back Kachchativu. After 3 and 5 March 2003 incidents, the leaders of the All India Anna Dravida Munnetra Kazhagam, the Dravida Munnetra Kazhagam, the Tamil Manila Congress and the Chief Minister of Tamil Nadu, called upon the Indian government to intervene and deal firmly with this issue, even to the extent of suggesting that a permanent solution to the problems faced by Tamil Nadu's fishermen can be achieved only if the Centre takes steps to get back Kachchativu from Sri Lanka.[60]

How far can conflict spread in the sea borders of India and Sri Lanka? Is there any limit under which its spread and speed can be counted? It is quite disturbing to find that the conflicts are exceeding all their local boundaries and are becoming a common habitat in most of the concerned areas. In many instances, the conflicts are a part of the material conditions relating to the economic life of the fisherfolk concerned, the terrain on which they work, their daily lives and borders, as against that of the fisherfolk from the other side and so on. The actual arrest, firing, killing could differ from one local event to another and give each or some of them a particular colour. What is common to them all, however, is the manner in which the conflict has been warped in the regular working and living space of the whole region. 'Fishing vessels crossing over by mistake cover only a small percentage of the cases. The vast majority of border crossings is intentional and involves travelling deep into Sri Lankan waters. It is an open secret that Rameswaram fishing vessels, especially trawlers, find good fishing grounds only on the Sri Lankan side and therefore do most of their fishing on that side. Every alternate day, around 500 Rameswaram trawlers routinely cross the IBL and go into Sri Lankan waters and conduct fishing operations', says V. Vivekanandan of ARIF. When asked about the Sri Lankan boats and fishermen being regularly captured by the Indian coast guards, he has similar disturbing observations, 'It is the growth of this multi-day fishing boat fleet that is behind the problem of Sri Lankan fishermen getting caught by the Indian coast guards. Except for the rare FRP boat that drifts accidentally towards the Indian coast in the Gulf of Mannar, the Sri Lankan vessels captured are all multi-day boats, which are found operating in the Arabian Sea and the Bay of Bengal. A number of them are caught near the Andamans and the Lakshwadeep Islands. It is worth mentioning that the Sri Lankan boats are caught even in Maldives and Seychelles.'[61]

A. J. Vijayan, in his overview of the marine fisheries and fishers in and around Rameswaram, clearly points to the fact that fishers in the region are increasingly depending on fishing in Sri Lankan waters for livelihood. And if they strictly follow the rules and do not transgress, then their jobs will be terminated, as they will not be able to bring any catch. 'It is the Indian fishermen who intrude into the Sri Lankan waters because the fish are there. All the shootings happen there. The fishermen who claim that they were shot in Indian waters might not be telling the whole truth', observes Vice-admiral R. N. Ganesh, the coast guard director general.[62] He adds, 'The fisherman can get compensation only if he files an FIR. He can file an FIR only if the event happens in the Indian Territory.' Oscar Amarasinghe has the same conclusion: 'Fishing inside the EEZs of other countries is purposive and is also common. It appears that crew workers aiming at high average incomes from multi-day fishing willingly accept to bear the risks of arrest, illness and even life.'

The circle of conflict reasoning is so much ingrained that even organisations like ARIF, which is an alliance of trade unions and non-governmental organisations for the release of innocent fishermen arrested on the Indo-Sri Lanka maritime border, sees the situation going nowhere:

> Sri Lanka does not normally arrest Indian fishermen for poaching. If it starts doing so, the numbers will be in hundreds, not scores, which is the case with Sri Lankan fishermen caught by our coast guard.... While the Sri Lankan fishermen are normally caught in the Gulf of Mannar and the Arabian Sea in the EEZ (beyond 12 nautical miles and within 200 nautical miles), the Indian fishermen in the Palk Bay are clearly violating the territorial waters (area within 12 nautical miles) of Sri Lanka.... Sri Lanka may or may not choose to retaliate. But we have to question the wisdom of punishing the Sri Lankan fishermen for an offence that the Indian fishermen have been so far getting away with rather lightly.[63]

Ethnic Conflict, Terrorism and Fisherfolk

Contemporary political conflicts between India and Sri Lanka, often involving political violence and armed battles are also taking environmental forms. Simultaneously, various environmental issues are getting regionalised and politicised. There is thus an 'environmentalisation' of certain conflicts and politicisation of environment in the region.[64] The contagion effects of political conflicts make the fisherfolk more vulnerable to the violence and domination of armed forces. It is the suffering and subjection of the coastal fisherfolk to a common source of violence coming from both sides, even before they know how to deal with this political situation. The striking developments of aggressive religious and political positions, rise of terrorism, continuum of authoritarian regimes and wars have further aggravated coastal conflicts and instability, as the causal links between these are not often indirect. Sri Lanka's ethnic conflict, the presence of LTTE militants in coastal Tamil Nadu and the killing of the Indian Prime Minister Rajiv Gandhi, have all taken a heavy toll on the livelihood of villagers on both sides of the Strait. Immediate fallout of the rise in militancy has been that since 1993, Sri Lanka's navy has been given *carte blanche* to open fire on all unauthorised boats in its territorial waters, extending from Trincomalee to Mannar. Lankan fishermen from Jaffna and Mannar face restrictions on the types of boats they can own, areas they can fish in and the time they can spend in the sea. Colombo promulgates emergency regulations, whereby its waters become a prohibited zone. The Indian government has also adopted tough measures to prevent infiltration and movement of LTTE guerrillas. In these situations, nobody makes a distinction between militants and fishermen.

With the intensification of Sri Lanka's ethnic conflict, Tamil Nadu became a centre of activity for the Tamil militants. According to V. Suryanarayan, the efficient network which the LTTE painstakingly built in Tamil Nadu—comprising smugglers, fishermen, political activists, transport operators, businessmen and corrupt officials—provided support for their war machine. Along the 'Prabhakaran trail'—stretching from the arid areas of Coimbatore, Salem, Erode, through Karur and Trichy on the Cauvery banks to the coastal village of Vedaranyam—explosives, hand grenades, food, medicine, fuel and diesel moved towards the Jaffna peninsula. Tamil Nadu's long coastline, with its innumerable fishing harbours, provided a safe haven for fast moving LTTE boats. The assassination of the Indian Prime Minister Rajiv Gandhi made Colombo, Delhi and Tamil Nadu take measures against the LTTE and its support base in Tamil Nadu. The enforcement of many regulations, meant to prevent the flow of arms and militants to and from Tamil Nadu, by the Sri Lankan navy, which cannot distinguish between Tamil militants and fishermen, has hit the Indian fishermen badly.

In Rameswaram it is felt that the majority of the fisherfolk do not support Tamil militants from across the border, but there are a small numbers of fisherfolk and mechanised boats, mostly owned by people outside the fishing community that are involved in supplying goods to the militants. A. J. Vijayan, an activist of the NFF, explains:

> Fishers do not consider the operations of such people as political in nature, but act for just making money like smugglers. Diesel is in great demand by the militants and since fishers also use it as a fuel, it is very difficult to find the miscreants. While some miscreants indulge in such shady deals and make a lot of money too, it is often the innocent fishers who face the repercussions.

The repercussions are of course severe. Since 1983 till the end of August 1991, there have been 236 incidents of attack by the Sri Lankan navy on Tamil Nadu fishermen. Three hundred and three boats have been attacked affecting 486 fishermen. Fifty-one boats have been destroyed. One hundred and thirty-five fishermen have been attacked and injured and over 50 fishermen have been killed; 57 fishermen have been injured in firing incidents. The Sri Lankan navy has seized 65 motor boats and arrested 205 fishermen.[65] According to a report in *Indian Express*: 'In the last three years, 25 Tamil Nadu fishermen had been killed in firing by the Sri Lankan navy. Besides, 109 were injured. A total of 136 attacks had taken place on fishing boats, 15 of these had been sunk.'[66] The victims do not agree with the official figures. Says one angry Tamil Nadu fisherman, 'The government figures of deaths and injuries are quite partial. We estimate that since 1990, 700 Indian fishermen have been shot dead and an equal number of them have been injured. What is this? Are we being asked to abandon fishing and take to begging?'

Indian fishermen are a regular target of attack allegedly by the LTTE. On 23 April 1997, a number of Indian fishermen were injured when the LTTE attacked a Sri Lankan naval camp in northern Talaimannar, using Indian fishing vessels as cover. The militants virtually dragged the fishing vessels along with them. Muruganandan, president of the Ramanathapuram District Fishermen's Association, complains: 'LTTE men regularly take away our fishing boats and send the crew back. People belonging to Rameswaram have lost at least 40 boats. As recently as March 1998, LTTE members came as close as Tondi on the Indian side of the sea and took away a fishing boat.' In March 2007, 11 fishermen from Tamil Nadu and one from Kerala were reportedly abducted by the LTTE. This not only lead to accusations-counter accusations by the governments of both the countries, but also created a furore among Tamil Nadu fishermen.

Military has become integral to the sea borders between India and Sri Lanka, where talking about the suffering of the fisherfolk and their security frequently leads to the constant presence and consideration of the role of the military. The military solely justifies its action in the name of anti-terrorism and national security. In addition to the conflicting and war times, their presence in the non-conflicting and non-war times influences the entire landscape. There is thus a state of continuous low-intensity warfare with cumulative impact on fisherfolk. Thus at Kankesanthurai (Jaffna), J. H. U. Ranaweera, commanding officer (North) of the Sri Lankan navy sees trespassing Indian fishermen as 'one of the biggest security problem' for the Sri Lankan navy. 'Several times a week, up to 200 Indian boats could be spotted in high security waters around the islands off Jaffna peninsula, like Delft, Nainathivu, Karainagar and Kovilan Point. We are on high alert all the time for LTTE boats. When we see such a large number of Indian fishing boats, it is impossible for us to tell whether they are really fishermen or Sea Tigers', says he and cites a few examples of how sometimes Sri Lankan navy crafts were badly damaged when they went close up to inspect what looked like Indian fishing boats, but in reality they were Sea Tigers suicide boats.

In this kind of an atmosphere, the concerns for the fishermen mainly stem from an understanding of security of the nation-states and its borders, developed within the discourse of conflicts, war and related machinery. First, a particular risk of terrorist activities is being referred to as the sole concern of security. And then there comes a particular object or area to be secured. The security issue in the coastal borders between India and Sri Lanka is a power and war word, a state act that is paving the way for state monopolisation of responses to a multi-faceted situation, labelled now as a security issue. These states no longer see this issue as one to be dealt with through mainstream institutions, but one that requires extraordinary measures. Thus we see that a confidential document on this issue reads like a military paper:

> Since 1983, with the escalation of terrorist activities in the North and the East and the ferrying into Sri Lanka of terrorist cadres, arms

and equipment from bases in Tamil Nadu, the incidents of violations by Indian fishermen assumed a new dimension, as they now constituted a serious security problem to the Government of Sri Lanka. In view of the grave security threat posed by these continuing violations, a decision was taken by the security authorities in August 1984, that any future violations of Sri Lankan waters by Indian vessels would be dealt with firmly under the laws of Sri Lanka and if necessary, Sri Lankan naval craft will open fire on any boats violating Sri Lankan waters. This decision was taken ... in the expectation that the Indian authorities would take preventive action on the Indian side of the Maritime Boundary.[67]

The year 2007 have witnessed an escalation of attacks, firings and killings between Indian and Sri Lankan fisherfolk, Sri Lankan navy and Indian fisherfolk and LTTE and Indian fisherfolk. Serious conflict has been witnessed not only in and around Kachchativu, but also in the deep Sri Lankan coastal zones like Kankesanturai and Point Pedro, Mannar and Talaimannar, killing at least four Indian fisherfolk and injuring several. In the wake of ethnic violence in Sri Lanka, these clashes have led to proposals for joint monitoring of the International Maritime Boundary Line (IMBL) by the Indian and Sri Lankan navies, deploying of surveillance systems and enhancing the presence of coast guards and navy for intensive sea and air patrolling with additional manpower and state-of-the-art vessels and aircrafts.[68] However, all these measures further the rigid line of mindless securitisation of the coastlines without taking into account deeper issues at stake.

In the same way that the US is now engaged in a 'war against terror', suggesting a response of a kind equivalent to war; labelling a particular challenge as a security issue scripts that challenge as a threat to the country, consequently excusing the state from the normal checks on its behaviour. The 'securitisation' of the coastal issues between India and Sri Lanka and ethnic conflicts and terrorism has given different players in the field enough opportunities to justify drastic and unaccountable actions against the fisherfolk.

What is to be Done?

There have been a plethora of suggestions by specialists, policy analysts, academics and activists: to develop a database on Sri Lanka

and the Indian Ocean and undertake in-depth studies and policy
measures on the impact of the changing international
environment;[69] to get the island of Kachchativu and adjacent islets
on 'lease on perpetuity' solely for fishing, drying nets and pilgrimage
by Indian fishermen while upholding the Sri Lankan sovereignty
over the island;[70] to introduce a system where licensed Indian
fishermen could be permitted to fish in Sri Lankan waters up to
five nautical miles, and the number of fishing boats, the type of
fishing vessels, the number of fishing days, the amount of catch
and the licence fee should be settled after detailed negotiations.
Simultaneously, Sri Lankan fishermen could be permitted to fish
in the Arabian Sea and near the Minicoy Islands on the same terms
and conditions.[71] In one of his recent books, V. Suryanarayan
argues from an Indian perspective that any meaningful solution
will have to address the deep sense of dismay that the government,
political parties and above all, fishermen of Tamil Nadu harbour
towards the governments of India and Sri Lanka that their vital
interests were sacrificed at the altar of good neighbourly relations,
when the maritime agreements of 1974 and 1976 were concluded.
There is a need, states he, to find a solution, which will guarantee
the livelihood of thousands of fishermen on both sides of Palk
Bay, to rectify the enormous damage caused to the marine
environment by the unrestricted and unregulated use of
mechanised trawlers by Indian fishermen, to provide alternate
means of livelihood to Indian fishermen by expeditiously
implementing long-pending projects like the Sethusamudram
Canal, to neutralise the Sea Tigers who have emerged as the third
naval force, posing a threat to Indian and Sri Lankan security, and
to work out a new vision and a new deal to jointly enrich marine
resources.[72] 'The need of the hour is the creation of consortia for
development of deep sea fishing', suggests V. Suryanarayan.[73]

On the other hand, it is also being suggested from the Sri
Lankan perspective that the solution lies with Sri Lanka taking
effective steps to develop the fisheries in the North, so that Sri
Lankan fishermen could effectively harvest the prawns and other
catches in these waters. 'If the fish stock is adequately utilised,
there will be no inducement for fishermen from Tamil Nadu to
encroach on these waters.'[74] A number of other options are also
being suggested to solve the problems associated with border
crossing by the fishermen. Vivekanandan offers various solutions:

Free access and freedom for the fisherfolk to fish in each others' waters. On the Sri Lankan side, such a free access policy actually exists in the Palk Bay and on the Indian side, in the Arabian Sea, the multi-day Sri Lankan fishing boats are not seen as outsiders by the small fishermen of Tamil Nadu and Kerala.

Returning fishermen without any litigation. After establishing the bonafide of the fishermen, they could be sent back within a week or two.

Strict enforcement, but with a humane approach. After establishing the bonafide of arrested group of fishermen, the crew should be repatriated without any delay. Subsequently, the skipper should be charged, presented in a court of law and if he pleads guilty, no elaborate trial is called for and a clear set of graded fines can be enforced: Rs 20,000 for a first-time offence, Rs. 50,000 for a second offence and boat may be confiscated in case of the third time. And in no case should the skipper be punished with imprisonment.

Reciprocal access. Sri Lanka could formally allow Indian vessels to fish on its side of the Palk Bay and in turn, ask for reciprocal access to its multi-day fishing boats in the Arabian Sea, the Gulf of Mannar and the Bay of Bengal. If 500 Rameswaram boats are regularly fishing in the Palk Bay, Sri Lanka could also be allowed to send around 500 multi-day fishing boats into Indian waters.

Separate management regimes for each ecosystem as well as a joint system of regulation and management. Restrictions on fleet size, gear regulations, each country's fleet fishing on alternate days, etc., or India promoting joint ventures between fishermen of both countries as an alternative to the ventures that are usually between large corporations.[75]

Regular exchange of information between Indian and Sri Lankan navy on missing fishermen and other events; 'coordinated patrolling' by Indian and Sri Lankan navy along the international maritime borders; and governments of India and Sri Lanka taking up joint naval exercises to eliminate the threat of unauthorised operations by the sea arm of the LTTE are also being suggested and practised at times by the Indian and Sir Lankan coast guards and navy.[76] Another expert on fisheries, V. S. Somavanshi, points out that the focus of cooperative development and sharing of know-how has to be on the 'fishing community and fish stocks of the region, appropriate technologies to be used through practice of Code of Conduct for Responsible Fisheries and suitable management and conservation measures.'[77]

Indian and Sri Lankan governments have met many times to solve the problem of arrests and deaths of fishermen and have sometimes proposed few solutions. For example, on 1 June 2001 a meeting was held between Mahinda Rajapaksa, Minister of Fisheries and Aquatic Resources Development, Sri Lanka and Nitish Kumar, Minister of Agriculture, India in Delhi on the problems relating to the jailed fishermen of both countries. They agreed for a joint monitoring committee consisting of relevant officials and ministers' representatives of both countries to be set up without delay; a meeting of the joint monitoring committee once in two months, alternatively in Colombo and New Delhi to resolve the problems faced by the fishermen; freeing all the fishermen held in detention; granting of safe passage to the Arabian Sea for Sri Lankan fishermen through the EEZ of India.[78] Evoking a spirit of 'kindness', 'compassion' and 'humanity', the meeting also decided in detail 'the simplified procedures for the release of fishing vessels which inadvertently stray into each other's waters'; 'precautionary measures'; and the principles of 'using minimum force' by navy/coast guard of two countries. Some of these initiatives have also desired a move towards regional cooperation and policy-making on coastal resources. 'With the bilateral [agreement] between India and Sri Lanka, we wanted to move towards managing the Indian Ocean together in this part of the world. There should be common policy on sustainable use of coastal resources in the South Asia region. The arrest of Indian and Sri Lankan fisherfolk should not be taken as a territorial problem, but it is a human terrain problem', says Mahinda Rajapaksa, President of Sri Lanka and Fisheries Minister for three years.[79] However, Rajapaksa admits that all his initiatives have been spoiled because of different perceptions of the foreign ministry, changes in government and frequent elections. A number of documents also show that there have been several proposals and counter-proposals, submitted by both governments in these years, which have proposed arrangements and obligations on the fishermen as well as the navy/coast guards of both countries.[80]

The increasing number of killings and arrests on both sides has led various NGOs, labour support groups, trade unions, and individuals to get involved in ensuring the release of the arrested fisherfolk, supporting legal processes and proposing several long-term policy measures. On the Indian side, a trade union and NGO initiative led to the formation of ARIF (See Box 4.1).

Box 4.1: V. Vivekanandan on ARIF

1. *What are the initiatives and activities of the ARIF in the past 5 years?*
ARIF has been continuing to work on the release of Indian fishermen from Sri lankan jails and Sri Lankan fishermen from Indian jails. This is done on a case by case basis rather than on the basis of any common advocacy or policy intervention. As soon as we hear of an arrest, we try to lobby for release without prosecution. If this fails, we get into the legal system, fight the case and obtain a release. This is being done on both sides of the border by ARIF. Of course, we have collaborators on the Sri Lankan side, but we cannot sit back and let them do the work as the Sri Lankan side is not organised like us and will not put resources in this work. They only support our guys who go there to do the work.

Getting the boats back has been more difficult than getting the fishermen back. Recently we have managed to get court orders to release 83 Indian boats in Sri Lanka but many of them are in bad shape, some damaged during the tsunami. We have managed to get tsunami compensation for 15 boats so far and hope to get a similar benefit for the rest as well. We have now excellent working relationship with the Indian High Commission in Colombo, the Sri Lankan Deputy High Commission in Madras and the Fisheries Departments of Sri Lanka and Tamil Nadu. All acknowledge ARIF as a common link and fishermen on both sides come first to us rather than the government agencies.

In terms of advocacy, we have focussed on the long-term solutions. On the Indian side, this can only mean a reduction in our trawl fleet. This is too major a step for which there is no precedence in India. So we have been spreading this idea among the fishery policy-makers and now there is some interest in this idea. The idea of a trawler buy-back has been proposed by us for Rameswaram and this is now getting accepted as an idea for sorting out the trawler problem at the national level as well. In a recent meeting of the fisheries working group for the XI Five Year Plan, the idea of a buy-back scheme has been mooted. It might not go through, but the idea has been seeded. The South Indian Federation of Fishermen Societies (SIFFS) is planning a workshop in collaboration with the Tamil Nadu Fisheries Department in which the FAO has agreed to bring resource persons who can explain experiences with buy-back schemes elsewhere.

(Contd.)

(Contd.)

2. *How does ARIF perceive the current situation of arrests, harassment and killings of Indian and Sri Lankan fishermen? Do you see any change?*
   Arrests, as such, are routine affairs. However, the shootings are a result of the civil war once again breaking out in Sri Lanka. It is difficult to entirely prevent such incidents but we are able to minimise them by making noise. The Sri Lankan Deputy High Commissioner has agreed to take up such incidents if ARIF can give full particulars.

3. *After the 'historic goodwill', have you been able to implement the decisions in any way? What has been the follow up of the 'goodwill' and how?*
   The immediate follow up was weak and got completely derailed by the tsunami. The SIFFS got fully sucked into tsunami relief and ARIF activities were put on the back burner. On the Sri Lankan side, the return visit was also cancelled due to the tsunami. However, the recent spate of shootings has resulted in ARIF's services being once again in demand and the fishermen themselves are keen to revive the process. While the 'goodwill' visit has not been followed up meaningfully till now, the impact of the mission still continues. Now with more focus on the fishermen of Tamil Nadu and Sri Lanka as a result of the tsunami, the ideas generated by the mission are finding a wider audience and giving us the credibility to take the advocacy to a higher level. At the time of the mission, our strength was the rapport with the fishermen organisations, but the solutions required government interventions. Now we have higher credibility with the government and have a greater clout with them. This is also the result of SIFFS' work in the tsunami in Tamil Nadu where we are perhaps the largest local NGO involved in rehabilitation, building 2500 houses and undertaking many other initiatives. Even though we did not follow up the goodwill mission immediately, it appears that the delay was not a loss as we are now back with more vigour and power to influence.

4. *What are the concrete, as well as other broader outcomes, of ARIF's interventions?*
   ARIF was inspired by the SALF initiative on Pakistan and was seen more as a policy advocacy forum. However, it has become more of a permanent mechanism to release fishermen and boats that are captured regularly from time to time by both sides. At the same time, the policy advocacy part, though slow in evolving, is now once again becoming important, as we sense the possibility of a breakthrough. Since SIFFS is the main anchor of ARIF, we

(Contd.)

(*Contd.*)

have used ARIF's activities to get into fisheries policy advocacy. We have now FAO support for a pilot project to create community-based management systems in three locations in South India. Rameswaram is one of the locations and the trawl fleet reduction is a key agenda here. The FAO is also sponsoring a study by the Centre for Economic and Social Studies (CESS) in Hyderabad to undertake a study on the Rameswaram situation and analyse the consequences of a buy-back scheme.

Very concretely ARIF has been responsible for timely release of a large number of fishermen (the figure runs into hundreds) over the last 10 years and scores of boats. It has become an established institution for this and both fishermen and government departments use us for this. This gives us power and credibility to influence changes at fishermen level and policy level.

5. *How do you see the solution from the perspective of fisherfolk and their organisations?*

We see the problem as a fisheries problem and want a solution that allows the fishermen to pursue their livelihoods peacefully and legally. The fleets and technologies used should not harm the resources and not harm the livelihoods of small fishermen. Within this framework, border crossing should not be considered illegal and should be a permitted activity with some controls to ensure that resource management principles are adhered to and security concerns properly addressed.

Source: Email communication and interview with V. Vivekanandan, Convenor ARIF and Chief Executive, SIFFS, 9 December 2006.

Besides ARIF, initiatives like SALF, and organisations like the Centre for Education and Communication and the South Indian Federation of Fishermen Societies (SIFFS) too have been active. On the Sri Lankan side, there has been no particular organisation or network to take up the issue; instead a number of interest groups have got involved and have taken effective action. While the Forum for Human Dignity has been providing legal assistance to Indian fishermen, other NGOs, trade unions and fishermen's organisations like the National Fisheries Solidarity, and Social and Economic Development Centre have been giving various kinds of information and support.[81] Since Sri Lanka is a much smaller country and most things get decided at Colombo, its NGOs have been at times more effective in getting Indian fishermen released.

In the last three to four years the NGOs have been very proactive, and they have acquired considerable knowledge and information about the nature of the problem.[82]

As alternatives and prevention, it is being suggested in Sri Lanka that under a bilateral agreement, the arrested Sri Lankan and Indian fishermen should be immediately repatriated, taken into custody by their own authorities, and prosecuted for illegal fishing under their own national law.[83] In May 2004, a goodwill mission of Indian fishermen to Sri Lanka and a dialogue between the Tamil Nadu and Sri Lankan fishermen of the Palk Bay resulted in working out a compromise solution. Its report stated:

> The Indian side had agreed in principle that trawling has to be stopped in Sri Lankan waters, given that Sri Lankans are banning their own trawlers. No agreement was, however, reached on the time frame for stopping trawling, as the Indian side wanted a much longer period than what the Sri Lankans found acceptable. A three-month period has been given for further dialogue on the issue and for a mutually acceptable time frame; a Sri Lankan delegation will visit India during this period to carry forward the dialogue. As an interim measure, the Indian trawlers will keep a distance of three miles from the Sri Lankan coast in the Palk Bay and seven miles on the northern coast (the Jaffna-Vadamarachi stretch). The Indians will not use the four types of trawl nets earlier identified. Any violation of the above understanding by Indian boats will be reported to the Indian fishermen's organisations, which will take suitable action against the erring boats; the Sri Lankan fishermen will not take direct action. Both sides will work for the speedy release of fishermen and boats currently detained by both countries.[84]

Further, at the behest of ARIF and SIFFS on 28 October 2006 the Sri Lankan Deputy High Commissioner P. M. Amza hosted a dinner for fishermen leaders from districts, which had problems with the Sri Lankan navy. Around 12 fishermen from Nagai, Karai, Rameswaram and Pudukottai districts along with members of SIFFS were present. He promised to take up the issue of shooting by Sri Lankan navy, and to intervene in processes for release of Indian fishermen and boats.[85] Even before these path-breaking initiatives, there had been some efforts to organise dialogue between the affected fisherfolk of both countries: Rameswaram Fishermens' Cooperative Society of India and North Vadamarchchi

Fishermen's Cooperative of Sri Lanka organised the talks between fishermen of Tamil Nadu and Jaffna to work on the problems of fishing rights off the north-eastern coastline of Sri Lanka.[86]

Conclusion

Coastal fisherfolk on the borderlines of India and Sri Lanka cannot be appropriated within the narratives of borders and capital. Even when both states and the dominant civil–social institutions have taken recourse to descriptions confined to their borders and markets, the coastal fisherfolk continue to lead a subterranean, subversive life within them, as they refuse to be 'bonded' in any way. These insecure, militarised and terrorised states are only ready to recognise a single, demarcated, bordered form of coast, even at the cost of subjugating and suppressing aspirations of coastal communities. The struggle between coastal communities and capital in both countries, along with the defiance of coastal borders will continue. The aspirations of coastal communities can only be addressed and claimed by working on an alternative livelihood system, with rights to coastal spaces beyond national borders. To re-envision the coastal communities and spaces of India and Sri Lanka along pluralist and sustainable directions, the monological imagination of the fisherfolk aligned with national territory and identity in a singular and final fashion has to be changed. Further, coastal autonomy and devolution of power within the coastal areas should be an important step in mitigating the contemporary violence among the fisherfolk. Such autonomy, combined with efforts at creating joint management of resources will make coastal communities more earthy and real.

Every geographical coastal unit in South Asia is a combination of centuries of mixings, adulterated histories, cultural interminglings, natural migrations and multiplex affiliations. If provincial boundaries can be created on linguistic or other parti-cularity, surely coastal borders can be concretised on the coastal identity of coastal people, by the creation of coastal enclaves and by the promotion of cultural, economic, political and social linkages amongst them.

5

Ironies of Identities: India and Bangladesh

I belong nowhere. I am a people without a country. I have my roots in Bangladesh, but I have grown in India. I do not know what to say when I am asked as to where do I belong to. If pushed, I can say that I think of myself as an Indian, but I am still considered an outsider in India. Years back, I felt it safer to come to this side of the border for my livelihood since I was a Hindu. I feel more religious affinity to people in India. Few Muslim fishermen migrated. But I still feel attached to Bangladesh as well.

—Haribhakta Das[1]

These Bangladeshi fishermen come to our land and usurp our fish, our land, our livelihood. Why can't our government be more strict with these fishermen? They belong to Bangladesh. The Bangladeshi navy mistreats us so much if they catch us when we enter their territories. We are Indians and moreover Hindus. We are humiliated more because of our religion. Muslim fishermen of India, if caught, are treated differently by Bangladeshi authorities.

—Ramhari Das[2]

Haribhakta Das, a fisherman from Chittagong, Bangladesh, came to India 18 years ago. Some of his family members are still in Bangladesh. In India, he still does not have a ration-card and his name is not on the voters' list. Ancestors of Ramhari Das too had been fishermen. He was born in West Bengal and was caught once by the Bangladeshi navy while fishing. There has been a steady decline in his fishcatch over the period. The narratives by these two fishermen carry within them complex narratives of identities, linked to migrations, religious attachments, community constructs, national affiliations, ecological crisis and border crossings. Their discourses of sameness and difference reflect multilayered contradictions, which are an integral part of crossing of fishermen on the fluid borders of India and Bangladesh.

The 4,000 kilometre long porous India–Bangladesh border is a man-made one. It has been witness to a spectre of large-scale 'unauthorised' mass movements, of both short- and long-term immigrants, across the sea (and land) borders of West Bengal and Bangladesh, including a substantial number of fisherfolk. Migration was legal until 1952, although India and Bangladesh disregarded illegal migration until 1971. Since then, a discourse has developed in India in which migrants are depicted as infiltrators. According to Indian state officials, there are more than 20 million illegal Bangladeshis in India. This huge diaspora of mostly poor labour migrants has created political problems like anti-foreigner movements and pogroms, mass deportations and conflicts between India and Bangladesh, as well as economic benefits for both Indian and Bangladeshi economies.

This flow of people has been prompted by historical and social affinities, geographical contiguity and economic imperatives. Pitted against the natural urge for survival, 'nation' and 'border' have been easily marginalised in the minds of these migrants and they have found 'illegal' ways to tackle this obstacle in the path of their well-being.[3] What is also significant and different about crossings by fisherfolk across India–Bangladesh border is that unlike in the case of India and Sri Lanka or India and Pakistan, the fisherfolk here are not just temporary, short-term migrants; long-term migrations are an intrinsic part of coastal and marine fishing in this region.

Intense scale of ecological crisis and environmental disasters like famines and cyclones in Bangladesh, which have caused considerable human displacement, have resulted in large-scale movement of fisherfolk towards West Bengal. Gravely affected by ecological imbalance, these fishermen have desperately sought alternative domiciles, even if temporarily. Thus, there is an intrinsic relationship between migration and coastal ecosystems.[4] Most of the migrant fisherfolk are small-scale fishers, working either for a wage or for a share in the catch. They usually work on board vessels that are 10 to 12 metres in length, barely enough to stretch their backs. But they perceive that migration would give them the power to transform their circumstances.

Simultaneously, in the last 59 years, two partitions have produced a grotesque reality in the border zone between India and Bangladesh. There have been attempts from both sides to transform mixed villages on the border into exclusive Hindu/Muslim solidarities.[5] Fishing communities too have been drawn in this scenario. Moreover, there have been many other irritants and disputes between India and Bangladesh. Apart from the 'illegal' immigrants, Farakka barrage, handing over the enclaves, and fencing along the land and maritime border have been major sources of discontent between Dhaka and Delhi.[6]

Politics of Borders and Maritime Disputes

The careful balancing of maritime zones through UNCLOS III was regarded as reversing a disturbing trend in the marking of maritime boundaries in which some states claimed territorial seas up to 200 kilometres in order to create a monopoly over coastal resources or for purposes of security.[7] Since the convention entitled coastal states to exercise jurisdiction over a large part of the sea, even states that could own a tiny island of 7 miles radius could automatically obtain EEZ of an extraordinarily large area.[8] However, though UNCLOS III determined the precise limits of various maritime zones, it failed to agree on any single universal set of principles by which these boundaries were to be delimited. Consequently, the process of delimitation of the EEZ or the continental shelf between adjacent and opposite states, and subsequent demarcation of maritime boundaries continued to remain in dispute, and this is reflected in various maritime disagreements between South Asian countries. Articles 74 and 83 of UNCLOS III vaguely state that the delimitation of the EEZ or the continental shelf between states with opposite or adjacent coasts shall be affected by an agreement on the basis of international law, as referred to in Article 38 of the statute of the International Court of Justice, in order to achieve an equitable solution. As no distinction has been made in terms of delimitation between the EEZ and the continental shelf, or between adjacent or opposite coasts, such a formulation has considerable potential for misinterpretation. In effect, it is widely agreed that this does not constitute a reliable guide to negotiators or even arbitrators of delimitation questions.[9] As the 'median' or the 'equidistance' line between two coastal states had been sufficient to determine maritime boundaries in the past, this principle has largely been followed in UNCLOS III, for both adjacent and opposite coastal states. The international law of the sea also stresses that neither of the two states is entitled, failing agreement to the contrary, to extend its territorial sea beyond the 'median' line. However, this is not to apply where it is necessary, by historic title or other special circumstance, to delimit the territorial sea between two states in a manner different from this provision.[10]

In pursuance of UNCLOS III,[11] Bangladesh and India promulgated laws with regard to their EEZ, in order to explore marine resources in the Bay of Bengal. But these laws sometimes overlap and encroach upon one another's EEZ, due to the geographical and geo-morphological nature of coasts in the Bay of Bengal.[12]

Bangladesh has special reasons to be interested in the evolution of the law of the sea. Bangladeshis have historically been sea-faring people. The limited land-based food and fuel resources available to its people, and the disparity between resources and subsistence needs of a large population makes it imperative for Bangladesh to recognise the potential of oceans as a tangible promise for the future. Hence, the government of Bangladesh through an act of parliament enacted the Territorial Waters and Maritimes Zones Act, 1974 (Act no. XXVI of 1974).[13] This Act, however, did not specify the breadth of the EEZ of Bangladesh in the Bay of Bengal in clear-cut terms.

Bangladesh's coastal waters are said to have the following characteristics:[14]

1. The dynamic estuary of Bangladesh is such that no stable water line or demarcation of landward and seaward areas exist.[15]
2. The continual process of alluvium and sedimentation from many banks has made her coastal area so shallow as to be non-navigable by other than small boats.
3. The navigable channels of land through aforesaid banks are continuously changing their courses and require sounding and other detailed geological analysis for boundary demarcation so that the latter pertain to the character of river mouths and inland waters.

Bangladesh has a small coastline, but it has a huge continental shelf. However, as both India and Bangladesh explore their off-shore resource options in the Ganges delta through increased emphasis on the fishing sector and the exploration for hydro-carbons, overlapping claims and other resource disputes have become increasingly irritant factors in their bilateral relations.[16] In the absence of a 200 kilometre area as EEZ, the confusion over sea boundary has increased. Besides this technical aspect, the dispute over maritime boundary has important economic ramifications for Bangladesh because it affects Bangladesh's territorial sovereignty over the sea, fishing rights and ownership of seabed resources.

The India–Bangladesh maritime dispute primarily focuses on differences in the principles by which the maritime boundary is to be demarcated, as well as disputed sovereignty over a small island. The basis for conflicting claims lie in the choice of methods for lateral definition of the continental shelf around the Ganges delta. The Indian claim of maritime boundary demarcation and EEZ is based on the equidistant/median-line principle. Bangladesh, on the other hand, favours the application of the equitable principle.

The configuration of the coast of Bangladesh is concave, whereas that of India convex. According to a scholar from Bangladesh, if the sea zones are delimited by equidistance principle, the state with the concave coast will lose in having the sea zones, against the convex coast country. Where the coastal configurations are identical, the sea zones delimited by equidistance principle between coastal states will somewhat be equitable. This gives rise to a point that delimitation of maritime zones between Bangladesh and India by equidistance principle will not result in an equitable principle and this cannot be imposed on a coastal state by another coastal state in the delimitation of sea zones between them. Further, by nature equidistance principle is specific and rigid, while the equitable one is more open-ended and abstract.[17]

Bangladesh, to mitigate the negative effects of its concave coast, prefers to have a 10-fathom base-line for the measurement of its 200 nautical miles EEZ from this line. This would lead to enclosing hundreds of square miles of continental shelf within its internal waters. It has also been lobbying for the drawing of straight base-lines along the farthest seaward extent of a submerged sedimentary delta, in area where the greatest part of coastline is constituted by a continuous process of sedimentation of fluvial deposits rendering the low-water line unstable.[18] Moreover, by the application of the 'median line' principle between India and Bangladesh, as well as between Myanmar and Bangladesh, it is seen that Bangladesh will get self-locked, and thereby will be unable to claim the full extent of its EEZ or continental shelf.[19]

In the case of Indo–Bangladesh EEZ boundary demarcation in the Bay of Bengal, India claims that the block awarded to Ashland actually falls in her EEZ. Bangladesh, on the other hand, to overcome the disadvantage of its recessed coastline, announced unilaterally a 10-fathom base-line, except west of Cox's Bazar where there is deep landward indention of isobaths. Bangladesh declared that under this criterion, Ashland region came within its EEZ. It maintained that wide fluctuations in the low-water mark and extensive areas of shallow water meant that the area could not be charted in the usual way. It was also argued that apart from the channels leading to the ports of Chalna and Chittagong, most of the area in question was not navigable. By claiming this base-line, Bangladesh has also sought to convert 6,200 square nautical miles of its potential EEZ into the country's internal territorial water.

On 30 April 1982, the Burmese and the Indian delegations rejected this defence of Bangladesh's actions, arguing that there was no possible justification for these base-lines. They stated that even if the coast of the Ganges delta was considered to be shallow and liable to retreat, that was no excuse for fixing the base-line as much as 50 nautical miles seaward of the nearest land. Because this base-line is not anchored to the coast, it would be technically possible to sail into the internal waters of Bangladesh without crossing the straight base-line.[20]

Bangladesh has no agreed sea boundary with its neighbours. The delimitation of maritime boundaries has created a conflict between Bangladesh and its neighbours. Disagreement arose mainly with India when the Bangladesh government in 1974 signed contracts to share production with six international oil companies, granting them oil and natural gas exploration rights in its territorial waters in the Bay of Bengal (see Box 5.1). Thus, the Bangladesh line moved towards the south from the edge of its land boundary, while the Indian line took a south-easterly direction, thus creating an angle within which lie thousands of square miles of the Bay, claimed by each country as its economic zone. This conflicting claim has become a critical problem between these countries. Thus, the delimitation of maritime boundaries is an all-important matter for Bangladesh and its authority in the seas. For example, the territorial sea, EEZ and the continental shelf will depend on how this dispute is resolved.[21] Harekrishna Debnath, chairman of the NFF observes:

> Since the mid 1970s, after the International Conference on the Law of the Sea, a sense of EEZ and maritime boundary has deeply got involved with questions of sovereignty of a nation. All nations, particularly those with coastal lines, are engaged therefore in demarcating their maritime boundaries. However, while theoretically this has been realised, unlike land, it is not easy to demarcate sea boundaries. The process is also tied closely to the lives of millions of fisherfolk all across the globe. India–Bangladesh are no exception to this. Between them, there is less than 400 kilometres area in the sea. Thus there is an absence of the 200 kilometres EEZ on both sides, though it theoretically exists. This has lead to a great amount of confusion. In this situation it is not only difficult but near impossible to maintain the LOS decision.[22]

Although negotiations have been going on since 1974, Bangladesh and India have been unable to settle the delimitation problem, mainly because of the concave nature of the Bangladesh coast. Bangladesh's position is that no right principle can be applied in the present case and that the basic guideline should be equity. India on the other hand, applies the equidistance principle in delimiting the boundary, ignoring the physical features of the coast.[23] It is imperative that an amicable solution be reached regarding this problem, even if it is based on the equitable principle.

Box 5.1: Coastal Geography and Conflict in Bangladesh

Bangladesh cannot settle its maritime boundary dispute without taking into account the concerns of its neighbours—India and Burma. As a small and weak state, it must be cautious about its security interests in the Bay of Bengal. As an adjacent state, Bangladesh faces the task of delimitation of sea zones with India extending from the coast of the latter's mainland to the states of West Bengal and Orissa. Moreover, with respect to the continental shelf/margin, the country requires to fix the boundary with India as an opposite state taking into account the Andamans and Nicobar Islands. India is in an advantaged position because of its convex coast. When it comes to delimiting the continental shelf/margin with Bangladesh, the Andamans and Nicobar Islands also place India in a favourable position. The most active jurisdictional dispute that exists among the Indian Ocean littoral states is between India and Bangladesh in the Bay of Bengal where an area of

(Contd.)

(*Contd.*)

4,000 square nautical miles is under dispute in the Bengal Basin. This dispute arose when Bangladesh issued exploration right to six companies in 1974, which was viewed in India as an encroachment upon the 'Indian-Claimed' seabed areas, particularly around the Ashland block. The territorial sovereignty issues with respect to the newly emerged islands within the Bay of Bengal further complicated these overlapping claims.

Source: R. C. Sharma and P. C. Sinha, *Maritime Boundary Delimitation and India in India's Ocean Policy*, Khama Publishers, New Delhi, 1994, p. 115; M. Habibur Rahman, 'Delimitation of Maritime Boundaries: Some Pertinent Issues for Bangladesh', in M. G. Kabir and Shaukat Hassan (eds), *Issues and Challenges Facing Bangladesh Foreign Policy*, Dhaka, Bangladesh, 1989, p. 115.

Further, both India and Bangladesh claim an island covering an area of 2 square miles, lying in the estuary of the Haribhanga and Raimangal rivers in the Bay of Bengal. This U-shaped island known as New Moore or Purbhasha in India and South Talpatti in Bangladesh lies 5 nautical miles off the Ganges delta from Bangladesh's coast and 2 nautical miles off India's coast. This island, a no man's land between India and Bangladesh, emerged in 1970 due to acute volcanic activity in the area and was discovered by the Indian navy in the following year. India claims the island on the grounds that the flow of the Haribhanga river is to the east of the island and the island lies on the natural prolongation of Indian territory. Meanwhile, Bangladesh claims that the river flows to the west of the island, as a result of which it is not possible to clearly distinguish the natural prolongation of the Indian territory.[24] The sovereignty over Talpatti is becoming very important because of growing crime by the sea pirates on this island, which remains unresolved. Bangladesh's failure to vigorously assert its ownership over it only strengthens India's claim over the island by virtue of its actual control. And as long as the 'Shanti Bahini' finds sanctuary and arms across the border, it is unlikely to agree to a negotiated settlement of the Chittagong Hill Tracts (CHT) issue. Thus the insurgency in the CHT and the land and maritime boundary issues constitute a direct threat to Bangladesh's territorial security.[25] Sub-divisional police officer (SDPO) of Kakdwip, Amitabh Verma, thinks that this is of equal, if not more, concern for India. He says in an interview:

> Bangladesh Rifles (BDR) and sea pirates from both the countries basically create the question of maritime conflict. Talpatti is a no man's land. It is a part of Bangladesh. This is a huge area of around 21 kilometres. In the India–Bangladesh map, we can see a river named Raimangal. This river was basically the demarcation line between India and Bangladesh. But after certain natural developments in that zone, Talpatti became a centre for pirates. Kakdwip police of district 24 South Parganas encountered 16 pirates in the Kedo islands in 1989, and some of them were also caught under the 14 Foreigners' Act.[26]

In May 1981 there was a brief scuffle over its possession—three Bangladeshi gunboats threatened an Indian survey ship in the area. This ended with the dispatch of an Indian frigate, the *INS Andaman*, to the island.[27] The issue was again discussed in 1990, but no tangible solutions could be found. Thus, despite a series of negotiations, Bangladesh and India have still not been successful in settling the dispute over the island. Claims and counter-claims have been made. Both countries claim that the island lies in its territorial sea and thus its settlement is linked to the marking of territorial sea boundary first.[28]

The dispute over the island has more to do with the extent of the maritime zone to be potentially acquired in the oil rich Ganges–Brahmaputra delta, than the island itself.[29] If India is given sovereignty over the island, it can claim an additional 16,000 square metres of continental shelf.[30] However, if Bangladesh is given sovereignty over the island, it will get a much lesser area of the continental shelf.[31] This complex intertwining of questions concerning the new international laws of the sea and coastal geographies of neighbouring states, combined with conflicting and contested spatialities, have added further elements of discord in the South Asian maritime affairs.

The maritime borders between India and Bangladesh therefore are neither 'natural', nor can they be always clear-cut and stable even if they are drawn. Rather, borders like the meanings of any signifiers are always in a flux here. The boundary as a physical and geographical marker actually signifies an experimental, liminal space here, filled with border-crossing encounters. Besides the boundary disputes, the ecological crisis in the region has added to the problems.

Harsh Habitations: Poverty, Fishing, Ecological Malaise and Migrations

Bangladeshis live in extreme poverty. It is one of the world's most densely populated countries. Its population is over 120 million and will double in 35 years at its current 2 per cent growth rate. While the country has made noteworthy economic and social strides since Independence in 1971, its long-term challenges are immense. Bangladesh has limited natural resources and is highly vulnerable to devastating cyclones, floods, and droughts. Its per capita income is under US $ 250, and over half of its population is below the poverty line. Eighty per cent of its population live in rural areas, where the incidence of poverty is greater. Two-thirds of children under six in Bangladesh suffer from moderate to severe malnutrition. The country faces a future of mounting stress on the carrying capacities of its natural ecosystems and its human service systems.[32]

At the same time, about 34 per cent of the area of Bangladesh is under water almost six months each year. The country has extensive riverine systems, as well as productive coastal and marine fishing grounds. It has rich and diverse natural resources for fisheries and many fish species. It has one of the largest freshwater fisheries in the world. Estimates of the total yearly harvest range from 750,000 to 1,500,000 metric tonnes. The fisheries sector makes important contributions to employment, income, food consumption, nutrition, trade, commerce and foreign exchange earnings. Fish and other aquatic products account for 6 per cent of the country's gross domestic product and more than 12 per cent of its export earnings. Fish supply approximately 80 per cent of the animal protein and 7 per cent of the total protein intake in the average Bangladeshi diet.

The number of fisherfolk here is more than the total population of many countries. A majority of the country's 120 million people live in river flood-plains and engage in some fishing activities. There are estimated to be about 2.4 million full-time professional fishermen and 11 million part-time, mainly subsistence fishermen, whose numbers peak in the June–October monsoon season (see, Table 5.1). Altogether, these fishermen and their families represent about 50 per cent of Bangladesh's population. For subsistence fishermen and their families, the fish they catch is often their only source of protein and essential minerals. Fisheries are vital to the life of the people here. Thus, a fisherman of the region remarks: '*mache to jeevano* (fish is my life).'

Table 5.1: Employment and Trade in Fisheries in Bangladesh

Estimated Employment (1997)	
Primary Sector:	
Full-time Fisherfolk	570,000
Part-time Fisherfolk	1,196,000
Secondary Sector:	NA
Gross Value of Fisheries Output (1997)	
(At Ex-vessel Prices, Estimate)	US $ 1,000 million (= 3.12% of GDP)
Trade (1994/95)	
Value of Imports (Estimate)	US $ 590,000 (Average 1994–1995)
Value of Exports	US $ 325.11 million
	(9.38% of Total Export)

Source: http://www.fao.org/fi/fcp/en/BDG/profile.htm.

The fishing activity in this region shows promise. According to a World Bank report:

The natural resources to support a growing fisheries sector are abundant. More than 1 million ha. of perennial inland water bodies, and over 3 million ha. of flood plains (30% of total area of Bangladesh), provide an extensive and highly fertile area suited to inland fish production, while some 4 million ha. of coastal and offshore waters contain productive areas and fish stocks to support marine fisheries.[33]

Table 5.2: Overview of Fisheries Sector in Bangladesh

Commodity Balance (1995)	Production	Imports	Exports	Stocks Variat-ions	Total Food Supply	Per Caput Supply Kg/Year
		'000 Tonnes Live Weight				
Fish for Direct Human Consumption	1,170	0.3	38	0	1,128	9.5
Non-Food Uses	5					

Source: Same as Table 5.1.

However, despite their contribution to the national income, the fishing community faces increasing problems, including depletion from overfishing and coastal pollution. Since 1980, notwithstanding its rich resources, fish production in Bangladesh has grown at only 3 per cent per year.[34] The inland fisheries particularly have suffered; thus, marine fisheries have had an important role in compensating for the decline in catches from inland fisheries. The share of marine fisheries in total national landings has increased from 10.6 per cent in 1970 to 28.2 per cent in 1993. Around 95 per cent of marine fish production is estimated to come from artisanal fishing, practiced on the extensive continental shelf. Industrial trawlers produce the remaining 5 per cent. Industrial trawling first started here with an introduction of seven trawlers in 1971. Presently, some 53 Bangladeshi trawlers fish in the Bay of Bengal, 40 of which are engaged in shrimp trawling and the others in fish targeting. The Government of Bangladesh, through the Bangladesh Fisheries Development Corporation (BFDC) operates a small fleet of fish and shrimp trawlers; others are privately owned.[35]

Ecological problems abound in this region. Gobal climatic change is the most serious of the major long-term environmental concerns likely to affect the country over the coming decades. The rise in greenhouse gas emissions and consequently in temperature may also cause the sea level to rise, enough to affect up to one-third of the coastal area by the year 2050. Although the impacts of global warming are still far from precisely predictable, the prospect is sufficiently likely and alarming to warrant precautionary action at the national as well as the international level.[36] Bangladesh also suffers from disasters like floods and famines, endemic ills like land degradation, desertification, salinity, water crises and deforestation.

The coastal regions of Bangladesh have seen growing ecological threats. Indiscriminate killing of hilsa fry, popularly known as *jhatka*, continues unabated despite a ban on it. According to reports, about 3,200 fishing trawlers and over 10,000 fishing boats fitted with 'current nets' are on the ceaseless hunt for *jhatka* in different rivers and in the Bay of Bengal. It is alleged that a section of the unscrupulous staff members of the fisheries department in collaboration with policemen are engaged in illegal *jhatka* trade.[37] Bangladesh earns a considerable amount of foreign exchange from the export of shrimp and prawn. The government has declared shrimp cultivation a priority industry and to boost its production, specific support programmes, both technical and financial, have been designed. Recently the estimated amount of shrimp export was about 38,000 metric tonnes and it is increasing every year. As a consequence of the shrimp trade, a vast area in the coastal zones of Khulna, Satkhira, Bagherhat and Cox's Bazar has been converted into shrimp farms.[38] However, many farming and fishing communities throughout the region are protesting against the intrusion into the lands and the despoliation of their land and water resources by aquaculture farms. Alongside farmers, fishing communities too have been badly hit as aquaculture ponds have blocked their access to the sea from their village and displaced the places where the fisherfolk land and park their boats and spread their nets. The fisherfolk's catch is also depleted by pollution from the ponds and by the capture of young shrimp by the aquaculture farms for their hatcheries. If one takes into account sustainability and the total household economy, shrimp farming has not resulted in tangible local benefits. Instead, income distribution from it has been heavily biased in favour of the owners or controllers of the field.[39]

The biggest ecological threat that Bangladesh faces is to its 6,000 sq kilometre Sundarbans, which are considered the largest mangrove wetlands in the world and a world heritage site. Parts of the Sundarbans also belong to India. They represent 53 per cent of Bangladesh's total forest area, forming a natural shield against nature's fury, cyclones and tidal surges from the Bay of Bengal that often devastate Bangladesh's coast. They are a source of livelihood for three to four million people in south-western Bangladesh. The most eloquent description of areas in and around them comes in the new novel by Amitav Ghosh, which also highlights how Sundarbans offer the classic case of blurred boundaries:

> Until you behold it for yourself, it is almost impossible to believe that here, interposed between the sea and the plains of Bengal, lies an immense archipelago of islands. But that is what it is: an archipelago, stretching for almost 300 kilometres, from the Hoogly River in West Bengal to the shores of the Meghna in Bangladesh.
> The islands are the trailing threads of India's fabric, the ragging fringe of her sari, the *achol* that follows her, half-wetted by the sea.... The

rivers' channels are spread across the land like a fine-mesh net, creating a terrain where the boundaries between land and water are always mutating, always unpredictable....

There are no borders here to divide fresh water from salt, river from sea.... The currents are so powerful as to reshape the islands almost daily....

When the tides create new land, overnight mangroves begin to gestate, and if the conditions are right they can spread so fast as to cover a new island within a few short years....

There is no prettiness here to invite the stranger in: yet, to the world at large this archipelago is know as 'the Sundarban', which means, 'the beautiful forest'.[40]

Sundarbans are vital to fish production, animal grazing, and production of natural fuel and manure.[41] There are more species of fish in the Sundarbans than in Europe. They provide a living for fishermen and thousands of families who collect timber, firewood and honey. However, studies on water management in Bangladesh have shown how the successive Flood Action Programmes (FAP) have affected the wetlands, fisheries and *char* (sandbed) lands, leading to further erosion, salinity, and decline in the employment potential of fishermen and women particularly (see also Box 5.2). Further, Sundarbans have been subject to large-scale poaching and timber smuggling.[42]

Box 5.2: Protecting While Exploiting Fisheries and Wetlands

Bangladesh has some of the world's most important wetlands (e.g., the world's largest mangrove wetland, the Sundarbans). In a sense, almost the entire country can be considered to be a vast network of wetlands which include rivers, lakes, floodplains, ponds and even seasonally flooded agricultural lands. Practically the whole country, except for a few highland areas, is seasonally flooded during the monsoon and can therefore be considered to be wetlands of one kind or another. In addition to having very important natural ecosystem functions, as important habitats in their own right, the wetlands of Bangladesh also constitute important fisheries, which is a major source of protein and micronutrients to the people, particularly the poor, as well as generate employment for large numbers of people. These wetlands and their associated fisheries are increasingly coming under threat from both natural causes, such

---

(*Contd.*)

(*Contd.*)

as siltation and raising of the lands, as well as human interventions such as building embankments to protect agricultural land from monsoon flooding. At current rate, most of the large inland wetlands are likely to be soon lost forever, as happened to the Chalan Beel in Rajshahi over the last two decades. Many of the major fish species, most notably the Indian carp, have been also considerably depleted over the last few decades in the open water catch of the rivers and floodplains.

The fisheries sector of Bangladesh, comprising open water capture fisheries (both fresh water and marine) and closed water culture fisheries, which includes export-oriented shrimp cultivation, offer enormous promises for a breakthrough in terms of production, export earnings as well as employment generation. In the case of open water fisheries the experience with projects trying to re-stock them with major carp species have shown that production can indeed be raised significantly if done properly. An important factor in protecting the open water fisheries will be the role of embankments in future as these could have a negative impact on open water fisheries.

The failure to maintain the wetlands in the face of radical engineering interventions is undermining natural fish production by silting up of the canals and estuaries. It is estimated that within the next 10 years the annual loss in fish production would be the equivalent of 12 per cent to 18 per cent of today's catches.

Source: Bangladesh Development Series, *Bangladesh 2020: A Long-Run Perspective Study*, World Bank and Bangladesh Centre for Advanced Studies, University Press Limited, Dhaka, 1998, http://www.worldbank-bangladesh.org.

Another major problem in this region is the cyclones, which affect the Bangladeshi fishermen particularly, though even West Bengal fishermen do not escape it (see, Box 5.3). The fishermen in the region constantly face insecurity and fear of death. Amitav Ghosh, while referring to fishermen in the Sundarbans area, remarks:

When the menfolk went fishing it was the custom for their wives to change into the garments of widowhood. They would put away their marital reds and dress in white saris; they would take off their bangles and wash the vermillion from their heads. It was as though they were trying to hold misfortune at bay by living through it over and over again. Or was it merely a way of preparing themselves for that which they knew to be inevitable?[43]

Box 5.3: Monsoons, Cyclones and Fishermen of Bay of Bengal

The biggest problem that the coastal fisherfolk of both West Bengal and Bangladesh face is continuous cyclones in the Bay of Bengal region. Many lives have been lost due to this.

On 11–12 November 2002, 34 fishermen were feared dead and 560 were reported missing in the Bay of Bengal after a cyclone. Their trawlers capsized. These included fishermen from West Bengal and Bangladesh. West Bengal's Fisheries Department Minister, Kiranmoy Nanda, stated that nine trawlers sank off the Digha coast during the storm and only 66 fishermen were rescued. The cyclone lashed the southern coast of Bangladesh, destroying fishing villages and rice farms.

Source: '34 Fishermen Feared Dead, 560 Missing in Bay of Bengal', *Deutche Presse Agentur*, 13 November 2002.

Again, in July 2003, 173 fishermen went missing off Bangladesh's coast after 20 trawlers sank in rough weather in the Bay of Bengal. In the Borguna district on the southern coast, 77 fishermen on 12 trawlers were unaccounted for after a sudden and heavy downpour, said chief of the local trawler owners association, Golam Mostafa Chowdhury. Borguna's police superintendent Fazlur Rahman noted that such incidents were normal during Bangladesh's monsoon.

Weather authorities had warned fishermen of a medium level storm but the fishermen apparently ignored the warning as the monsoon is prime catch season. Trawler accidents are frequent in the turbulent Bay of Bengal. Fifty-three fishermen were reported dead in boat capsizes in the Bay in June.

Calamity-prone Bangladesh, criss-crossed by 230 rivers, has been hard hit since heavy rains began in April, submerging stretches of the country and setting off flash floods. Bangladesh's Relief and Disaster Management Minister, Chowdhury Kamal Ibne Yusuf, called last week for the country to study ways to limit the human and material damage of disasters, saying some 500,000 people have died in natural calamities in the past 40 years.

Source: Aroop Talukdar, '173 Fishermen Missing, 20 Trawlers Sink in Bengal Sea', *Agence France-Presse*, 28 July 2003.

Fishermen in Bangladesh also tend to suffer more due to cyclones because they use traditional modes of fishing, and are not very familiar with modern technologies, which in any case are expensive and sometimes questionable. Fish catching methods are generally based on traditional fishnets, boats and icebox. These fisherfolk often lack proper information on oceanic disturbances that can create havoc in the coastal zone, particularly when a cyclone hits it.

Box 5.4: Artisanal Coastal Fisheries in Bangladesh

Artisanal coastal fisheries include both commercial and subsistence fishing. The last survey (1988) showed that of 67,300 artisanal fishing boats, only 6,000 were mechanised. Most people living in coastal communities make their livelihood from fishing and—unlike inland fishing communities—are almost totally dependent on it. Fisheries in Bangladesh, particularly marine and brackish-water fisheries are faced with a dilemma. On the one hand, fisheries provide the people of Bangladesh with protein at a reasonable price, and generate employment, income and foreign exchange. On the other hand, fisheries—particularly the in-shore marine and estuarine fisheries— are under stress due to over-fishing, environmental and habitat degradation and competing uses of water systems. The Government of Bangladesh has committed to preserve and conserve the aquatic resources of the country and the related environments, while seeking sustainable ways of exploiting the resources to benefit the population. To this end, the government has drawn up a Perspective Development Plan for the period 1995–2010 to give direction to *inter alia* the fisheries sector and its development. A National Fisheries Policy for fisheries development and management was drafted in 1998 and approved by the government. Sustainable management of aquatic resources and the management mechanisms necessary to achieve it form an important part of the plan.

Source: National Workshop on Fisheries: Resources Development and Management in Bangladesh, Madras, 1997, http://www.fao.org/docrep/X5625E/X5625E00.htm#Contents.

In India too coastal sea fishing has suffered, though in Bangladesh the ecological problems are much more severe. The growing facilities given by the Indian state governments are mainly supporting inland fishing, where over 78 per cent of production is from aquaculture. India's big 'blue revolution' has failed to touch the lives of reverine and marine fisherfolk.[44] Ninety per cent of traditional fisher people live below poverty line.[45] For about

10–15 per cent of the Indian population living in the coastal area fishing is the sole means of livelihood. The total catch of marine fish in India, estimated at 2.7 million tonnes in 1994–95 is far less than the estimated sustainable yield of approximately 4 million tonnes in the EEZ.[46] There has been a decline in fish catch also due to the indiscriminate use of nylon nets to catch *chingrir meen*, the spawn of tiger prawn. The nets are so fine that they catch the eggs of all the other fish as well.

The necessity for sustainable fisheries is now being increasingly recognised, due to the gradual decline in open water fish production because of resource depletion. The gap between supply and demand for fish has widened, with a decline in production and increasing human population. The per capita fish availability has decreased; thus, fisher community has become impoverished.[47] The field-work in Midnapur and 24 South Parganas districts—in the areas of Kakdwip, Kalinagar, Gangadharpur, Sankarpur and Contai—revealed the pathetic condition of fisherfolk. In such a scenario, when India too is facing an ecological crisis on its coastal waters and the condition of its fisherfolk is bad, the migration of fisherfolk from Bangladesh results in greater insecurities. While there have been various reasons for the migration of fisherfolk from Bangladesh to India, environmental factors have been crucial in compounding the water problems in Bangladesh, leading to large-scale migrations, mainly to India. 'Floodplans', as the official approach towards water management in Bangladesh has succinctly been described, speaks of the deep connection between water and migration.

However, even Indian fishermen drift towards Bangladesh. Like their Bangladeshi counterparts, West Bengal coastal fishermen too live like nomads, constantly facing the dangers of oceanic disturbances. As in the case of India–Pakistan and India–Sri Lanka, they too enter into another's arenas knowingly and unknowingly. Often they accidentally drift into neighbouring waters because of engine failures or strong currents.[48] Simultaneously, unprecedented migration of fishing vessels across sea borders has been facilitated by technological developments in the small-scale fisheries sector. Improved and affordable technology has made it possible for such sectors to target fishery resources in distant waters, especially since the 1990s. Global positioning systems (GPS) and radio communications; hulls, nets, hooks and ropes made of stronger and lighter material; and growing markets for fish and fish products, have emboldened the small-scale fishermen to venture out into distant fishing grounds.[49]

Harekrishna Debnath, who is originally from Bangladesh and came to India at the time of 'liberation' adds another critical dimension to these crossings of borders:

> Only Contai produces dry fish. Some Bangladeshi fishermen therefore come here to produce dry fish in the months of September–November. While the production of dry fish is here, its consumption is very much in Bangladesh. For poultry farms, dry fish is very important, and this has also led to some piracy, especially from 1990. On the other hand, Hilsa is available more readily in Bangladesh, but its real consumer is in West Bengal. Most of the migrated Bangladeshi fisherfolk know this fact, and thus are always trying to catch Hilsa available on the Bangladesh side, to improve their earnings.[50]

Insecurities in this area have become more acute[51] due to a combination of environmental migrations, declining fish catch, social conflicts, concerns for national security, piracy, trafficking and illegal trade on the Indo–Bangladesh border, making crossing of sea boundaries and fishing major issues in the recent years.

It needs to be however remembered that crossing the sea in this region is closely related to its socio-economic environment, which has been very poor since centuries. East Pakistan, presently Bangladesh, was in all respects the worst of the three regions. It had been one of the most neglected parts of the Empire, whose economy had been greatly damaged at the end of the 18th century.[52] Between the first partition from India in 1947 and the second from Pakistan in 1971, life here was relatively tranquil.[53] After Independence, this region remained undeveloped. The increasing dependency on fishing and other agricultural activities here is because of the poor development of industries and service sectors. This is combined with environmental problems, floods and increasing costal disturbances. Thus the migration of fisherfolk largely from Bangladesh to West Bengal has taken place against a historical background. There are other significant dimensions to migrations too, to which we now turn.

Shifting Terrains of Nationalism and Communalism: Paradoxes of Crossings

Religious identities too seem to have played a significant role in these migrations, as discourses around it have shaped the everyday politics of boundary crossings among the fisherfolk of this region. Traditionally, most of the professional fishermen in Bangladesh had been the low caste Hindus, the Dalits, particularly of the Rajbanshi, Bapari, Dhibar, Bagdi and Halder communities. They belonged to the poorest segment of the population, oppressed and exploited both by Muslim fundamentalists and by upper caste Hindus. In the social stratified society of Bangladesh, fishing was considered a taboo for most Muslims. But in the last few decades, the number of Muslim fishermen, has increased. This has happened despite intense social pressure from their co-religionists who regarded the involvement of anyone from their village in fishing as impinging on the status of the community. Because of this social stigma, people who have overcome this social barrier fish occasionally but relatively intensely during the period when fish is easily available.[54] Many Dalit fishermen started feeling somewhat discriminated against and marginalised in this scenario and migrated to India. Thus most of the coastal fishermen in West Bengal are low caste Hindu refugees, belonging to the castes mentioned above and also to Jalada and Malo castes.[55] This became apparent during fieldwork in Kakdwip, a coastal area of West Bengal, which was dominated by Dalit Hindu fishermen, most of who migrated from Bangladesh in 1971 or after. Due to their minority status in Bangladesh, they felt it easier to stay and work in India.

A poem eloquently says, 'life is lived in transformation'.[56] Migrations by Hindu fishermen of Bangladesh to West Bengal have lead to transformations in their discourses of social identities, where they increasingly express and mark their religious identity much more than their national one. Their narratives are seeped in multivocality in terms of their geographical space, while adopting a univocal language for their religious affiliation. While their place and spatial structure is not fixed but shifting, they emphasise their religious identity and social and economic relations rather than geographical fixities. They 'fix' their religion, but leave 'open' their territory. Manik Das, one such fisherman, states: 'Fishing is my only occupation. I was not feeling nice in Bangladesh, and so I came to India some 22 years ago. But I cannot deny my past or my roots also. At present however, I feel more comfortable here among my co-religionists. Now I have even got a ration-card and I am also an Indian voter.'[57] Because of their circumstances, these fisherfolk have developed new mechanisms of adaptation that draw on sources of collective religious identity and solidarity, while at the same time attempting to relate to notions of formal nationality and citizenship.

There has almost been a demographic revolution in the border areas of West Bengal since the 1970s particularly, which has transformed the region's social geography. Bindu Das, secretary, Sundarban Samudrik Matsyajibi Shramik Union, Kakdwip, notes that many fishermen in the Kakdwip region are from Bangladesh, but for all practical purposes are now settled here. He remarks: 'In Kakdwip, there are more than 10,000 fisherfolk who have come from East Bengal, both before and after 1971. Most of them are Hindus. All of them neither have ration cards, nor are they in the voters' list. It becomes therefore difficult to classify them as citizens either of Bangladesh or of India. It is near impossible to say as to where they belong to.[58] These fishermen thus simultaneously belong to two nations or rather to none of them. But while the identities of these fisherfolk are free to an extent from geographical boundedness, there are other identifications which are taking place across spaces. As has been pointed out, 'In the world of contemporary theory, identity is widely understood as lived and imagined in ways that break down its contiguousness with geographically bounded locality.'[59]

What makes the situation more complicated is that many of the fisherfolk of Kakdwip caught by the Bangladeshi navy on charges of crossing the maritime boundary are/were actually 'Bangladeshi'. The rhetoric of religious divide again gets played up here, combined with anger against Bangladesh authorities. Haribhakta Das originally from Bangladesh was once arrested by the Bangladeshi navy. He shouts angrily: 'The Bangladesh navy behaves like our enemy [shatru]. I was physically examined by them as they wanted to know if I had had circumcision [khatna] or not. They thus wanted to determine if I was a Hindu or a

Muslim fisherman. Other Bangladeshi prisoners kept abusing me, though I too am from there originally. I could not get any meat in the jail as they only served beef once a week, and this really hurt my religious sensibilities as well.[60]

The emotional evocation of religious identification provides a poignant glimpse of ways in which changing social contexts destablise fixed and unitary notions of community, culture and nationality. Manik Das, another Hindu fisherman originally from Bangladesh was caught and detained in the Bangladeshi jail, and had painful experiences to narrate:

> Fishing is my only occupation. I came to India from Bangladesh 22 years ago. Now I have a ration-card and I am also an Indian voter. I have some bonding with Bangladesh, but am more at home in India now as I am a Hindu. I had been working on a boat owned by Kalinga Das. Due to low and high tides, it is sometimes difficult to control the movement of our boats. In any case, wherever there is fish, there are fisherfolk. On the morning of 29 February 1999, I was arrested and kept in the Bagerhat jail, near Khulna in Bangladesh and I was freed only on 8 August 1999. At the time of my arrest, I was severely beaten up by the navy, and this continued in the jail. I got only a quarter of my normal food intake. They gave me one bread [ek ta roti] in the morning, four in the afternoon and very little rice [alpa bhat] at night. I was not allowed to write a single letter at home. I kept telling them that I too had lived in their country for a long time, but they would not listen to me. Even other Bangladeshi prisoners behaved very badly with me, and my religion had a great deal to do with it. There were 21 more of such fisherfolk with me at that time.[61]

The anger of Haribhakta Das and Manik Das perhaps also contains within it an attempt to form an alternative community based on sectarian divisions. In this new imagined community, their religious identities become more important while their national identities are elided. These fishermen, by their very status and nature, are simultaneously fishermen, Bangladeshi, Indian and Hindus, which has led them to express multiple, paradoxical and at times oppositional identities.

What are the stories and the narratives of the Indian fisherfolk, who live amidst the migrated Bangladeshi fisherfolk? Ironically, we find that for many of the Indian fisherfolk, the Indian state and even the fishermen's bodies, it is the national identity of these migrated fishermen from Bangladesh which remains the focus and their religious affiliation is underplayed. However, if these immigrant fishermen are Muslim, then both their religious and national identity is seen as a threat. For them, Bangladeshi fishermen are a menace, as they have entered their geographical spaces and usurped what was rightfully 'theirs'. As the quote in the beginning by Ramhari Das emphasises, many of them resent the presence of these migrated fishermen in their midst, whom they see as 'illegal aliens'. The regulation of immigration, appeals of security, national cohesion and keeping the 'alien' at bay have a popular appeal as well. Thus the imagined communities are played out differently by the fishermen.

Contradictions abound here as well. The discourse of Indian fishermen, who have at some point illegally crossed the international maritime boundary, and have been arrested, detained and even faced bullets from the Bangladesh side, is of course tragic. It is simultaneously however seeped in a communal language as well, reflecting religious solidarities. There is also not a surpassing of the nationalist sentiment, but rather a recycling of different forms of nationalism in their narratives.

In most interviews, there is a shared rhetoric of Hindu/Muslim divisions, which extends mostly into anger against authorities. There is thus the story of a boat-owner Sunil Kumar Das. He states:

> In 1994, about 40–50 mechanised boats were taken away by the Bangladesh navy, including my boat. The demarcation lines in the seas are not present, and in any case all fishermen from Kakdwip were on the Indian side. My boat has still not been recovered, and I have a strong suspicion that it has been sold or auctioned by the Bangladeshi government. I had four boats; now I only have three. The cost of my boat was around 1 to 1.2 million rupees. That time, insurance was not compulsory and thus my loss is huge. All the fishermen in my boat were caught. They were in the jail for around one month, and at that time I paid Rs. 500 to every fisherfolk family. The Bangladesh navy really mistreated these people and there were gross violations of human rights. I prefer to have a free movement of fishermen on both sides. I do not have any confidence in the present government of Bangladesh. I particularly fear the regime of Khalida Zia, while perhaps that of Sheikh Hasina is a little better. The Muslim authorities of Bangladesh are very cruel towards our fishermen.[62]

His narrative is endorsed by Bishnupada Jana, another arrested fisherman: 'I was heavily beaten up by the Bangladeshi navy in 1999, as a result of which I got serious spinal injuries. They kept abusing me, saying that I was a Hindu. Because of my injuries, I have not been able to catch fish since then'.[63] Communal feelings have crossed lands and the deep sea. The rhetoric of religious divide is implicitly used to divide India and Bangladesh. There is a negative stereotyping of Bangladeshi authorities and people in many narratives. Hariram Das, a Hindu fisherman stated:

The Bangladesh navy caught us illegally in February 1998. They beat us severely and many fishermen fell unconscious. They were ruthless with us. We were thus forced to surrender. They then looted our fish, which was worth more than Rs. 2,00,000, and included shrimps. I am not a Muslim. I am a Hindu fisherman from India. But I was forced to offer the *namaz*. I felt very humiliated in doing so. These Muslim authorities of Bangladesh always use religion as a weapon to degrade us further.[64]

The 'us'/'them' divide is thus constructed and reconfirmed here. Tejendra Lal Das a boat-owner, and secretary of Kakdwip Fishermen's Association and Dakhin Bengal Matsyajibi Forum— a state unit of the NFF—recounts the December 1999 incident:

Fourteen fishermen were arrested by the Bangladeshi navy, of which two were Muslims. These two were taken separately by the navy and were told that they will not be punished. They were even offered permanent shelter in Bangladesh, but they had to refuse since their families were in India. All the rest of the fishermen were severely beaten up. One of the navy personals even asked a Hindu fisherman as to who was bigger—Allah or Krishna? They asked another Hindu to read the *kalma* (Islamic doctrine). However, the presence of the two Muslim fishermen made it possible for the other Hindu fishermen to be freed. All these fishermen from Kakdwip however continue to face serious health problems.[65]

Kanahi Lal Pradhan, manager, Sankerpur Fishermen and Fish-traders Association recounted the tale of a murder during fishing: 'In February 2000, two Bangladeshi Muslim fishermen posed themselves as Hindus. They became crew members and once on the sea, they hijacked the boat and killed the head crew [manjhi], throwing his body in the sea. They took the boat to their area near Chittagong. All the other fishermen were sent to jail and everything on the boat (including boat machine, nets and fish) was robbed.[66] While religious divides are often articulated, there are other tales of simple human tragedies. Nanda Gopal Das and his family had once such experience to share (see Plate 5.1). He narrated: 'I was both a boat-owner and a fisherman. On 29 February 1999, the Bangladeshi navy caught me, along with seven other fishermen. There was a dense fog that day and I could not see if I was crossing the sea border. I stayed in the jail till 8 August 1999, and kept thinking of my family. I have lost all my money, my boat, my net, and my will to live.'[67] His wife Radharani Das recounts her experience:

> After 15 days of my husband's arrest, there was a phone call at the Kakdwip Fishermen's Association office, and then only I came to know of this incident. Initially I was very upset but then I realised I had to rely on my own power to get my husband released. Thus began a series of my attempts to secure hearings from the BDO, the fish department, the CM and the police. I sold a part of my land to raise money to get him freed. I even paid money to all the other families of fisherfolk who had been arrested. It was a long struggle.[68]

Their 3-year-old son, Nayan Raj Das, states: 'I cried every day, and kept asking my mother as to when my father will be back. I prayed to God to get my father back.'[69] Another fisherman, Nathu Ram Jana, describes: 'In December 1998, around the Sundarban area, when we were 30–40 kilometres away from the Bangladesh border, we were caught by their navy in broad daylight and thrashed. We were beaten up by hammers and iron sticks. They looted all our fish. We are very afraid to go to that side now.'[70]

Gangadhar Das, president, Kakdwip Fishermen's Association, recites a similar tale. His boat *FB-Ship Durga* was caught and looted by the Bangladesh navy. Interviews in Contai revealed that most fishermen, besides suffering from monetary losses and mental strain, became physically unfit for fishing after torture in Bangladeshi jails. Many boat-owners lost their boats and became poor. The emotional charge of the account of these fisherfolk reveals that they perceive injustices in multi-layered ways, including in religious terms and of how their 'own people' are being disadvantaged (see Plate 5.2).

Plate 5.1: Members of Nanda Gopal's Family
in Sukanya, Contai

The feeling of nationalist jingoism and the enemy 'other'
however operates even at a subconscious level, not sparing even
fishermen's organisations. Thus Harekishna Debnath, while
gravely concerned with the welfare of the fisherfolk, says:

> For the Bangladeshi coast guards and navy, everything is related to
> questions of national security. Thus for example, the Jeneva camp in
> Bangladesh has 1.5 to 2 million refugees, most of them fisherfolk
> from Bihar and West Bengal. The Indian navy in comparison has
> been lax against the fisherfolk from Bangladesh, while it has been
> strict with Pakistani fisherfolk. More Bangladeshi boats are coming
> to our side, but due to political pressures or some bilateral
> negotiations, most of the Bangladeshi fishermen are set free and return
> back.[71]

However, many Bangladeshi fishermen are often caught by
Indian coast guards. In December 2002, 112 Bangladeshi

Plate 5.2: Fisherfolk Making Fish Nets in Contai

fishermen were arrested.[72] A year later 46 Bangladeshi fishermen were caught and jailed. The Indian government is fearful of the migrations, and this has led to a strengthening of its national security perspective, turning it into a national security state,[73] where it has increasingly articulated the need for a fenced border between India and Bangladesh. To suit its interests, the Indian government plays up the differing national allegiances of the fishermen. Boundaries in its definition are the primary sources of identity and the markers of imagined communities. For this, it invests places and people with new meanings, attempting to fix and keep people in specific places and geographical locations. It is in favour of punitive measures, designed to discourage unauthorised migrations of fishermen. This line of argument is persuasive, as it appeals to the 'national habitus', an exclusivist notion of belonging and political and economic rights, central to which is the assumption that these Bangladeshi immigrants are not entitled to share in 'national' resources and wealth, especially when these are apparently becoming scarce. This discourse is also deeply embedded in power relations.

Bangladesh, on the other hand, has a more ambivalent attitude in this case. The Foreign Secretary of Bangladesh, Syed Muazzem Ali, stated in 2001: 'Fencing will widen the gap between the two friendly neighbours. We do not want to create a gap. Instead, we want a border, which will be a bridge of friendship.... We need to resolve all border issues in a spirit of goodwill. Both the sides should try hard to resolve these. Political will is required for this'.[74]

While fishermen, fishermen's bodies and governments speak in parallel, similar and contradictory voices, there is another side of the picture as well, which is more chaotic, defying the logic of religious or national identities. Despite the rhetoric of divisions, in their everyday discourses, conversations and narratives, many fishermen of India and Bangladesh also share stories and memories across borders. It needs to be remembered that the fishing culture of the West Bengal fisherfolk is very closely related to that of Bangladesh. In many cases the divides are artificial. This is reflected in language, dialects, singing, dancing and food habits, and provides a basis for harmony between fisherfolk of the two countries, who also have shared histories. Thus while there is the language of division, there is also a reality of increasing intermingling across the porous sea borders between India and Bangladesh. The World Forum of Fisher People (WFFP) has thus been campaigning for a more lucid structure in boundary crossings. In a letter written to various governments of South Asia it states: 'We have been fishing for centuries in these waters, which have now become borders of each other's countries. Since there is a demarcation of border of each country, it has become a problem for the fisher people to cross over each other's territory, and we are arrested for many reasons like no passport and visa, violation of customs etc. We have been fishing there for our livelihood and survival. We cannot go anywhere else'.[75]

Some of its spokespersons also argue that actually the flow of people, including fisherfolk, across borders is often good for development and for the labour supply. They hold that de-legitimising migration is counterproductive and they reject the 'coerced identity' of 'infiltrators'. Many of the fisherfolk feel that their identity cannot be neatly bounded in state territories and national boundaries. A fisherman remembering the two partitions states: 'After the partition in 1947, East Bengal became East Pakistan and after the 1971 war, East Pakistan became Bangladesh. Our hearts have been repeatedly divided. We lost half of our heart the first time, and then another half the second time. I do not know where I belong. I have been part of India, Pakistan and Bangladesh at different points of time, and even at one and the same time.' These fisherfolk are neither part of the sea nor of land. There is danger in the deep sea, around the sea and out of the sea and they are safe nowhere. They are neither Indian nor Bangladeshi. They are people living in a world of fear and uncertainty.

Many of the fishermen of both India and Bangladesh define themselves in terms of attachments at local, regional and trans-national levels. Their public worlds shift across borders. They express hybrid loyalties and overlapping cultures.[76] Everyday activities lead to a natural accessibility of the space on either side, downplaying the role of the border which divides them. It has been observed that 'Borderlands... tend historically to be zones of cultural overlap and political instability where the national identity and loyalties of the people often become blurred.'[77] Daily life has an immediacy that nations or even religions do not have. It is located in the local, in the nearby, and not necessarily bound by national and religious boundaries. Thus despite articulations in terms of nations and religions, many of these fisherfolk have a more dynamic and ambivalent attitude. Thus remarks Keshav Das, a fisherman from Kakdwip: 'My daughter is married to a Bangladeshi fisherman. I met him while fishing, and thought him suitable for her. I could share my language, food and songs with him and felt an affinity with him. I sometimes feel closer to the fishermen from across border as I have more in common with them than other occupational groups or elites of my own country'.[78]

Thus the cross-border activities of fisherfolk allow the creation of overlapping transnational spaces, where the significance of border and religion often gets underplayed. They also have a more fluid, de-nationalised, transnational discourse of cooperation and interaction, because they operate on the edges and not the core of their respective countries. For them, the existing maps often do not provide directions for their movements, and the routes, bound-aries and territories demarcated are not the one they often know.

The stories of these interviewees thus provide evidence for flexibility across and beyond different socio-political spaces. In their everyday lives, these fishermen construct and confirm their identities in contradictory ways, as they are surrounded by volatile socio-political environments. Both positive and negative strategies are visible in their discourses, revealing different layers of experiences, and also their dilemmas of dislocations and divided loyalties. They simultaneously talk of their proximity and distance across borders.[79] The stories which emerge in the interviews involve life histories, social and individual memories, and social and political analysis. While each one has his/her individual narrative about borders and crossings, it is also interspersed by some master narratives of Muslims versus Hindus, Bangladesh versus India, the authoritarianism of Bangladeshi authorities, the pathetic situation of fishermen in Bangladesh and so on. These interviews simultaneously revealed similarities, tensions and conflicts that exist across borders. The fluctuating narratives of fisherfolk mark their victimhood, shared and disparate identities, and reflect the highly mobile and contextualised construction of their identities. These fisherfolk are caught in paradoxes and dilemmas in their relationship with the border. Their discourses highlight the multiple transitions that they are undergoing, making it a complicated and messy reality.

Actions from Above and Visions for Future

Both Indian and Bangladeshi governments need to formulate certain policies to protect fisherfolk and even their own interests in the coastal Bay. It should be remembered that the densely populated Bangladesh will have to increasingly depend on its sea resources, and it is time for a plan to rehabilitate its vast population. Certainly, the islands emerging in the Bay of Bengal could be a place for its population to be rehabilitated. Such optimism for the future, however, depends on the government's policy. Policy-makers should use and extend the existing international laws and practices to articulate their maritime interests. It is commonsense to adopt the sea zones on the basis of internationally recognised principles, state practices, judicial decisions, and principles of equity and good conscience.[80] Theoretical steps are not enough to solve this problem.

Bangladesh has a vital stake in seeing that its neighbouring countries remain peaceful, stable and friendly towards it. It has a more direct interest in making sure that hostilities between countries do not occur, that the region is peaceful and that destabilising factors and disputes are eliminated through peaceful settlements.[81] Bangladesh's security primarily depends on its relationships with South Asian countries. Although Bangladesh's immediate direct strategic interests continue to include stability, safety and friendly dispositions of the closest countries, it is not in Bangladesh's interests to see any country become a dominant power in South Asia.[82]

Several rounds of talks on the Indo–Bangladeshi maritime dispute have taken place since 1974, but to no avail. Even the implementation of the so-called Gujral doctrine, could not solve this complex and contentious issue.[83] During the nine-year period in which the international negotiations on UNCLOS III were being conducted (1973–1982), India began the difficult task of delimiting its maritime borders with states on its opposite coasts. This led to a series of maritime boundary agreements in the 1970s and 1980s, which finally culminated in the bilateral agreement with Thailand and the trilateral agreement with Thailand and Myanmar in 1993. However, a trilateral maritime agreement with Myanmar and Bangladesh is pending, although this can only take place after the delimitation of India's maritime boundary with Bangladesh. The delimitation of the Indo–Bangladeshi maritime boundary is fraught with problems, with considerable economic consequences for both countries. Nonetheless, a resolution of this dispute should not be prevented by political complications. In the interim period, a joint development of the area between India and Bangladesh could take place.[84]

The Government of Bangladesh recognises the institutional bottlenecks and the public sector's over-involvement in fisheries activities. It has thus expressed its intentions to reorganise and restructure the fisheries institutions by encouraging the private sector and the NGOs to play a greater role in them. It also recognises the need for greater coordination within and among government agencies concerned with fisheries' development and management, in order to reduce duplication and overcome hurdles posed by multiple-jurisdiction situations. A comprehensive National Fisheries Policy Paper addressing many of these issues has recently been issued; it provides a framework for addressing these matters. However, implementing this policy will require certain institutional changes. The capacity of both government agencies and NGOs to deal with this sector, in terms of skills, resources and coordination between institutions has to be improved. The importance of involving resource-users in management has also been emphasised.[85]

Thus, maritime strategy includes national policies and objectives to promote sovereign rights in maritime fields in which the sea/ rivers are substantial factors. Naval strategy is but that part of it which determines the movements of the fleet when maritime strategy has determined what part fleet must play in relation to the commercial activity of the country. It must affect or dominate every aspect of national, political, economic, diplomatic as well as military considerations, for it scarcely needs saying that it is almost impossible that a war can be decided by naval action alone. Since men live on land and not in sea, great issues between nations at war have always been decided, except in the rarest cases, either by what the army can do against the enemy's territory and national life, or by the fear of what the fleet makes it possible for country's sustenance. Although Bangladesh is not a military power to reckon with at present, as a nation-state it definitely has the right to protect itself. It is essential that every citizen is capable of thinking about its economic interest in the Bay of Bengal, coastal belt and its adjacent areas including defence posture. One should have such power at the disposal of its state that would allow it to pursue a policy free of intimidation or adverse influence of other nations in their sea areas.[86] The same can be argued for India.

We must recognise many factors that contribute to the accidental or intentional movement of fishermen across boundaries. A judicious mix of compassion, recognition of traditional rights and development of legal regimes to facilitate formal movement of small-scale fishing vessels could contribute significantly to put an end to the shameful drama that is now a feature of the Indian Ocean.[87] Ex-assistant secretary of the Marine Fisheries Department, K. K. Nag who is now a special officer at the Sankerpur fish harbour, argues: 'If they take our boat, we should also take their boat. The number of coast guards is very less but the BDR is very active. There should be a demarcation line in the sea. Any such arrangement will be helpful for the poor fishermen—be it by big floaters, lighting in the night, or by buoy.'[88] Utpal Kumar Sar, assistance director of Fisheries (Marine) in West Bengal, stated in an interview: 'Till such a time that we clearly demarcate our coastal boundary, we should stop harassing fisherfolk from both sides. We have to have a joint policy. There should be a buffer zone of around 20 kilometres. At present it is probably just 5 kilometres and this needs to be increased definitely. The fishermen can be charge-sheeted, but then they must be immediately sent back to their respective countries if they have an identity card showing thus.'[89]

Recently the WFFP in a letter to the governments of India, Pakistan, Bangladesh and Sri Lanka, states:

> In order to save the innocent poor fisher people of all the countries we request all the governments to hold a meeting of all the four governments, including representatives from WFFP, so that we can find a permanent solution. In order to achieve this WFFP is placing before you the following proposals for your consideration.
> 1. Hold a meeting of all the governments and WFFP representatives within 6 months.
> 2. Our concern is to protect the fisher people of all the 4 countries that are depending on fishing for their livelihood.
> 3. Issue an identity card to those fisher people who have no record of smuggling, terrorism, or participation in divisive politics.
> 4. Do not arrest those fisher people who are holding an identity card.
> 5. We agree that the fish resources are shared by the fisher people for their livelihood.
> 6. Until we have a permanent solution, we request you to release all the detained fisher people and fishing vessels.[90]

Coastal proximity has been seen as a matter of insecurity for a country in this age of terrorism. From the point of view of the nation-state, it is important. At the same time, there is a humanitarian side to this, based on the poor, socio-economically deprived status of the fisherfolk in the coastal regions. Cases of piracy, murder, loot and heavy migration are there, but in general, fisherfolk are concerned only with fishing. The solution to this problem warrants a joint approach. Policy-makers should not only think on the basis of the nation-state, but on humanitarian and historical grounds as well. Fisherfolk who do not have any fixed national identity, food or shelter, are the real sufferers as a result of policy failures and negligence in the last few decades. Vote bank politics and unjustified economic policies of hunger and unemployment are linked to the issue of the fisherfolk in a wider sense. The 'welfare-ism' of the government has failed here. Half of the population in the coastal regions of India and Bangladesh is below the poverty line. But neither Indian nor Bangladeshi governments seem to be interested in looking at these problems. Governments have always been emphasising only the problems of national security. Before introducing any international negotiations on this issue, governments should address the basic needs of the people. Agendas to uplift the poor fisherfolk need to be taken up first. They should not only see the sea, they should also see the other side of the sea, which is inside their own country.

   At the local level, different fisherfolk associations have expressed their anger against the atrocities of the government. Officials steps should also be taken to prevent such atrocities. The Principal Secretary, Fisheries Department, Government of West Bengal, had written a letter to the concerned authorities, urging them to take the necessary action for compulsory registration of fishing vessels and issuing of photo-identity cards to the coastal fishermen. Different local fisherfolk forums, like the Kakdwip Fishermen's Association and the West Bengal United Fishermen's Association, are working hard for a solution to the basic problems of the fisher-folk in this region. They are against imprisonment and detention of fisherfolk. These associations have written many letters to the governments and the concerned authorities in this regard. However, much needs to be done.

Conclusion

Each slow turn of the world carries such disinherited
ones to whom neither the past nor the future belong.
                                   Amitav Ghosh, *The Hungry Tide*[91]

This chapter reveals the contradictory nature of sea borders and how they are viewed by fishermen. While the border areas of West Bengal and Bangladesh are places of contrast between two cultures and economies, they are also places where fishermen work out everyday accommodations between two cultures. It is a place where nationalists impose their prejudices, but it is also a place where pragmatic fishermen develop a spirit of solving and getting along. The coastal borders thus represent a spectrum of different encounters and human interactions and this needs to be taken into account, rather than just marking rigid divisions.

These coastal fishermen represent the need to negotiate and to express multiple forms of identity, where on different occasions their national or religious identities can reassert themselves episodically. They straddle, obfuscate and deny various identities at different points of time, cutting across the bipolar historio-graphical constructions. They reveal the vicissitudes of their own complex locations. Their crosscutting identities highlight the arbitrariness and violence of discourses of nationhood, citizenship and sovereignty.[92]

6

'Unruly' Fisherfolk in the Eyes of Law

The chapters in this book have shown that coastal fishermen of South Asia are migratory subjects on an everyday basis. For them, crossing of sea borders is a part of their daily existence. However, both international and national laws related to the seas and maritime zones have fallen short in recognising the complexities of issues involved, or of giving space to such movements. Sea laws move seamlessly between punishment, protection and prevention, all in the name of safeguarding the nation. These fishworkers, through their journeys, on the one hand disturb the universalist premise of international ocean laws, and on the other hand question the limitations and the basis of national maritime laws. However, these fishermen have been treated as the constitutive 'others' and have been curtailed, restricted and arrested by the state using the premise of law, supported by arguments of security, ecology and sovereignty.[1] While examining the historical evolution of the law of the seas, this chapter, although recognising the importance and need for it to an extent, simultaneously questions the rigidities and lack of contextualisation and reasoning in its structure. It also attempts to offer a critique on the way maritime laws have evolved in various South Asian countries, where even basic agreements have not been reached. The implications have been far reaching for the fisherfolk.

A critical arena of law has been to map geography, which despite its territorial permanence has been contextually changing in terms of its importance and meaning. The law thus formulates a set of norms and modalities to draw the use of boundaries and their legal regulation. Sea laws, both national and international, have been regarded as absolutely essential for the progress and development of nation-states, for the establishment of peace and for national security. Their stated purpose is to set norms on the operational and juridical control over the marine world, like conflict over access to the marine resources and the increasing complexes of the modern technologies. In support of greater need for their implementation, it is argued that the technological advancements and the economic and political conditions of individual states, with unilateral designs, have been derailing the tranquillity of the ocean world. As human civilisation has progressed, the potential wealth of the marine environment has been unlocked, making it necessary to adopt a composite view on ocean administration, in consonance with national and multinational interests in marine resource share and management. Legal embodiments thus set the nature of authority, exclusivity of territorial rights, fishery zones and jurisdictional laws, pertaining to the oceans, which apply both within and outside the countries. Thus sea laws are viewed as markers of progress, order and peace, as they draw legitimate borders in the seas.

However, there is another side of these sea laws. They need not apply an uncomplicated and linear march towards progress.[2] These laws have also been used both in the international arena and by the nation-states to uphold and sustain unequal structures of power, by marginalising the voices of the weak states and by suppressing the voices of the subalterns of the seas—the fisherfolk, the sailors and the boatmen. International and national sea laws have intersected in their interests, unquestioningly taking the nation-states as their epicentre, and negotiating between them, without giving any space to alternative voices and visions of the people who actually live on the sea and earn their livelihood through it. In the name of security and peace, sea laws have served the interests of the state. They have also been the corrosive tools, used by the omnipotent states, to arrest, detain and jail the fisherfolk. These subalterns are subject to a spectrum of legal rules and criteria, designed to question the very legitimacy of their livelihood. Simultaneously, the actions and journeys of these fishworkers pose a challenge to sea laws and regulations formulated to draw sea borders. They also question the assumptions about universality, neutrality and objectivity of sea laws. Their disruptions emphasise the need to create new imaginations and possibilities that go beyond the rigid ways in which sea laws have till now been classified.

Historical Evolution of the Law of the Seas

For a long time, the bulk and the essence of the law of seas could be summed up in a single phrase, i.e., 'freedom of the seas'. This of course had two-fold implications. For the fishermen, sailors, enterprising navigators and migrants this meant unrestricted freedom of movement, and traditional and customary rights over the sea. However, with the advent of imperialism and colonialism, this also meant that countries that had technological capabilities, maritime strengths and naval power, could rule and exploit the seas at their will, with no consideration for the interests of others.[3]

The genesis of ocean laws, however, goes back to the early seventh century when a Dutchman Hugo Grotius and an Englishman John Seldon were engaged in a historic argument over the law of the sea. The former called for 'freedom of the seas' in his book *Mare Liberum*, and the latter made a case for sovereignty of the nations over their coastal waters. Grotius won. Freedom of seas was established and territorial waters were confined to three nautical miles, the distance of cannon ball shot in those days.[4] The concept flourished in the age of colonial expansion, as it was suited to its needs. 'Freedom of the seas' was used by the West and the European powers to include each other but to exclude the colonised. However after the World War II, international economic, political and technological developments demanded a modification in the sea laws. The discovery of technological techniques to exploit the oceanic resources, along with the evolution of many newly independent states, made it important to restrict maritime passages, under the pretext of economic progress of various nations and security. A search for an international consensus on ocean interactions began earnestly.

Most of the dialogues on legalised ocean interactions were taken up in the United Nations Organisation's Conventions. These recognised the desirability of establishing, with due regard to the sovereignty of all states, a legal order for the seas and the oceans, which would facilitate international communication, promote a peaceful use of the oceans, an equitable and efficient utilisation of their resources, and conservation and protection of marine environment. It was also stated that the achievement of these goals would contribute to the realisation of a just and equitable international economic order, which would take into account the interests and needs of mankind as a whole and in particular, the special interests of developing countries, whether coastal or land-locked. It was thus believed that the modification and progressive development of law of seas would contribute to the strengthening of peace, security, cooperation and friendly relations among all nations, in conformity with the principles of justice and equal rights of the UN.

The 1958 Geneva Convention on Ocean Laws was the first major step in this direction, taking up issues of control—of access, of resources and over specific objects. Access was defined as freedom of movement in the ocean by various vehicles, manned and unmanned. Resource use involved not only the harvesting of living organisms and recovery of minerals and power fuels from the seabed and subsoil, but also other uses such as navigation, recreation, scientific investigation and disposal of sewage and industrial wastes.[5] A significant issue in the convention was of the contiguous zone. According to its norms the coastal states could exercise control to prevent infringement of its customs, fiscal, immigration and sanitary regulations within its territorial sea. Many issues however remained unresolved for example, questions related to the breadth of the territorial sea and the existence of exclusive fisheries zones beyond territorial limits. The convention was seen as lacking in clarity and enforceability. From this conference thus, there emerged various other conventions on sea laws: on the territorial sea and the contiguous one, on the high seas, on fishing conservation of its resources and on the continental shelf. Over the years, a complex body of international laws concerning jurisdiction over the oceans grew.

A major change in the making of ocean laws came with the involvement of the developing countries. For proper ocean governance, the African-Asian countries were the first ones to raise the issue of an EEZ.[6] At the January 1971 session of the Asian African legal consultative committee, Kenya's representative Njenga suggested the extension of coastal state jurisdiction to 200 miles as its EEZ; in June 1997, the EEZ Act was postulated. Finally in August 1980 the concept of EEZ was endorsed in the Draft Convention on Law of the Sea.[7] The most important development, however, was the UNCLOS III in 1982.[8] It was seen as an attempt to establish true universality in an effort to achieve a 'just and equitable' international order governing the ocean space. It established the means by which the coastal nations could extend their sovereignty over adjacent marine resources and enjoy immediate benefits of tangible fishing and navigational rights—a just and equitable framework to protect and conserve the resources of the world ocean for the welfare of the world community. The preamble of UNCLOS III signified: 'Prompted by the desire to settle, in a spirit of mutual understanding and co-operation, all issues relating to the law of the sea and aware of the historic significance of this convention as an important contribution to the maintenance of peace, justice and progress of all peoples of the world and conscious that the problems of the ocean space are closely inter-related and need to be considered as a whole.'[9]

It was one of the longest, most complex and important diplomatic negotiations conducted after World War II. On 10 December 1982, it opened for signatures at Montego Bay, Jamaica. After 15 years of negotiations and preparations involving 150 countries, the treaty was to come into force one year after 60 countries had ratified it. The 'magic figure' was reached when Guyana ratified the convention in November 1993 and on 16 November 1994 it came into force. Its text comprised 320 articles, divided into 17 parts and annexes. It covered a large number of aspects of ocean space: establishment of a clear set of maritime zones, breadth of the territorial sea, EEZ, contiguous zone and continental shelf, freedom of navigation and overflight, laying of cables and pipelines, rights of transit, right of states to conduct marine scientific research, fishing rights, creation of marine parks for protecting migratory fish, marine mammals and so on, and duties of states to protect marine environment.[10] These arenas were seen as upholding the security and resource interests of coastal states, balanced against the interests of maritime nations, to have relatively open access to the oceans. It incorporated the extension of territorial sea to 12 nautical miles, contiguous zone to 24 nautical miles, a new concept of EEZ of 200 nautical miles and a continental shelf which could even extend to more than 200 nautical miles in the case of countries possessing a wide continental margin like India.[11] This Treaty was regarded as a historic agreement, as the developing states, also known as G-77, had their views endorsed for the first time in a sphere which had been known for superpower exclusivity. It was considered a revolutionary development in establishing a 'just oceanic order' in the world.[12]

During UNCLOS III, debates over the right of innocent passage had become strongly evident, which had been a popular part of the customary international law, and under which all foreign ships enjoyed the right of innocent passage through the territorial sea as long as it was not prejudicial to the peace and security of the coastal states. The politics of 'innocent passage' became increasingly controversial as the Third World countries became more vocal in their demand for prior notification or authorisation when the developed world was intransigent. UNCLOS III was alleged of being accommodative towards the big powers.[13] At the global level, a compromise was worked out between the security interests of the coastal states and the navigational and military interests of the maritime states.

The 1982 sea laws, particularly the provisions of Article 73 gave considerable enforcement powers to the coastal states. Its basic tenets were:

1. The coastal state may, in the exercise of its sovereign right to explore, exploit, conserve and manage the living resources in the EEZ, take such measures, including boarding, inspection, arrest and judicial proceedings, as may be necessary to ensure compliance with the laws and regulations adopted by it in conformity with this convention.
2. Arrested vessels and their crews shall be promptly released upon the posting of reasonable bond or other security.
3. Coastal state penalizes the violation of fisheries laws and regulation in the EEZ, but it may not include imprisonment in the absence of agreements to the contrary by the state concerned or any other form of corporal punishment.
4. In cases of arrest or detention of foreign vessels, the coastal state shall promptly notify the flag state, through appropriate channels, of the action taken and any penalties subsequently imposed.[14]

Regarding the EEZ it stated: 'In exercising its rights and performing its duties under this convention on the EEZ, the coastal state shall have due regard to the rights and duties of other states and shall act in a manner compatible with the provisions of this convention.'[15]

The stated basic objectives of these international sea laws have been to deal with conflicts over access to marine resources and to reach a consensual understanding in inter-state relations. However, these laws are flawed as they take questions of security, formation of nation-states and boundaries as given. These laws give extensive powers to coastal states and restrain the freedom of fishermen to navigate within the EEZ. While claiming to be universal and considerate to all nations, the negotiations also bring into sharp relief the exclusions that are inbuilt in their very structure and in the format of various conventions. As has been remarked, universality is always accompanied by 'the other side of universality'.[16] The conventions take into account the interests of states as geographical entities and physical territories, but not of people inhabiting these domains. The inhabitants of coastal areas are expected to conform to these rules, as they are assumed to be for their benefit. They have to follow the laws to achieve full citizenship of their respective nations. Implicit in the way these conventions make nation-states their focus is also an assumption that the subjects, the fisherfolk, to whom these laws affect in the most fundamental ways, are incapable of thinking for themselves, and their states have the power to decide their fates and movements. In fact, the supposed backwardness of these children of the sea implies that the states can intervene on their behalf as well and pose as their defender.

The situation is further exacerbated due to the way in which these laws have been interpreted, partially accepted/rejected and imposed in South Asian coastal countries. Moreover, in many cases not even basic maritime agreements have been reached between them, as the previous chapters have revealed.

Maritime (F)laws in South Asia

After the World War II, the strategic importance of the water world of the South Asian region grew in the international arena, having wide implications for both international politics and regional power set up, making legal confirmation of its oceanic interaction all the more pertinent. The emergence of new states in the region also challenged the western basis of the 'traditional international law'. As was remarked, 'Present international law developed during the last four centuries. Asian and African states had very little to do with it because they were conquered and colonised and made to serve the interests of the metropolitan states. It is not, therefore, surprising to find that states that were victims and passive objects of such an unequal position rebelled against their application.'[17] However, their position was also mixed up with partial rejection and acceptance. Some of the previous provisions, particularly those dealing with sovereignty, state territories and non-interference in domestic affairs, were seen by the new states as giving them the required stability, status and protection. Later, UNCLOS III was particularly regarded as taking into account the interests of new states, developing countries, land-locked states and even the coastal archipelagos.

If we look at the historical evolution of maritime laws in the South Asian region, we see that the coastal countries particularly have evolved them to protect their sea borders and resources. However, in this region, the balance of power is asymmetric, heavily weighing in India's favour, which shares common borders with almost all other states. Due to its sheer size and power, India has been a huge beneficiary of various sea laws. India's first formal claim to the continental shelf was made by a presidential proclamation on 30 August 1955, whereby it claimed 'full and exclusive sovereign rights over the seabed and subsoil of the continental shelf adjoining its territory and beyond its territorial waters.'[18] In 1956, India extended its territorial sea limits from three miles to six miles. Occupying a central position in the Indian Ocean, with a coastline extending to 5,700 kilometres, having about 1,200 islands and islets (667 in the Bay of Bengal, including the Andaman and Nicobar archipelagos and 508 in the Arabian Sea, including the Lakshadweep group of islands), and lying on the most important international maritime routes of the Indian Ocean, India added a lot of prime maritime areas to its sovereign jurisdiction.[19]

The maritime boundaries of India are governed by the Maritime Zones of India (MZI) Act 1976 and the MZI (Regulation of Fishing by Foreign Vessels) Act 1981. In accordance with the international court, in the 1976 Act India redefined its continental shelf as extending throughout the natural prolongation of its land territory to the outer edge of the continental margin or to a distance of

200 nautical miles from the baseline.[20] It also declared its EEZ in 1977 through an Act of Parliament, extending to 200 nautical miles, in which it would have 'sovereign rights for the purpose of exploration, exploitation, conservation and management of the natural resources, both living and non-living, as well as for producing energy from tides, winds and currents.' The MZI Act of 1981 provided that no foreign vessel shall be used for fishing within any maritime zone of India except under and in accordance with a licence or permit granted under the provision of the Act. It also provided for heavy penalties and confiscation of such vessels that did so.[21] India's claims regarding its maritime jurisdictions were endorsed by the 1982 UN convention, and in fact it became a great beneficiary because of its large coastline and wide continental shelf. It gained at least 587,000 square nautical miles of real estate within its sovereign jurisdiction as part of its EEZ. These laws give immense powers to the Indian state to stop and control any movement of cross-border fisherfolk. Other coastal countries have not lagged behind in enacting similar laws. Let us examine them.

Pakistan has a small coastline of 440 miles, 12 miles of territorial sea and 200 miles of EEZ.[22] Pakistan's maritime boundaries are governed by the EEZ (Regulation of Fishing) Act 1975 and the Territorial Waters and Maritime Zones Act 1996, almost similar to those in India. It too has been a strong advocate of sea laws, taking into account the interests of respective states.

The island state of Sri Lanka has a coastline of 650 nautical miles, an EEZ of 150,000 square nautical miles and a narrow continental shelf. In Sri Lanka there is the Fisheries (Regulation of the Fishing Boats) Act No. 59 of 1979 and the Fisheries and Aquatic Resources Act No. 2 of 1996. To protect her own national rights over sea resources, Sri Lanka has been an advocate of a cut off point of actual demarcation of the water world interactions. Regarding its continental shelf it has argued that limiting the outer edge of the continental margin according to the thickness of the sedimentary rock or 60 miles from the foot of the continental slope would deny it more than half of its margin, which would otherwise belong to it, since continental margin consisted of the shelf, slope and the rise.[23] Sri Lanka's premise can be traced to a law its government had passed in 1976 defining its legal conti-nental shelf as extending to the outer edge of the continental margin, which is in conformity with the general international law on the recognition of sovereign rights of the coastal states as extended throughout the national prolongation of the land mass into and under the sea. The issue was brought to light in UNCLOS III. Sri Lanka supported the extension of sovereign rights beyond the 200 nautical miles on extra payment and contribution, as mentioned in Article 82 of the 1982 Convention.[24] Responding to Article 76, Sri Lanka had suggested an additional method of delimitation, applicable to special geological and geomorphological conditions.

Bangladesh faces continuous erosion and shoaling both on land and in sea due to heavy rainfall, tides and cyclones. The presence of deltas and islands off its coast add further complexities to the delimitation of maritime zones.[25] Bangladesh stated that the continental shelf should be co-extensive with the economic zone. It argued for special consideration because of the geographical and geo-morphological nature of its coastal seaboard. The basic claim of Bangladesh on the delimitation of continental shelf was based on the idea that depth rather than objects on the coast, which in its case was heavily indented and ever changing, should determine the continental shelf. Thus, Bangladesh supports delimitation of EEZ and continental shelf on the basis of the principle of equity, which had been established by several rulings and judgements in the international court of justice when settling maritime boundaries.

The maritime laws and the viewpoints of coastal countries of India, Pakistan, Sri Lanka and Bangladesh reveal a number of things for coastal fisherfolk and have important implications. They endorse and enforce the biases inherent in the international laws and make national interests their primary focus. They give tremendous powers to the states to curtail crossings of fisherfolk. The sovereignty of the state is central to these laws, the only determining factor, giving no space to the traditional and customary rights and centuries of movements of the subaltern subjects. It is ironic that these South Asian countries which fought against the biases of international laws with regard to third world countries, refuse to extend the same privilege to their coastal fisherfolk. A close analysis reveals that there is a disregard for actual realities and avoidance of issues relevant for human enforcement of the statutes. In defining and fighting for their sea borders, these countries fail to recognise the porosity of these very borders. In the name of protecting national interests, these sea laws fail to come to terms with the much deeper roots of affiliation that exist among coastal fisherfolk in the South Asia region, or their blurred religious and regional identities. The legal frameworks and tools thus fail to engage with the everyday reality of these subaltern workers.

The need to enforce these laws has led to a more stringent monitoring of the borders. Thus, Satyavir Singh remarks:

> India's concern for its economic, political-strategic and security interests in the maritime zones along its coastline and around the island groups is but natural. The major security problems related to these maritime zones of India are threats to onshore and offshore economic and strategic installations, poaching and pollution, growing menace of smuggling and illegal immigration, delimitation of maritime boundaries and neighbouring maritime states, increasing nexus between drug trafficking, smuggling and offshore terrorism, and military uses of the oceans.[26]

Similarly, the deputy chief of the naval staff of the Government of India, S. V. Gopalachari opined that terrorism seemed to have found a perfect haven in maritime environment.[27] Such fears have led to more laws. India thus enacted the Coast Guard Act in 1978 to combat poaching by foreign ships in its waters. The Act was meant to enable the country to organise a specially trained and equipped maritime force to tackle sea problems. The 1981 MZI Act further empowered the maritime forces—the navy and the coast guard—to stop, detain, board and search any foreign vessel in the economic zone and to impart punishment to them.[28] Other coastal countries too have invested heavily in the maintenance of naval coast guards and enacted laws around it, making border controls more rigorous. These laws have been repeatedly used to arrest and convict the fisherfolk. They have been left at the mercy of the marine security, and subjective interpretations of laws and boundaries.

It can be argued that to protect their EEZ, marine resources and territorial waters, some level of enforcement measures are necessary by countries. Poaching activities by foreign fishing vessels are detrimental to the interests of fishermen as well.

Fishermen too need to comply with some fishing regulations. At the same time, EEZ has given coastal states jurisdiction over large areas of water, which they have used mainly to develop large-scale fisheries and exploit maritime resources at the cost of traditional, small-scale and subsistence fishers. Thus in practice EEZ has proved to be a double-edged sword. In no other part of the world have there been as many incidents of fishermen being killed, fired on, arrested or detained as in the Indian Ocean, consequent to countries of the region adopting the 12-nautical mile territorial sea and the EEZ regime. Nonetheless, these nations have not recognised the gravity of these problems sufficiently enough to deal with them with alacrity.[29] If there are EEZs, it is also critical to have regional and bilateral agreements, ensuring community and traditional fisherfolk rights.

Simultaneously, what we are arguing for is that these processes need to differentiate between fishermen, smugglers, terrorists and mechanised trawlers. Often it is the fisherfolk with traditional and minimal mechanised boats who are caught and penalised, whereas the industrial fishing vessels and big trawlers are poaching at will. The language of the state, borders and law produce rigid definitions of criminality, without recognising that fishermen movement across borders of South Asian countries may be illicit but is not part of an organised crime.[30] This confusion becomes an important reason for the arrest of fisherfolk. The governments have sought simplistic and unrealistic solutions in order to stop smuggling, terrorist activities and for exploitation of sea resources for their own exclusive use. It is believed that arrests of fishworkers will dissuade them from moving in each other's territories, but this is not going to happen given their complex subjectivity. The enforcement laws fail to recognise that often these crossings of fisherfolk are outside their control, due to lack of navigational skills or wind currents.

The various laws enacted by the South Asian coastal countries and their views on continental shelf, EEZ and sea boundaries further reveal that they are attempting to implement laws that suit their national interests best and each of them is trying to extend its jurisdiction in the seas. In the process, there have occurred obvious clashes, as various chapters in this book have revealed. The 1982 UN convention had left various regional specificities to the states, to be evolved in mutual consultation.

But the South Asian countries have been unable to resolve a large number of issues regarding their sea laws, maritime boundaries and coastal resources amicably, leading to increasing conflicts. International sea laws, foreign policies and domestic interests have often cross-cut each other in this process.

For example, maritime agreements between India and Pakistan remain unresolved, as a previous chapter has shown. Further, Pakistan has advocated that in disputes on the continental shelf, in extreme cases a third party involvement may be necessary to reach a settlement. This has been seen by India as detrimental to its interests in the region. India and Sri Lanka amicably completed the process of their boundary delimitation in 1977 through several agreements. In 1974, the conflicting claims of the two countries regarding the small, half-coral, half-sand island of Kachchativu, about 3.75 square miles in area, lying in the Palk Strait about 12 miles from the nearest Indian coast and 10.5 miles from Sri Lanka, was resolved by India seceding the island to Sri Lanka.[31] Subsequently, there were various agreements on fishing as well, through which a sizeable amount of quality fish had to be given by India to Sri Lanka. However, the tensions have resurfaced around Kachchativu and other issues. Bangladesh and India share 52 mighty rivers that flow in both countries and they too have had differences on issues of water sharing and ocean boundaries. The lack of coherency and the absence of stated agreements has led to subjective interpretations of boundaries and laws, with arrested fisherfolk paying the price. The absence of agreements or procedures to handle expeditiously and humanely the problem of fishermen captured for poaching has resulted often in gross violation of the spirit of the UNCLOS III, which clearly discourages incarceration as punishment for poaching.

It was thought that the 200 mile extended jurisdiction in the sea would bring peace to the countries and their people—externally through delineation and demarcation of maritime boundaries with neighbouring countries, and internally through development policies, as the EEZ gives enormous space and scope for national appropriation and proper management of resources. But on both counts there have been failures. External failures are because among the various countries of South Asia, there is a lack of political will to negotiate on maritime boundary demarcations. Thus, India has failed in negotiating border demarcations

with Bangladesh and Pakistan. Even where these have been
worked out, as for example with Sri Lanka, the agreed rules are
not followed. The internal failures arise from the absence of political
will to foster a vision of development, which contributes to the
long-term sustainability of resources, ecology and the people who
depend on both.[32]

Moreover, in the context of fisherfolk, these countries have been
so caught up in marking their jurisdictions and nautical miles that
they have not come to terms with the fact that these children of
the sea would continue to move in the ocean in clandestine ways
as a strategy of survival. The sea laws of these countries have failed
in addressing the push factors that compel such 'unsafe' journeys
on an everyday basis. The fisherfolk move in the seas, crossing
EEZ of another country with or without their knowledge, for a
variety of reasons. Since these countries have not adequately
addressed problems of sustainable resource use, they have failed
to recognise why these people move, and instead have tried to stop
their movement through more border controls, and by displacing
the problem onto individuals and their families.

The clash over maritime interests and sea laws has also to be
seen in the context of growing tensions and conflicts between
countries of South Asia at other political, economic, social and
religious levels. Kashmir, LTTE, terrorism, other border disputes,
declining resources—all have been pulled inside the discourse
on sea laws. And it is the fisherfolk who are suffering for this.
They are repeatedly questioned about their alleged links to
terrorists. They are targeted as the 'other', the dangerous and the
unruly. The laws implicate these fishworkers, and by extension
their families, as criminals. In fact, as these chapters have shown,
as tensions escalate between countries, the arrests of fishermen
also increase. Inherent in the arrest of these fisherfolk are also
fears of intermingling across borders, and concerns with securing
the nation's borders from the threat posed by the dangerous
'other'.

Sea laws, however, are also twisted to suit the nations' needs
in different times. Thus during peace initiatives, these fisherfolk
become pawns and are often represented and treated as victims.
However, at another time they become threats to national security.
The prosecution of the fisherfolk thus keeps shifting, depending
on the relations between respective countries. Fundamentally,

these laws just fail to address the complex, fragmented and blurred realities and identities of these subaltern people.

Moreover, these countries endorse international laws only partially, not implementing the ones unsuitable to their interests. Many of the enforcement measures implemented by each country to protect its marine resources, EEZ and territorial waters, do not fully adhere to the international laws of the sea. For example, in case of contravention taking place in any area within the territorial waters of India, Section 10 of MZI Act 1981 provides for heavy penalty. It includes imprisonment for a period of maximum three years, or a fine not exceeding 1.5 million rupees, or even both. Section 9(2) provides for the seizure and detention of such vessel which an authorised officer has a reason to believe is a foreign vessel and which is being used for committing an offence under the MZI Act. He may also require the master of the vessel so seized or detained to bring such vessel to any specified part and arrest any person who such an officer has a reason to believe has committed such an offence. Section 12 lays down the penalty for contravention of permit with a fine not exceeding Rs. 500,000 in case of contravention relating to the area of operation or method of fishing and in any other case with fine not exceeding 15,000 rupees. Much of this does not adhere to international laws and violates the spirit of UN convention, particularly Article 73.

There are certain grey areas of ocean governance, which increase the intensity of the troubled water world. Section 3 of UNCLOS III establishes the right of innocent passage through the territorial sea. Further, Article 17 specifically discusses the enforcement of fisheries laws and regulations of the coastal state in its EEZ. It is of particular significance in view of the human hardship that has been created by the seizure of vessels and crew, which have been found to fish illegally in other countries' EEZ. While law enforcement requires deterrence, Article 71 (2) and (3) clearly state the prompt release of arrested vessels and their crew upon the posting of reasonable bond or other security and that penalties for violations of fisheries laws and regulations in the EEZ may not include imprisonment and, in the absence of agreements to the contrary, no form of corporal punishment be given. These provisions are clearly violated in South Asian countries.

Further, the restrains if any that can be imposed under international laws of the sea have to be reasonably fair and just, and in accordance with the international conventions on civil, political, economic and cultural rights. For example, Article 59 of the international sea laws clearly specifies that if there is a conflict regarding EEZ, it should be resolved on the basis of equity and in light of all the relevant circumstances, taking into account the respective importance of the interests involved of the parties, as well as of the international community as a whole. Implementation of legislation to deal with the arrest of fishworkers should not violate the spirit of Article 73 of the 1982 convention, or contravene the appropriate articles in the UN International Covenant on Civil and Political Rights, 1976 and the UN International Covenant on Economic, Social and Cultural Rights, 1976, among others.[33] Penalties for illegal fishing should be based on principles of proportionality.

Many of the sea laws in South Asia fail on the above stated counts. Ocean affairs have been marked by frequent misuse and violation of ocean jurisprudence. There are still a large number of Pakistani and Indian fishermen in custody of each other's country, who have been deprived of basic human and legal rights for many years. Their punishment is analogous to imprisonment. No international law permits this. Basic human rights violations and sufferings have occurred in the name of sea laws, which regard these crossings as a law and order problem rather than a question of human rights. South Asian countries need to respect freedom of navigation and innocent passage, particularly that of the fishing community in conformity with international sea laws. Also, the changing contexts of globalisation and transnationalism require that the rules and laws be modified and made more flexible. However, the sea laws delegitimise the crossing of fisherfolk, without contextualising or understanding the reasons for it.

The South Asia Labour Forum, a platform of various labour groups of South Asia including fishworkers' bodies has taken up this issue in an earnest fashion. Despite various limitations in its vision, as it too takes up national categories as given, it has proposed certain significant measures which can be regarded as the initial steps to resolve the issue. It has suggested that India and Pakistan mark out their maritime boundary so that various marking devices would be visible to fishermen, while they are in the seas. It emphasises the need for a long-term solution and an agreement among the SAARC countries that would enable their fishermen to fish in the Arabian Sea, the Indian Ocean and the Bay of Bengal without hindrance. It points out that the provisions of the Maritime Zone of India Acts, 1976 and 1981 under which the fishermen are detained and punished, do not correspond with those of the UN convention of the law of the sea, of which India is a signatory. The SALF has demanded that these acts be amended so that they are in consonance with the UN convention. It has also requested that fishermen's organisations and trade unions be represented at and consulted on bilateral negotiations on this issue. It has further demanded that there should be separate courts for the speedy trial of cases like these. The fishermen ought to be deported immediately after they complete their period of conviction.

However, while these measures are useful, they do not question the fundamental premise of sea laws, whether national or international. In maritime agreements and disputes, power balance, and political and security interests of national governments have taken precedence over the rights of poor fishermen. The sea laws constantly blur the lines between fishworkers, smugglers and terrorists, leading to confused strategies that are basically anti-fisherfolk. They refuse these people the right to movement or right to earn a living. They do not acknowledge the identity of these fishworkers as daily migrants; instead, they are treated as criminals who by breaching sea borders are regarded as a threat to the nation's security. These laws of the seas, and the legal norms and institutions pertaining to them, stigmatise, penalise and criminalise these subaltern workers. They have been another method used by the 'democratic' countries to legitimate and perpetuate policies and practices of political exclusion and marginalisation of minorities and economically disadvantaged groups, denying them their traditional and customary rights, or even recognising contemporary realities of ecological crisis.

While no exact numbers exist, due to the clandestine nature of these activities, the number of coastal fisherfolk who voluntarily or involuntarily engage in cross-border movements in South Asia appears to be very high. Their excursions are deeply embedded in their right to livelihood and the shrinking resources of the ocean. This is a reality which cannot be ignored. Seeking simple and unrealistic solutions—by arresting them, marking further borders or drafting more laws—have not curbed these movements. However, these measures make the life of fisherfolk very difficult and make their activity further underground. These fishworkers are brave, aware and smart, and know what is good for them, for their livelihood and for their very survival. Fishing is the sole source of livelihood for them and their families. Many of them choose to move, to fish where there is maximum catch and exercise control over their life and body. Their crossings challenge nation-states and sea borders and reconfigure the map of national, political and cultural identity.

Conclusion

In such a scenario, it is imperative to interrogate the present sea laws, both national and international, the role of enforcement agencies, and the responsibilities of the state, especially in ways in which they define (il)legal and (il)licit.[34] They need to realise that sea borders particularly are not impermeable. They should also recognise that these coastal fisherfolk are transnational subjects; they are temporary, very short-term migrants, who cannot be scrutinised under concerns of security, terrorism or loyalty to, and identification with a particular nation. There is an urgent need to realise the gap between our reliance on analytical categories that presuppose social fixity, and the mobile practices and phenomena we are observing. The voices, actions and journeys of these subaltern subjects in a way challenge the claims of completeness and finality of sea laws, which are supposed to be based on foundations of universality and inclusivity. They also point to the urgent need to write resistances into international sea laws and make them recognise subaltern voices.[35] The complexities of the journeys of these fisherfolk require equally complex legal and political responses to address the issues raised by such movements.

7

Conclusion

The chapters in this book explore various dimensions and notions of national anxieties, frontiers, border insecurities, ecological crisis and fisherfolk identities in South Asia. They highlight elements of inequality, domination and exclusion, and their rationalisation through the control of sea frontiers. Woven together, the case studies in this book underscore a kind of social panopticon of surveillance and coercion, whereby the movement of coastal fisherfolk is restricted in multiple ways. Simultaneously, however, the book also reveals the desires of fisherfolk to cross borders. These coastal fisherfolk represent transnational histories and movements, a world of nowhere. The tension between these two views provides the pulse and the rhythm of this book. While addressing the problems of coastal fisherfolk, we also offer a critique of national historiographies. We try not to sidestep the tyranny of the national; instead we attempt to problematise it.

Questioning National Angst

Many countries like India, Pakistan and Bangladesh share a single colonial past and have their roots in a single colonial state. However, their postcolonial trajectories reveal various moments of tensions. The discourses and practices concerning the coastal fisherfolk reveal these tensions and fears of the nation-states of the region, which are further aided and abetted by the media and the professionals of security. The state restrictions on the cross-border movements of coastal fisherfolk expose the augmentation of national identity through border setting. The result has been harsh surveillance and repeated control by the state over maritime borders and the bodies of fisherfolk and denying them their move-ment and civic rights by using geo-political arguments. These countries not only attempt to block the fisherfolk at constructed, and often blurred, sea borders but also treat them as criminals.

The anxieties of these nations also reveal their obsession with borders and boundaries. The notion of border is very often considered a materialised line between two spaces. Borders are associated with differentiation between inside and outside, with control of who crosses the line. It is embedded into a theory of the territorial state that inhibits the capacity to understand the passage of frontier controls beyond the national territory. Thus borders, control and state are by definition intertwined.[1] Borders are tied with territories. Thus as these chapters show, territorial nationalism has asserted itself in South Asia in multi-faceted ways where there are disputes over minor pieces of land. The disagreements that India has around Kachchativu with Sri Lanka, on Sir Creek with Pakistan and over Talpatti with Bangladesh reveal that questions of territoriality have complex histories.

Sea borders particularly become arenas of anxiety in this context because while land limits movement and is encompassed often in fixed boundaries, seas and oceans are an unlimited space of possibilities, of fluidity. It is for this reason perhaps that for the state, ocean represents more of a threat than land, as it makes national boundaries fluid. The state firmly believes that crossing of fisherfolk across seas has to be controlled and this is only possible by securing their borders against illegal entries. The push towards more secure and neatly defined borders has a complex and disturbing relationship to attitudes towards the fishermen and their perceived superfluity. It is on the bounded bodies of fisherfolk that larger national projects have got played. The fisherfolks' daily search for a livelihood in over-harvested waters becomes increasingly risky as a result of these border-making processes. But this also raises the question whether the claim to the monopoly on the circulation of movement by a state apparatus is legitimate or not. It often appears to us that states do not have the right but simply a habit to control.

Coastal fishing occupations also help us in tracing the intersections of the logic of capitalism and state building. Transformations in the fishing industry and capitalist practices, combined with border enforcements in a space that is by definition fluid and which these fisherfolk have customarily navigated, have introduced new dangers, new insecurities, and a new economic tenuousness, increasing the hardships of fisherfolk.

Quotidian Life of Fisherfolk: A Paradigm for Rhythms of Movement

Simultaneously however, borders and boundaries are locations that may separate or may link, but most often accomplish both functions at one and the same time. Thus, there may be a creation of boundaries (the articulation of difference or experience of unfamiliarity) and collapsing of boundaries (the reduction of difference or the sense of familiarity) simultaneously. Thus borders also provide us with spaces where one can articulate fragilities and limitations of territorial nationalisms.

For the South Asian fishermen, who constitute a 'silent' transnational population, polarised nationalisms pose a threat, not a temptation. They desire to cross sea borders, as it provides them better opportunities to fish. Many of them find it difficult to identify where they 'belong'. Their identities stretch across national borders. They forge and sustain multi-stranded social relations. They build social fields that cross geographic, cultural and political borders. The lived and fluid experiences of many of these fisherfolk challenge conflations of geographical space and social identity.

The movement of fisherfolk across sea borders signifies life and freedom, rooted in the practicality of everyday life. It also emphasises the quotidian aspects of performed citizenship. The citizen and its vehicle, citizenship are unstable sites here that mutually interact to forge local, often changing (even transitory) notions of who the citizen is and the kinds of citizenship possible at a given historical political movement.[2] Movement, Arjun Appadurai suggests, is a social, economic and imagined condition.[3] The movement of coastal fisherfolk dislodges the entrenched categories of nation and state, and as a conceptual tool resists easy notions of community or nation.

'Order' and 'Disorder': Being National, Defying National

The articulation of coastal fisherfolk, however, also reveals multiple paradoxes. While in everyday life, their movement signifies spatial unity, there is also at times a heavily nationalised discourse that has seeped in the narratives of fisherfolk. These are not just ideological dilemmas in the discursive constructions of the borders. They also point to the complex, mixed and contradictory processes of identity formation. Fishing communities across borders have had to re-negotiate their status not only with regard to each other, but also with regard to the region, the state and its system. The ecological malaise, decline in fish catch and increasing capitalisation of the sector, have also aided this rise of new mode of identity construction that exacerbate conflict and, ironically, promote the same national projects that create the fisherfolks' hardships. The paradoxes and contradictions in the narratives concerning the state, nation and borders are an indication of the multiple transitions going on within the fishing communities. Thus discourses of ambiguity sit next to heavily nationalised discourses, shifting according to circumstances.

Overall however it can be said that on the seas and in the coastal areas, notions of national identity and citizenship are often blurred and subject to constant mutation and recombination. This is not to say that these fisherfolk do not have certain popular notions of national affiliation, but to suggest that for all the ideological claims made by the agents of the state and the historical claims made by the interpreters on different sides of the borders, most fishermen are more likely to have a flexible and a fundamentally instrumentalist sense of national affiliation than an adherence to a simple sense of being either 'Indian', 'Pakistani' or 'Bangladeshi'.

Where Do We Stand?

The nations need to learn from fishermen, who provide unprecedented latitude in selecting which boundaries to accept, which to reject and which to translate into terms that are meaningful to their everyday lives. The continuing social, cultural and economic intermingling on the coastal borders of South Asian countries provides us hope, as they reveal the deep ambivalences about relationships with nation-state and the national community. They also point to the need to show responsibility towards fragments and minorities. There is a deep need to remould ourselves and think creatively in new directions vis-à-vis state, security and borders.

New Governance

The governance of coastal borders and fisherfolk is filled with misconceptions: a) The fisherfolk are ignorant of maps and boundaries. b) Sea bordering, policing and other security measures address the border crossings and arrests of fisherfolk. c) Growth is the solution for the elimination of suffering of fisherfolk and sea degradation. Each link in this chain of arguments is faulty, making policies and measures that are based on it futile.

Rightly, the coastal fisherfolk of India, Pakistan, Sri Lanka and Bangladesh are also pushed to overfishing and overexploiting the sea, but in general they have proved to be reliable protectors of sea resources and coastal ecosystems. The long coastline provides the fisherfolk a habitat for a wide range of productive activities. Fishery is life here, providing survival and sustainable livelihoods, as well as giving joy, celebration and culture. Sea is not above human society and human security. No coastal security is possible without the security of coastal fisherfolk and this in turn is linked to the guarantee of livelihood security. The coastal fisherfolk in the border areas do not own land, water or forest. They rely on common property resources, the seabeds, which are owned by the community or the state, as their vital means of survival. It is thus a matter of fundamental human rights that the South Asian coastal fisherfolk enjoy a right to these common property resources. They should not be dispossessed of these resources by way of any kind of arrest, detention or jail. The rights of coastal fisherfolk to their resources in the coastal borders should be integrated in the national and regional laws. Similarly, the right to their natural habitat should be incorporated into the sea laws, which is an issue of human rights for coastal communities.

The suffering of coastal fisherfolk cannot be caught only in the realm of coastal laws. Several human rights instruments need to be revoked in South Asia. For example, the International Covenant on Civil and Political Rights and the Covenant on Economic, Social and Cultural Rights affirm the rights of people 'to freely dispose off their natural wealth and resources...based upon the principle of mutual benefit, and international law. In

no case a people be deprived of its own means of subsistence.'
The Biodiversity Convention underlies the principles of 'full and
effective participation', 'access on mutually agreed terms', 'benefit
sharing', and 'prior informed consent', to resolve the resource
conflicts between states, communities and corporations. With
these important reference points, fair access to border coasts by
the coastal fisherfolk and equitable benefit sharing for them must
be the benchmarks for any sea laws within and between the countries.
The South Asian countries and their regional bodies should begin
negotiations towards a South Asian Agreement on Community
Resource Rights in coastal borders. Further, in the realm of coastal
governance, the sovereigns of the state should lie with the
fisherfolk, instead of the political elite or the bureaucracy, where
a powerful few decide on coastal policies. If we take into account
coastal agreements in South Asia, the general trend has been that
the state takes over all decision-making powers, often in secrecy,
where political and economic stakes are high. Fisherfolk
participation and coastal democracy are the credible and long-term
solutions to coastal conflicts.

There can be at least six principles, applied immediately, to
respect the rights and freedoms of fisherfolk. First, the *principle of
prevention*: fisherfolk should not be arrested in the coastal borders.
Even when they have to be stopped for fishing in other's waters,
there are other simpler and harmless ways to do so. A complete
prevention of arrest, jail and detention of fisherfolk is an essential
basis for pro-fisherfolk strategies. Second, the *principle of precaution*:
decisions and actions must be taken nationally, bilaterally and
regionally, to avoid possibilities of conflicts between the fisherfolk
of different countries. This principle is about responsible decisions
of the states, in the face of changing laws, agreements and sometimes,
incomplete knowledge of the seas and its borders. Third, the *right
to information*: without any discrimination of citizenship, nationality,
religion or residence, coastal fisherfolk should have access to all
the information on coasts. Informed environmental and livelihood
choices can only be done on this basis. Various official or trade
secrets acts, operating in the name of security, terrorism or
intellectual property rights should be confronted. Fourth, the right
of *participation in decision-making*: the coastal fisherfolk and their
organisations should be given the rights to participate in all aspects
of decision-making on coastal borders. They should have the

right to suggest alternatives to proposed plans and policies and also to mobilise necessary information to stop anti-fisherfolk policies. Fifth, the principle of *access to justice*: coastal fisherfolk should be able to challenge any violation of their human and environmental rights in judicial bodies. The judicial procedures should be easy, free and fast. The fisherfolk should also have the right to challenge acts, activities and agreements that contradict environmental sustainability, rights to natural habitat and their community and environmental rights. And sixth, the *perpetuator-pay principle*: the coastal fisherfolk suffer a lot because of the states' high-handedness in terms of arrests and confiscation and destruction of fisherfolk's productive assets that are easily measurable and identifiable. Since it is the state that causes maximum harm, it must pay for it. To ensure justice and redress to the victims is simple, especially when the cause and effect in terms of time and space is clear. Mechanisms for immediate damage-pricing in the short term will compel the states to prevent harming fisherfolk in the long term.

De-bordering Coasts

It is by now a truism in India, Pakistan, Bangladesh and Sri Lanka that coastal borders, EEZs and laws of the seas have radically changed the coastal areas. The term—coastal conflicts—has become a menacing qualifier amongst us. It is clear as to how and why borders have affected fisherfolk who lived within its cartographic confines. It is equally agonising to find how these have also deeply affected those thinkers and policy-makers who live elsewhere, but who mostly see the solution within the confines of the existing borders. Thus, they are more concerned with cross-border policing and managing cross-border infiltration rather than coastal cross-border relationships and cross-border coastal conservation. More important, there is no effort to un-map and re-map the coastal borders, because the changes that have taken place are not only changes in the physical space but changes in ways of comprehending the region.

The imaginary of the coastal borders in the South Asian region was conceived primarily in reference to nation-building, relationships of nation-states within the region and natural resource management for a broader common good internationally. Coasts

were places where the 'geographic' and the 'management' could
be superimposed on one another to create powerful and secure
nations, with perceptions of nations' rights to harness their coastal
production. However, given the history of the region and community
relationships among the coastal fisherfolk, the coastlines have
been neither natural nor practical. Not allowing neighbouring
coastal territories of individual countries even an informal freedom
to interact, has made the coastal borders not only inimical to
livelihoods, but also to shared histories, religions, festivals,
sensibilities, languages and habits.

South Asian coasts need de-bordering and any process of de-
bordering entails a re-bordering from the perspective of coastal
fisherfolk. It is true that the function of the modern South Asian
coastal states has been to codify and territorialise the decoded,
deterrritorialised flows of the coasts, so as to prevent them from
breaking loose at all the edges and hems of national, environmental and coastal balances. But this has fatally failed the coastal
people. As certain sense-making machines become obsolete, new
ones need to be constructed. The South Asian states must rework
on their coastal borders, bilaterally and regionally, in such a
manner that a collective coastal community can come into being.

Coastal cohabitation is ideal, and the process of de-bordering
South Asian coasts entails more cross-border movements of
coastal fisherfolk, with a neighbourhood approach. If in the sand,
the mud and the rock, a 'no border' or a 'soft border' can be a
daily reality in South Asia—for example, the Nepal–India border
as mandated 'open' by the 1950 Treaty of Friendship, many points
between India and Pakistan, Punjab–Punjab, Sindh–Maharashtra–
Gujarat, between West Bengal and Bangladesh and others
individual cross-border points of contacts like Kerala–Sri Lanka,
Meghalaya–Sylhet, Nepal–Tibet/China, Jammu and the Pashtun
lands that straddle Afghanistan and Pakistan—then there is no
reason why the coastal borders of the region cannot be opened
to forge collaboration across waters. Since the coastal cross-border
movement of fisherfolk is an everyday practice, why not make it a
policy through bilateral and regional talks. The catalyst for such
a change in every region should be the dynamic interaction of
fisherfolk—their numbers, boats, catches, sustainability, mutuality,
quotas and months—in different borders. These fisherfolk live
and work in multiplicitous ways, but the political question is how

the depth and complexity of their living is ignored or how they are heard. De-bordering coasts in South Asia would result in an economic, cultural and social rejuvenation of multiple, inter-connected coasts. This can open up further possibilities of suggested regional groupings of states in the Indian Ocean, to forge collaboration across waters. Thus, coastal communities of South Asia can create a long-term constituency for regional integration.

Coastal Integration

Coastal cooperation and coastal integration are two different terms. Instead of coastal cooperation between two governments, coastal integration is the unleashing of a process that binds the coastal societies and economies of neighbouring countries more closely together. Any project of greater coastal bilateral and regional integration involves what are called 'sovereignty tradeoffs'. Integration often requires the establishment and maintenance of structures of authority and institutions that surpass national boundaries. The first condition that will make coastal integration possible in South Asia will be a new understanding of 'sovereignty' where the coasts do not symbolise control or power, but become spaces for interdependence, even though this may at first seem to compromise autonomy.

The second prerequisite condition for coastal integration is a commitment by South Asian states to liberalise not only the move-ment of capital, but also of people. A greater mobility of people in the coastal areas will initiate the idea of an integrated coastal common market, linking ideas of a liberal economy to opening of coastal borders. Further, since the coastal fisherfolk often live in two countries on an everyday basis, it is worth thinking of giving dual citizenship to them. However, this idea has only been mooted and materialised for the rich and the powerful of the South Asian region. If we look beyond coasts, regional economic integration has already been in the making in this region. In arenas of goods and products, some South and South-east Asian states have come together, and are forging new alliances and agreements. For India, the free trade zone now stretches from Kabul to Manila, and Sri Lanka has always been a pioneer in this respect, with a free trade agreement with India and a relaxed visa regime for all arrivals. Surely, coastal regions and its people can also have similar arrangements.

The third condition for the emergence of greater bilateral and regional coastal integration would be an acceptance by the South Asian states for a simultaneous dialectic of greater bilateral/regional integration and subregional power. In such a scenario, Sindh would likely develop extensive links with Gujarat. The coasts of Tamil Nadu will resonate vibrantly with their neighbourhood coasts of Sri Lanka, as might West Bengal and Bangladesh. On the ground, regional or bilateral coastal cooperation would gather momentum only when it is based on organic links between different coastal sub-regions of the subcontinents. Thus, not the centre of each country, but coastlines and surrounding areas would be the driving force behind policies and law making. By rediscovering and re-establishing cultural affiliations and working and living ties, the nations can actually emerge safer and more secure. This kind of coastal integration can also led to an emergence of new kinds of conflict management machineries and for that to happen there can be devolution of power locally. As coastal regions of India, Pakistan, Sri Lanka and Bangladesh will come together, coastal laws of all these countries too will begin to look more or less alike and work in integrated fashion.

Reconstruction

Along with the de-bordering of South Asian coasts and coastal integration, there should be reconstruction efforts or an enterprise to develop alternative systems of governance from the perspectives of fisherfolk and their organisations. It is worthwhile that some of the basic and broad principles for an alternative have been articulated in the last two decades in the wake of fisherfolk sufferings and it is now a question of translating these principles into concrete actions.

Many organisations and fisherfolk have contributed in diverse ways, in the past and the present, to work on alternatives. Fisherfolk-to-fisherfolk dialogue, self-regulation in the use of coastal resources, common coastal projects, redressal mechanisms on immediate issues like arrests and detention, visions for sustainable use of coastal resources and many other suggestions have been made, as various case studies in this book have shown, which may be synthesised as double efforts at countering globalisation and corporatisation impacts on the one hand and on the other hand, constructing humane systems for South Asian coastal governance.

What is reconstruction? It is of course not about withdrawing from the national–regional economy. It is about reorienting coastal economics from an emphasis on production for export, to production for local needs. It entails various things:

- Evolving policies and programmes for the development of a country's coastal resources from within, rather than leaning on corporate groups, multinational companies and foreign investment.

- Carrying out much-needed measures for coastal reforms, and ensuring rights to traditional, artisanal and small fisherfolk.

- De-emphasising growth and maximising equity, in order to radically reduce environmental disequilibrium.

- Subjecting fisheries policies, projects and investments to constant monitoring by the civil society.

- Building new production, distribution and market networks, bilaterally and regionally, which incorporate coastal cooperatives, fishers' organisations and private and public sectors and exclude multinational companies.

- Ensuring that production and distribution of coastal resources takes place at the community level so as to empower the fisherfolk.

We are seeking here alternative concepts and different scales for writing the histories, lives and livelihoods of South Asian coastal fisherfolk. We hope to see in this region deterritorialised coastal borders and transnational waters, providing not just livelihoods to many but also signalling spatial freedoms for the coastal fisherfolk, with their bodies unmarked and constantly in contact.

Notes and References

1. Introduction

1. Arundhati Roy, *The God of Small Things*, India Link, New Delhi, 1997, p. 53.
2. Amitav Ghosh, *The Hungry Tide,* Harper Collins, New Delhi, 2005, p. 254.
3. In the last 15 years, a rough tally through various press reports reveals that more than 300 coastal fisherfolk have been shot dead in the South Asian seas, many more injured, and several thousand arrested and detained.
4. P. R. G. Mathur, *Mapilla Fisherfolk of Kerala: A Study in Interrelationship between Habitat, Technology, Economy, Society and Culture*, Kerala Historical Society, Trivandrum, 1978; V. B. Punekar, *The Son Kolis of Bombay*, Popular Book Depot, Bombay, 1959; B. Raychaudhuri, *Moon and Net: Study of a Transient Community of Fishermen at Jambudwip*, Memoir No. 40, Anthropological Survey of India, Calcutta, 1980; S. K. Pramanik, *Fishermen Community of Coastal Villages in West Bengal*, Rawat Publications, Jaipur, 1993; Paul Alexander, *Sri Lankan Fishermen: Rural Capitalism and Peasant Society*, Sterling Publishers, New Delhi, 1995; Masakazu Tanaka, *Patrons, Devotees and Goddesses: Ritual and Power among the Tamil Fishermen of Sri Lanka*, Manohar Publishers, New Delhi, 1997; S. B. Kaufmann, 'A Christian Caste in Hindu Society: Religious Leadership and Social Conflict among the Paravas of Southern Tamilnadu', *Modern Asian Studies*, Vol. 15, No. 2, 1981, pp. 203–34.
5. S. Z. Qasim (ed.), *Indian Ocean in the 21st Century: Linkages and Networking*, Sai Publication, Delhi, 2000; Parvathi Menon, 'A Conflict on the Waves', *Frontline*, Vol. 20, No. 6, March 2003, pp. 15–28; Syed Ali Mujtaba, 'Fishing for Trouble', *Himal South Asia*, October 2003; Maarten Bavinck 'The Spatially Splintered State: Myths and Realities in the Regulation of Marine Fishermen in Tamil Nadu', *Development and Change*, Vol. 34, No. 4, 2003, pp. 633–57.
6. There is a vast literature on this. To mention a few: Eric Arnet, *Military Capacity and the Risk of War: China, India, Pakistan and Iran*, Oxford

University Press, Oxford, 1997; Praful Bidwai and Achin Vanaik, *South Asia in a Short Fuse: Nuclear Politics and the Future of Global Disarmament*, Oxford University Press, New Delhi, 1999; Sumantra Bose, *The Challenge in Kashmir: Democracy, Self-Determination and a Just Peace*, Sage Publications, New Delhi, 1997; Stanley Tambiah, *Leveling Crowds: Ethnonationalist Conflicts and Collective Violence in South Asia*, University of California Press, Berkeley, 1996; Peter van der Veer, *Religious Nationalism: Hindus and Muslims in India*, University of California Press, Berkeley, 1994; Gyanendra Pandey, *The Construction of Communalism in Colonial North India*, Oxford University Press, New Delhi, 1990.

7. Gyanendra Pandey, *Routine Violence: Nations, Fragments, Histories*, Permanent Black, Delhi, 2006.

8. Norman Meyers, *Ultimate Security: The Environmental Basis of Political Stability*, Norton, New York, 1993; Homer-Dixon and F. Thomas, *Environment, Scarcity and Conflict*, Princeton University Press, Princeton, 1999.

9. William van Schendel and Itty Abraham (eds), *Illicit Flows and Criminal Things: States, Borders, and the Other Side of Globalization*, Indiana University Press, Bloomington, 2005.

10. William Shakespeare, *Complete Works of William Shakespeare*, Vol. VI: *Pericles*, Thomas Nelson & Sons, New York, 1988, p. 91.

11. Meyers, *Ultimate Security*, see n. 8; Homer-Dixon and Thomas, *Environment, Scarcity and Conflict*, see n. 8.

12. Peter H. Gleick, 'Environment and Security: The Clear Connections', *Bulletin of the Atomic Scientists*, Vol. 47, No.3, April 1991, p. 18.

13. Meyers, *Ultimate Security*, see n. 8; Daniel H. Deudney and Richard A. Matthew (eds), *Contested Grounds: Security and Conflict in the New Environmental Politics*, State University of New York Press, Albany, 1999; Thomas Homer-Dixon and Jessica Blitt (eds), *Ecoviolence: Links among Environment, Population and Security*, Lanham, Maryland, 1998; Neville Brown, 'Climate, Ecology and International Security', *Survival*, Vol. 31. No. 6, November/December 1989, pp. 519–32.

14. Stephen Libiszewshi, What is an Environmental Conflict? ENCOP Occasional Paper No. 1, Zurich, 1992, http://www.fsk.ethz.ch/encop/1/libisz92.htm.

15. Jessica T. Mathews, 'Redifining Security', *Foreign Affairs*, Vol. 68, 1989, p. 162.

16. Thomas Homer-Dixon and Jessica Blitt, 'Introduction: A Theoretical Overview', in Homer-Dixon and Blitts (eds), *Ecoviolence*, see n. 13.

17. Food and Agricultural Organization Fisheries Department, *The State of World Fisheries and Aquaculture*, FAO, Rome, 1997.

18. World Resource Institute, *World Resources 1996–97*, p. 309.

19. For example, even a sound scholar like N. D. Chhaya, who has worked on Gujarat's coastal resources, remarks, 'Most of the earth's

environmental problems arise out of a lack of understanding of our demographic situation.... More population, more garbage, more effluents, greater stress on environment, greater degradation. It is a vicious cycle.' N. D. Chhaya, *Minding Our Marine Wealth: An Appraisal of Gujarat's Coastal Resources*, Centre for Environment and Education, Ahmedabad, 1997.

20. Nicholas Hildyard, 'Blood, Babies and the Social Roots of Conflict', in Mohammed Suliman (ed.), *Ecology, Politics and Violent Conflict*, Zed Books, London, 1999.

21. Suliman (ed.), *Ecology, Politics*, see n. 20.

22. This will be explored in detail in the next chapter.

23. Taken from the 2003 Calendar of *Saheli*, a women's group.

24. Benedict Anderson, *Imagined Communities*, Verso, London, 1983; E. Gellner, *Nations and Nationalism*, Cornell University Press, Ithaca, 1983; Eric Hobsbawn, *Nations and Nationalism Since 1780*, Cambridge University Press, Cambridge, 1990.

25. Gyanendra Pandey, *Remembering Partition*, Cambridge University Press, Cambridge, 2001, p. 152.

26. James Scott, *Seeing Like a State: How Certain Schemes to Improve the Human Condition Have Failed*, Yale University Press, New Haven, 1998, p. 65.

27. Anderson, *Imagined Communities,* see n. 24; Bernard S. Cohn and Nicholas B. Dirks, 'Beyond the Fringe: The Nation-State, Colonialism and the Technologies of Power', *Journal of Historical Sociology*, Vol. 1, No. 2, 1988, pp. 224–9; Michel Foucault, *Power/ Knowledge,* Pantheon, New York, 1980.

28. Etienne Balibar and Immanual Wallerstein, *Race, Nation and Class*, Verso, London, 1991.

29. Roger Brubaker, *Nationalism Reframed*, Cambridge University Press, Cambridge, 1996, p. 3.

30. Lawrence A. Herzog, 'Changing Boundaries in the Americas: An Overview', in Lawrence A. Herzog (ed.), *Changing Boundaries in the Americas*, University of California, San Diego, 1992, pp. 5–6.

31. Thomas M. Wilson and Hastings Donnan (eds), *Border Identities: Nation and State at the International Frontiers*, Cambridge University Press, Cambridge, 1998.

32. Michael Billig, *Banal Nationalism*, Sage Publications, London, 1995.

33. For example, it has been asserted by some that globalisation is not all bad and that it even encompasses claims of a common humanity.

34. R. D. Sack, *Human Territoriality: Its Theory and History*, Oxford University Press, Oxford, 1986.

35. Matthew Sparke, *In the Space of Theory: Postfoundational Geographies of the Nation-State*, University of Minnesota Press, Minneapolis, 2005.

36. Malcolm Anderson, *Frontiers: Territory and State Formation in the Modern World*, Blackwell Publishing, Oxford, 1996.
37. Timothy Mitchell, 'The Limits of the State: Beyond Statist Approaches and Their Critics', *American Political Science Review*, Vol. 85, March 1991, p. 94.
38. Anderson, *Imagined Communities*, see n. 24.
39. Saskia Sassen, *Losing Control? Sovereignty in an Age of Globalization*, Columbia University Press, New York, 1996.
40. Eric Hobsbawm and Terence Ranger, *The Invention of Tradition*, Columbia University Press, New York, 1983.
41. B. Kapferer, *Legends of People, Myths of State: Violence, Intolerance, and Political Culture in Sri Lanka and Australia*, Smithsonian Institute Press, Washington, DC, 1988.
42. Anil Kumar Singh, *India's Security Concerns in the Indian Ocean Region*, Har-Anand Publications, New Delhi, 2003, pp. 115–16.
43. K. M. Panikkar, *Geographical Factors in Indian History*, Bhartiya Vidya Bhavan, Bombay, 1955, pp. 95–6.
44. Ibid., p. 97.
45. K. M. Panikkar, *India and the Indian Ocean: An Essay on the Influence of Sea Power on Indian History*, George Allen & Unwin Ltd., London, 1945, p. 84.
46. See Chapter 4, in this book, particularly for this point.
47. Mohammad Ayub, *The Third World Security Predicament: State Making, Regional Conflict and International System*, Lynee Rienner, Boulder, 1995.
48. Sankaran Krishna, *Postcolonial Insecurities: India, Sri Lanka and the Question of Nationhood*, University of Minnesota Press, Minneapolis, 1999.
49. Schendel and Abraham (eds), *Illicit Flows,* see n. 9.
50. For details, see Chapter 2 in this book.
51. Fernand Braudel, *The Mediterranean and the Mediterranean World in the Age of Philip II*, 2 Vols., trans. Sian Reynolds, Fontana, London, 1972.
52. Homi K. Bhabha, 'Dissemination: Time, Narrative, and the Margins of the Modern Nation', in Homi K. Bhabha (ed.), *Nation and Narration*, Routledge, London, 1990, p. 315.
53. F.D. Colburn (eds), *Everyday Forms of Resistance*, Sharpe, New York, 1990.
54. For example, since times immemorial, Indian fishermen having been coming to Katchathivu for fishing. Similarly, Thalaimanar fishers of Sri Lanka used to go to Tamil Nadu in India for fishing during the lean season. For more details, see Chapter 4 in this book.
55. In the case of India–Bangladesh, it is different, where many of the fisherfolk have been long-term migrants. For details, see Chapter 5 in this book.

56. The term has been taken from the title of a recent book, Tony Ballantyne and Antoinette Burton (eds), *Bodies in Contact: Rethinking Colonial Encounters in World History*, Duke University Press, Durham, 2005.
57. Pablo Neruda, *Canto General*, trans. Jack Schmitt, University of California Press, Berkeley, 1991. These verses refer to the massacre of Chilean workers in 1946.
58. Walter Benjamin, *Illuminations*, Schocken Books, New York, 1969.
59. P. Levi, *The Drowned and the Saved*, trans. Raymond Rosenthal, Summit Books, New York, 1988. Also see, Chapter 4 in this book.
60. B. Muller-Hill, *Murderous Science: The Elimination by Scientific Selection of Jews, Gypsies, and Others, Germany 1933–1945*, Oxford University Press, Oxford, 1988.
61. T. De Lauretis, 'The Violence of Rhetoric: Consideration on Representation and Gender', in N. Armstrong and L. Tennenhouse (eds), *The Violence of Representation: Literature and the History of Violence*, Routledge, London, 1989.
62. For various efforts by fisherfolk bodies and trade unions, see different chapters in this book.
63. Partha Chatterjee, *The Nation and its Fragments: Colonial and Postcolonial Histories*, Princeton University Press, Princeton, 1993.
64. Navnita Chadha Behera, 'Discourses on Security: A Contested Terrain', in Navnita Chadha Behera (ed.), *State, People and Security: The South Asian Context*, Har-Anand Publications, New Delhi, 2002.

2. Beyond Borders: The Indian Ocean Region in South Asia

1. Sanjay Subrahmanyam, 'Introduction: The Indian Ocean between Empire and Nation', in *Maritime India*, Oxford University Press, New Delhi, 2004, p. xi.
2. For further details see Sugata Bose, *A Hundred Horizons: The Indian Ocean in the Age of Global Empire*, Permanent Black, Delhi, 2006.
3. David Parkin, 'Preface', in David Parkin and Ruth Barnes (eds), *Ships and the Development of Maritime Technology in the Indian Ocean*, Routledge, London, 2002.
4. Rahul Roy-Chaudhury, 'Maritime Cooperation in the Indian Ocean', *Journal of Indian Ocean Studies (JIOS)*, Vol. 4, No. 2, March 1997, p. 116.
5. Yevgeni Rumayentsev, *Indian Ocean and Asian Security*, Allied Publishers, New Delhi, 1998.

6. S. Z. Qasim, 'Physiography and Environmental Characteristic of the Indian Ocean', *JIOS*, Vol. 4, No. 2, March 1997.

7. Julia Gotthold, *A Bibliography of the Indian Ocean*, Clio, Oxford, 1988.

8. N. N. Vohra, 'Security in the Indian Ocean: An Overview', in Jasjit Singh (ed.), *Bridges Across the Indian Ocean*, Institute of Defence Studies and Analyses, New Delhi, 1997.

9. Brojendra Nath Banerjee, *Indian Ocean: A Whirlpool of Unrest*, Paribus Publishers, New Delhi, 1984.

10. On South Asia and the Indian Ocean, see Kenneth McPherson, *The Indian Ocean: A History of People and the Sea*, Oxford University Press, Delhi, 1993; Satish Chandra (ed.), *The Indian Ocean: Explorations in History, Commerce and Politics*, Sage Publications, New Delhi, 1987; K. N. Chaudhuri, *Trade and Civilisation in the Indian Ocean: An Economic History from the Rise of Islam to 1750*, Cambridge University Press, Cambridge, 1985; Bose, *Hundred Horizons*, see n. 2.

11. R. P. Anand, *South Asia in Search of Regional Identity*, Banyan Publication, New Delhi, 1991.

12. R. K. Mookerji, *Indian Shipping: A History of the Sea-borne Trade and Maritime Activity of the Indians from the Earliest Times,* Longman, London, 1912; V. K. Bhasin, *Super Power Rivalry in the Ocean*, S. Chand and Company, New Delhi, 1982.

13. K. Saigal, 'The Ocean in the Rig Veda', in R. Rajagopalan (ed.), *Voices for the Ocean: A Report to the Independent World Commission on the Oceans*, The International Ocean Institute, Madras, 1996.

14. Himanshu Prabha Ray, 'Shipping in the Indian Ocean: An Overview', in Parkin and Barnes (eds), *Ships and the Development,* see n. 3.

15. Devendra Kaushik, *The Indian Ocean: Towards a Peace Zone*, Vikas Publications, New Delhi, 1972.

16. Bhasin, *Super Power Rivalry*, see n. 12.

17. K. Sridharan, *A Maritime History of India*, Government of India, New Delhi, 1982.

18. M. Panikkar, *India and the Indian Ocean: An Essay on the Influence of Sea Power on Indian History*, George Allen & Unwin Ltd., London, 1945.

19. Ray, 'Shipping in the Indian Ocean', see n. 14.

20. Devendra Kaushik, *The Indian Ocean: A Strategic Dimension*, Vikas Publications, Delhi, 1983.

21. V. Suryanarayan, 'Glimpses into Maldivian History', *JIOS*, Vol. 4, No. 1, November 1996, p. 25.

22. K. A. Nilakanta Sastri, *The Cholas*, University of Madras, 1984.

23. K. A. Nilakanta Sastri and G. Srinivasachari, *Indian Ocean: A Historical Survey*, Allied Publishers, Bombay, 1961.

24. R. A. L. H. Gunawarda, 'Changing Patterns', in Chandra (ed.), *The Indian Ocean*, see n. 10.

25. K. N. Chaudhuri, *Asia before Europe: Economy and Civilisation of the Indian Ocean from the Rise of Islam to 1750*, Cambridge University Press, Cambridge, 1990.

26. Ashin Dasgupta and M. N. Pearson (eds), *India and the Indian Ocean, 1500–1800*, Oxford University Press, Calcutta, 1987.

27. On the role of Portugese and Dutch in the Indian Ocean and India, see M. N. Pearson, *The Portugese in India*, Cambridge University Press, Cambridge, 1987; Om Prakash, *The Dutch East India Company and the Economy of Bengal, 1630–1720*, Oxford University Press, Delhi, 1988; Sanjay Subrahmanyam, *Improvising Empire: Portugese Trade and Settlement in the Bay of Bengal, 1500–1700*, Oxford University Press, New Delhi, 1990.

28. Bose, *Hundred Horizons*, see n. 2.

29. Chaudhuri, *Trade and Civilisation in the Indian Ocean*, see n. 10.

30. A. Nizomov, 'A Zone of Peace: Good Neighbourliness and Cooperation', in Saral Patra (ed.), *Indian Ocean and Great Powers*, Sterling Publishers, New Delhi, 1979.

31. Rama Puri, 'Issues of Marine Pollution: The Regional Approach', in Akhtar Majeed (ed.), *Indian Ocean, Conflict and Regional Cooperation*, ABC Publishing House, New Delhi, 1986.

32. 'The Indian Ocean Conference: An Overview', in K. G. Kumar (ed.), *Forging Unity: Coastal Communities and the Indian Ocean's Future*, Proceedings of the Indian Ocean Conference 9–13 October 2001, International Collective in Support of Fishworkers (ICSF) and International Ocean Institiute (IOI), Chennai, 2003.

33. Nita Chowdhury, 'Managing the Indian Ocean Fisheries', in Kumar (ed.), *Forging Unity*, see n. 32.

34. D. Mazumder, Z. Samina and T. Islam, 'Freshwater Fisheries: Indigenous Knowledge and Issues of Sustainability', in Paul Sillitoe (ed.), *Indigenous Knowledge Development in Bangladesh: Present and Future*, University Press, Dhaka, 2000.

35. Menakhem Ben-Yami, 'Stealing the Common', *Samudra*, No. 19, January 1998, p. 11.

36. McPherson, *The Indian Ocean*, see n. 10.

37. Ibid., p. 65.

38. M. Channa Basavaiah, 'Fishing Along the Indian Coast: A Fishy Affair?' in Rama S. Melkote (ed.), *Indian Ocean: Issues For Peace*, Manohar Publishers, New Delhi, 1995.

39. Bhabananda Mukherjee, 'Comparative Study of the Fisherfolk: Coastal West Bengal and Orissa', in Surajit Chandra Sinha (ed.), *Research Programmes on Cultural Anthropology and Allied Disciplines*, Anthropological Survey of India, Government of India, Calcutta, 1970.

40. Maarten Bavinck, *Marine Resource Management: Conflict and Resolution in the Fisheries of the Coromondel Coast*, Sage Publications, New Delhi,

2001; M. Suryanarayana, *Marine Fisherfolk of North East Coastal Andhra Pradesh*, Archaeological Survey of India, Calcutta, 1977; U. Tietze (ed.), *Artisanal Marine Fisherfolk of Orissa*, Vidyapuri, Cuttack, 1985.

41. K. Sivaramakrishnan and Arun Agrawal (eds), *Regional Modernities: The Cultural Politics of Development in India*, Oxford University Press, New Delhi, 2003.
42. James Ferguson, *Expectations of Modernity: Myths and Meanings of Urban Life on the Zambian Copperbelt*, University of California Press, Berkeley, 1999.
43. Ben-Yami, 'Stealing the Common', see n. 35.
44. Vekatesh Salagrama, 'Coastal Area Degradation on the East Coast of India: Impact on Fishworkers', in Kumar (ed.), *Forging Unity*, pp. 143–55, see n. 32. For concrete examples and elaboration, see various chapters.
45. Salagrama, 'Coastal Area Degradation', see n. 44. The next few paragraphs are largely based on this paper.
46. Madras Fisheries Bureau, *Fisheries Statistics and Information, West and East Coasts, Madras Presidency*, Bulletin No. 9, Madras, 1916; Madras Fisheries Bureau, *Fisheries Reports for 1930*, Bulletin No. 24, Madras, 1933. Both of these are quoted in Salagrama, 'Coastal Area Degradation', see n.44.
47. Global Fishing Chimes, *Handbook on Fisheries*, Vishakhapatnam, 1994.
48. John Kurien and Antonyto Paul, *Social Security Nets for Marine Fisheries*, Working Paper No. 318, Centre for Development Studies, Kerala, October 2001, p. 8.
49. Indian Institute of Management, *Fishery Sector of India*, Oxford and IBH Publishing Co. Pvt. Ltd., New Delhi,1990.
50. Indian Council of Agricultural Research, *Handbook of Animal Husbandry*, New Delhi, 1997, pp. 769–70.
51. Chandrika Sharma, *Coastal Area Management in South Asia: A Comparative Perspective*, International Collective in Support of Fishworkers, Chennai, 1997.
52. ICSF Secretariat, 'The Indian Ocean Conference: An Overview', in Kumar (ed.), *Forging Unity*, p. 6, see n. 32.
53. Chowdhury, 'Managing the Indian Ocean Fisheries', see n. 33.
54. Kurien and Paul, *Social Security Nets*, p. 1, see n. 48.
55. Nicholas Hildyard, 'Blood, Babies and the Social Roots of Conflict', in Mohammed Suliman (ed.), *Ecology, Politics and Violent Conflict*, Zed Books, London, 1999.
56. Rajni Kothari, 'Environment Technology and Ethics of Environment and Development', in J. Ronald Engel and Joan Gibb Engel (eds), *Ethics of Environment and Development: Global Challenge, International Response,* Belhaven Press, London, 1990, p. 27.

57. For details, see Chapters 3–5 in this book.
58. V. S. Mani, 'Ocean Dumping of Radio Active Waste: Law and Politics', in R. C. Sharma (ed.), *The Oceans: Realities and Prospects*, Rajesh Publications, New Delhi, 1985.
59. L. Kannan, T. T. Ajit Kumar, A. Duraisamy and L. Natarajan, 'The Coastal Environment: Concerns and Challenges', *JIOS*, Vol. 6. No. 1, November 1998, p. 32.
60. R. Sen Gupta and S. Z. Qasim, 'The Indian Ocean: An Environmental Overview', in Sharma (ed.), *The Oceans*, p. 20, see n. 58.
61. Editorial, 'Indian Ocean Tensions', *Hindustan Times*, 7 July 1986.
62. M. G. Kabir and Shaukat Hassan (eds), *Issues and Challenges Facing Bangladesh Foreign Policy*, Bangladesh Society of International Studies, Dhaka 1989.
63. For further details, see Chapter 6 in this book.
64. EEZ is an area beyond and adjacent to the territorial sea of a coastal state.
65. Chowdhury, 'Managing the Indian Ocean Fisheries', p. 12, see n. 33.
66. J. R. V. Prescott, *The Political Geography of the Oceans*, John Wiley & Sons, New York, 1975, p. 124.
67. Ibid.
68. John Kurien, 'Forging Unity: The Agenda', in Kumar (ed.), *Forging Unity*, pp. 9–10, see n. 32.
69. Elisabeth Mann Borgese, 'Ocean Governance and the Fishing Village', in Kumar (ed.), *Forging Unity*, p. 18, see n. 32.

3. Fisherfolk as 'Prisoners of War': India and Pakistan

* The title of this chapter is taken from H. Mahadevan, Ashim Roy, K. K. Neogi, Mukul Sharma, Raghubir Mali, R. Venkataramani and Souparna Lahiri, *Fishworkers as 'Prisoners of War': A Fact Finding Report*, Centre for Education and Communication, New Delhi, 1998.
1. Interview with Shamji, a fisherman from Vanakvada village, Diu, 11 May 2002.
2. Interview with Late Premjee Vhai Khokhari, Secretary, NFF, Porbandar, 9 May 2002.
3. See Chapter 1 in this book for more details.
4. For details see Charu Gupta and Mukul Sharma, 'Blurred Borders: Coastal Conflicts between India and Pakistan', *Economic and Political Weekly*, Vol. 39, No. 27, July 2004, pp. 3005–15.

5. Ports and Fisheries Department, 'Port Policy', p. 1, http://www.gujaratindustry.gov.in/pol-port.html

6. The term has been borrowed from Anne Godlewska and Neil Smith (eds), *Geography and Empire*, Blackwell, New York, 1994.

7. Sankaran Krishna, *Postcolonial Insecurities: India, Sri Lanka and the Question of Nationhood*, University of Minnesota Press, Minneapolis, 1999.

8. For details of the dispute, see Alok Kumar Gupta, 'Other Territorial Disputes with Pakistan: Rann of Kutch and Sir Creek', in P. Sahadevan (ed.), *Conflict and Peacemaking in South Asia*, Lancer Books, New Delhi, 2001; Bharat Bhushan, 'Dividing up Swamps and Seas: Issues Mired in Maps and Methodologies', *Hindustan Times*, 9 November 1998, New Delhi; Atul Aneja, 'Talks on Sir Creek Today', *The Hindu*, 9 December 1998, New Delhi; Sandeep Dikshit, 'Sir Creek Dispute: India, Pakistan for Early Resolution', *The Hindu*, 8 August 2004; B. Muralidhar Reddy, 'Dialogue on Sir Creek Begins: India Pakistan Seek to Resolve Dispute over Coastal Strip of Gujarat', *The Hindu*, 29 May 2005; idem, 'No Progress on Sir Creek: Both Sides Agree to Meet Later', *The Hindu*, 30 May 2005. The following section is largely based on these sources.

9. Interview with Achyut Yagnik, SETU (Centre for Social Knowledge and Action), Ahmedabad, 14 May 2002.

10. For details on this, see Chapter 6 in this book.

11. Souparna Lahiri, 'The Elusive Line that Reduces Fishworkers to Mere Numbers', in K.G. Kumar (ed.), *Forging Unity: Coastal Communities and the Indian Ocean's Future*, Proceedings of the Indian Ocean Conference 9–13 October 2001, International Collective in Support of Fishworkers (ICSF) and International Ocean Institiute (IOI), Chennai, 2003.

12. A. G. Noorani, *Easing the Indo-Pakistani Dialogue on Kashmir: Confidence Building Measures for the Siachen Glacier, Sir Creek and the Wular Barrage Dispute*, Occasional Paper 16, The Henry L. Stimson Center, Washington, DC, 1994.

13. In December 2004, India and Pakistan agreed to begin a joint survey of the boundary pillars installed in 1924 to demarcate the area. See B. Muralidhar Reddy, 'Joint Survey of Boundary Pillars from Next Month', *The Hindu*, 16 December 2004. It was conducted in January 2005, whereby both sides deployed eight teams each for the survey of the horizontal segment of the Creek. India now wants Pakistan to accept land delineation on that basis. However, Pakistani officials state that they have yet to analyse the technical aspects of the survey. See Reddy, 'No Progress on Sir Creek', n. 8.

14. See Reddy, 'No Progress of Sir Creek' n. 8. The eighth round in May 2005 ended with both sides agreeing to meet at a later date. A joint

statement of 23 December 2006 stated that the two sides would
conduct a joint survey of the creek area, which may yield a common
map and a single set of data. This could be the basis for subsequent
discussions. See Manoj Joshi, 'India, Pak Closer to Sir Creek Solution',
Hindustan Times, 5 January 2007. The joint survey was conducted in
January 2007 and is now complete. It is in that light that the 10th
round of talks on Sir Creek dispute will take place. See Manoj Joshi,
'Creek Talks Inch Towards Settlement', *Hindustan Times*, 15 May
2007, p.14.

15. For example, see Thongchai Winichakul, *Siam Mapped: A History of
    the Geo-Body of a Nation*, University of Hawaii Press, Honolulu, 1994.
16. Material for this has been taken largely from Aly Ercelawn and
    Muhammad Ali Shah, 'Sustainable and Just Livelihoods for Coastal
    Fisherfolk: Securing Rights in Environmental Law and Policy', Paper
    presented at the 4th Sustainable Development Conference, held by
    the Sustainable Development Policy Institute at Islamabad, May 2000.
17. Jan Khaskheli, 'Anxiety-Ridden Fishing Community', *Samudra*, No.
    3, November 2004, p. 40.
18. Mohammed Moazzam, 'Fisheries of the Indus Estuarine System', in
    Azra Meadows and Peter S. Meadows (eds), *The Indus River: Biodiversity,
    Resources, Humankind*, Oxford University Press, Karachi, 1999.
19. S. H. N. Rizvi, M. Saleem and J. Baquer, 'Productivity of Gharo-
    Phitti Creek System', in A. Majid. M. Y. Khan, M. Moazzam and J.
    Ahmad (eds), *Proceedings of National Seminar on Fisheries Policy and
    Planning*, Marine Fisheries Department, Karachi, 1994, pp. 212–31.
20. M. I. Mirza, J. Ali and A. Rangoonwala, 'Marine Application of
    Landsat Images with Particular Reference to the Arabian Sea Coast
    of Pakistan', in M. F. Thompson and N. M. Tirmizi (eds), *Marine
    Sciences of the Arabian Sea: Proceedings of an International Conference*,
    American Institute of Biological Sciences, Washington DC, 1988.
21. Presented at a 'Seminar on Indus Delta', organised by the PFF on
    16 February 2002 at Ketti Bunder, Sindh, Pakistan. It was well
    attended by the local fisherfolk, including fisher women.
22. As quoted by Anwar Pirzado, 'Advancing Sea to Endanger Karachi',
    Daily Star, 18 February 2002.
23. Ibid.
24. P. J. Meynell, 'Possible Effects of the Indus Water Accord on the
    Indus Delta Ecosystem', Korangi Ecosystem Project, Issue Paper
    No. 1, IUCN, The World Conservation Union, Karachi, 1991.
25. Majid et al., *Proceedings of National Seminar*, see n. 19.
26. Khaskheli, 'Anxiety-Ridden Fishing Community', see n.17.
27. For this section on the ecological crisis in coastal Gujarat, we have
    largely relied on N.D. Chhaya, *Minding Our Marine Wealth: An
    Appraisal of Gujarat's Coastal Resources*, Centre for Environment and

Education, Ahmedabad, 1997; N. D. Chhaya, *Gujarat Fisheries: An Overview*, National Fishworkers Forum, Gujarat, 2001.

28. P. V. Khokhari, 'Problems of Fishers of Gujarat', in Kumar (ed.), *Forging Unity*, pp. 158–59, see n. 11.

29. Nalini Nayak and A. J. Vijayan, 'Gujarat: For a Few Rupees More', *Samudra*, No. 35, July 2003, pp. 3-6.

30. Interview with Ramesh Divandanriya, a Gujarati boat-owner, Porbandar, 9 May 2002.

31. Interview with I. C. Jadeja, Superindent of Fisheries, Porbandar, 9 May 2002.

32. Interview with R. K. Nair, Fishery Survey of India, Porbandar, 10 May 2002.

33. http://fisheries.gujarat.gov.in/fishataglance.htm

34. Ibid.

35. They are part of the Other Backward Castes (OBCs). Their political clout has substantially increased in the last few years, see interview with Yagnik, n. 9.

36. D. Hajra, 'Marine Fisherfolk of Gujarat: Preliminary Exploration', in Surajit Chandra Sinha (ed.), *Research Programmes on Cultural Anthropology and Allied Disciplines*, Anthropological Survey of India, Calcutta, 1970 pp. 60-4.

37. Nayak and Vijayan, 'Gujarat: For a Few Rupees More', see n. 29.

38. Interview with Vinod Bhai, boat-owner, Porbandar, 9 May 2002.

39. Nayak and Vijayan, 'Gujarat: For a Few Rupees More', see n. 29.

40. Interview with Divandanriya, see n. 30.

41. For example by 1997, 180 Pakistani fishermen had been kept in Indian prisons for more than five years. The corresponding number was 193 for Indian fishermen in Pakistani jails for that many years.

42. Diplomatic Correspondent, 'India Protests Killing of Fisherman by Pakistan', *The Hindu*, 17 February 2006.

43. For example in 1997, 195 Pakistani fishworkers from Indian jails and 193 Indian fishworkers from Pakistani jails were released in exchange. See H. Mahadevan, Ashim Roy, K.K. Neogi, Mukul Sharma, Raghubir Mali, R. Venkataramani and Souparna Lahiri. *Fishworkers as 'Prisoners of War': A Fact Finding Report*, Centre for Education and Communication, New Delhi, 1998.

44. For theoretical inputs on this, see Arthur Kleinman, Veena Das and Margaret Lock (eds), *Social Suffering*, Oxford University Press, Delhi, 1998.

45. Here too we often found it difficult, at various stages of our work, to determine the exact number of those who were still imprisoned in the two countries since government agencies did not release the figures.

46. Records of the Porbandar Police Station.
47. Mahadevan et al., *Fishworkers as 'Prisoners of War'*, see n. 43.
48. Interview with Ghani Rehman, fisherman, Porbandar Jail, 22 May 1997.
49. Interview with Muhammad Alam, fisherman, Karachi, Porbandar Jail, 22 May 1997.
50. Interview with Naushad Ali and Muhammad Iqbal, fishermen, Police Headquarters, Porbandar, 21 May 1997.
51. Lahiri, 'The Elusive Line', see n. 11.
52. Interview with Didaar and Muhammad Yakub, fishermen, Police Headquarters, Porbandar, 21 May 1997.
53. Express News Service, '156 Pakistan Fishermen Head for Home', *Indian Express*, 14 April 2005.
54. Zulfiqar Shah, 'Bordering our Waters: Fishermen of India & Pakistan Often Face Arrest on Charges of Violation of Sea Boundaries', *The News on Sunday*, 17 February 2002.
55. Ibid.
56. K.J.M. Verma, 'Pakistan Asks India to Probe Killing of its Fishermen', *Indian Express*, 21 May 2004; B. Muralidhar Reddy, 'Pakistan Protests Killing of Fishermen', *The Hindu*, 21 May 2004; Express New Service, 'Pak Crew's Bodies Returned', *Indian Express*, 26 May 2004.
57. Muralidhar Reddy, 'Pakistan Claims Fisherman Killed by Indian Coast Guard', *The Hindu*, 12 April 2006.
58. These letters are written in Gujarati. This particular one dated 18 April 2002 is in personal possession of his family.
59. Rajiv Shah, 'State's Fishermen Languish in Pak Jails, Reveal Letters', *The Times of India*, 26 July 2000.
60. Interview with Lakshman, Kanji Veera and Devji Nathu, Diu, 23 May 1997.
61. For example, 36 Indian fishermen were arrested on 8 April, 41 on 7 December and 55 on 17 December in 2004. See *Hindustan Times*, 9 April 2004; *The Hindu*, 8 December 2004; *The Hindu*, 18 December 2004.
62. Diplomatic Correspondent, 'India Protests Killing'; Express News Service, 'India, Pak Lodge Protests on Air, Sea Violations', *Indian Express*, 17 February 2006.
63. Interview with Kamta Devi, Vanakvada village, Diu, 11 May 2002.
64. 'Plea to Free 200 Indian Children in Pak Jails', *The Hindu*, 11 March 1997.
65. 'Pak Frees 38 Indian Minors', *The Hindu*, 16 March 1997.
66. Interview with Manji Dayar, Valangvara village, Diu, 23 May 1997.
67. Interview with Nanji Murji, Valangvara village, Diu, 23 May 1997.
68. Taken from a poster produced by *Jagori* and *Sangat*, and created by Kamla Bhasin and Bindia Thapar.

69. Amitava Kumar, *Passport Photos*, University of California Press, Berkeley, 2000, p. xiv.

70. The term has been used by Valentine E. Daniel, *Charred Lullabies: Chapters in an Anthropology of Violence*, Princeton University Press, Princeton, 1997.

71. Geetha Fernando, 'South-Asia Trans-Border Problem', Paper presented at an International Fisherfolk Workshop, 3 June 2002, Bali, Indonesia.

72. Interview with Shamji, fisherman, Valangvara village, Diu.

73. Here one is obviously inspired by the seminal work of James C. Scott, *Political Arts of the Powerless: Interpreting the Hidden Transcripts of the Powerless*, Yale University Press, New Haven, 1992. Also see James C. Scott and Benedict J. Tria Kerkvliet (eds), *Everyday Forms of Peasant Resistance in South-East Asia*, Frank Cass, Britain, 1986; F.D. Colburn (eds), *Everyday Forms of Resistance*, Sharpe, New York, 1990.

74. Interview with Daya Govind, a fisherman from Vanakvada village, Diu, 11 May 2002.

75. Interview with Hari Bhai, a fisherman from Vanakvada village, Diu, 12 May 2002.

76. Quoted by Bharat Bhushan, 'Fishermen Float Formula to Bridge the Creek', *The Telegraph*, 18 December 2003.

77. For theoretical inputs see Veena Das, Arthur Kleinman, Margaret Lock, Mamphela Ramphele and Pamela Reynolds (eds), *Remaking A World: Violence, Social Suffering, and Recovery*, University of California Press, Berkeley, 2001.

78. Interview with Kalavanti from Vanakvada village, Diu, 12 May 2002.

79. Sindhhu Suresh, 'After 18 Months, Families Wait to Welcome Back Fishermen from Pak Prisons', *Indian Express*, Delhi, 9 June 2001.

80. Sindhhu Suresh, 'Indian Fishermen Finally Return Home', *Indian Express*, Delhi, 10 June 2001. Similar ad-hoc releases have continued. For example, 266 Gujarati fishermen languishing in various jails of Pakistan were released on 6 January 2005. See, *The Hindu*, 7 January 2005; *Hindustan Times*, 7 January 2005.

81. 'Valley Truce Tied to Terror, says PM', *Hindustan Times*, 12 September 2005.

82. Express News Service, '156 Pakistan Fishermen Head for Home', *Indian Express*, 14 April 2005.

83. Amit Baruah, 'Kashmir: India, Pakistan to Find a 'Final' Solution', *The Hindu*, 29 June 2004; Express News Service, 'India, Pak Officials Talk Fishermen Release, Visa', *Indian Express*, 6 August 2004.

84. B. Muralidhar Reddy, 'Pak. Releases 269 Indian Fishermen', *The Hindu*, Delhi, 5 September 2003.

85. B. Muralidhar Reddy, 'Pak. to Restore Diplomatic Ties; Road, Rail and Air Links', *The Hindu*, Delhi, 7 May 2003.

86. B. Muralidhar Reddy, 'Indian Fishermen to be Released', *The Hindu*, Delhi, 23 February 2003.
87. Janice Thomson, 'State Sovereignty in International Relations: Bridging the Gap Between Theory and Empirical Research', *International Studies Quarterly*, Vol. 39, Summer 1995, pp. 213–33.
88. Interview with K. C. Pande at Army Inland Unit, Porbandar, 22 May 1997.
89. Quoted in Ritu Sarin, 'Match the Catch: Pak Still Holding 240 Fishermen, India 90', *Indian Express*, 21 July 2001.
90. Interview with Atul Karwal, Porbandar, 22 May 1997.
91. Atul Aneja, 'India, Pak. Naval Hotline?' *The Hindu*, 15 July 2001; Staff Reporter, 'Coast Guard to Have Hotline with its Pakistan Counterpart', *The Hindu*, 29 July 2004.
92. Sandeep Dikshit, 'India, Pakistan to Discuss Common Fishing Zone', *The Hindu*, 22 May 2004; Sandeep Dikshit, 'Fishermen: India-Pakistan Deal in Sight', *The Hindu*, 1 December 2004.
93. S. Keen, *Faces of the Enemy: Reflections of the Hostile Imagination*, Harper & Row, New York, 1986.
94. For efforts by SALF, see Mahadevan et al., *Fishworkers as 'Prisoners of War'*, n. 43; Lahiri, 'The Elusive Line', n. 11.
95. Quoted in 'News Round-Up: Boundary Fights', *Samudra*, No. 30, December 2001, p. 50.
96. Rathin Das, 'Pak Navy Inciting Fishermen to Sail into Indian Waters', *The Hindu,* 23 October 2000.
97. For example, the magazine *Hello! Saurashtra*, special issue, has on its cover photographs of some Indians behind bars, with the caption reading 'Torture in Pakistani Jails'.
98. Letter by Manish M. Lodhari, a boat-owner of Porbandar, to the Prime Minister of India, dated 11 April 2000.
99. Interview with Balubhai Socha, Kodinar, 11 May 2002.
100. Quoted by Bhushan, 'Fishermen Float Formula' see n. 76.

4.   The Killing Waters : India and Sri Lanka

1. W. H. Auden, 'Refugee Blues', in *Collected Shorter Poems 1930–1944*, Faber and Faber, London, 1962, p. 256.
2. Court proceedings in Kochi, Kerala, 9 February 2001.
3. For a brilliant critique of national anxieties in the context of India and Sri Lanka, see Sankaran Krishna, *Postcolonial Insecurities: India, Sri Lanka and the Question of Nationhood*, University of Minnesota Press, Minneapolis, 1999.

4. V. Vivekanandan, 'Crossing Maritime Borders: The Problem and Solution in the Indo-Sri Lankan Context', in K. G. Kumar (ed.), *Forging Unity: Coastal Communities and the Indian Ocean's Future*, Proceedings of the Indian Ocean Conference 9–13 October 2001, International Collective in Support of Fishworkers (ICSF) and International Ocean Institiute (IOI), Chennai, 2003.

5. The full text of the agreement and discussion are included in *Lok Sabha Debates*, 23 July 1974, cols. 197–201.

6. V. Suryanarayan, *Kachchativu and the Problems of Indian Fishermen in the Palk Bay Region*, T. R. Publications, Madras, 1994, p. 24. The author also concludes that every piece of historical evidence points to how Kachchativu formed part of the zamindari of Ramnad and how the Raja of Ramnad had exercised control and ownership of the island. The evidence includes documents of zamindari rights, lease agreements, court judgements, collection of revenues and the non-payment of revenue at any point of time to governments of Ceylon.

7. Ibid.

8. *Lok Sabha Debates*, 24 March 1976, cols 130–31.

9. For details see, W. T. Jayasinghe, *Kachchativu: And the Maritime Boundary of Sri Lanka*, Stamford Lake Publication, Sri Lanka, 2003; V. Suryanarayan, *Conflicts over Fisheries in the Palk Bay Region*, Lancer Publishers, New Delhi, 2005; Suryanarayan, *Kachchativu*, see n. 6; T. S. Subramanian, 'Island of Contention: Kachchativu and Fishermen's Rights', *Frontline*, 22 April 1994.

10. There were other arguments from the Indian side. For example, according to T. S. Balu, Reader, Department of International Law, Madras University, there is no mention of Kachchativu in the 1976 Agreement. It deals only with the Gulf of Mannar. In the Exchange of Letters in 1976, only the Gulf of Mannar and the Bay of Bengal are mentioned. Thus, the traditional navigational rights exercised by India and Sri Lanka in each other's waters remain unaffected. For details, see Subramanian, 'Island of Contention', n. 9.

11. S. D. Muni, 'Kachchativu Settlement: Befriending Neighbouring Regimes', *Economic and Political Weekly*, Vol. 9, No. 28, 13 July 1974, p. 1121; Partha S. Ghosh, *Ethnicity versus Nationalism: The Devolution Discourse in Sri Lanka*, Sage Publications, New Delhi, 2003; P. Ramaswamy, *New Delhi and Sri Lanka: Four Decades of Politics and Diplomacy*, Allied Publishers, New Delhi, 1987.

12. It has been argued by V. Suryanarayan that the main objectives of India's South Asia policy during this period were to consolidate relations by speedy conclusions of agreements, which had been under negotiation for some time; to improve political relations by providing legitimacy to governments friendly to New Delhi and to remove irritants in bilateral relations by gestures of goodwill. Since Sri Lanka,

under Sirimavo Bandaranaike, shared the larger foreign policy concerns of India, it was essential to assist Colombo in stabilising and consolidating its regime. For details, see Suryanarayan, *Kachchativu*, pp. 21–22, n. 6.

13. For details, see Fact Finding Team, 'India-Sri Lankan Fishermen's Problems: A Report', *Trade Union Record*, 20 June 1998, pp. 14-15.

14. Interview with R. Jayasinghe, Deputy High Commissioner of Sri Lanka, Chennai, 30 September 2001.

15. Interview with S. Gautama Dasa, then Deputy High Commissioner of Sri Lanka, Chennai, 22 May 1998.

16. Department of Fisheries, *Fisheries Development Mission*, Government of Tamil Nadu, 2002, p.6.

17. 'Lanka Fishermen', *Hindustan Times*, 4 June 2004.

18. Mukul Sharma, 'In Risky Waters', *Frontline*, 24 September 1999, pp. 65–70.

19. For example, 77 Indian fishermen were apprehended on 3 December 2003 and 23 on 12 February 2004. See, *The Hindu*, 4 December 2003; *The Hindu*, 13 February 2004.

20. Interview with Pathinathan, fisherman, Pamban village, Rameswaram, 22 May 1998. Fishermen have often resorted to hunger strikes. For example, in February 2004, 67 Indian fishermen detained in Jaffna prison went on an indefinite hunger strike. See *Indian Express*, 18 February 2004.

21. Interview with Susha Raj, boat-owner, Pamban village, Rameswaram, 22 May 1998.

22. Interview with Antony Doss, coolie, Vercode village, Rameswaram, 28 May 1998.

23. Interview with Sahayraj, fisherman, Vercode village, Rameswaram, 28 May 1998.

24. Interview with M. Sahayam, fisherman, Vercode village, Rameswaram, 28 May 1998.

25. Interview with Felix Gomez, Assistant Director, Rameswaram, 21 May 1998.

26. Oscar Amarasinghe and Herman Kumara, 'The Process of Globalisation and Sri Lanka's Fisheries', Paper presented at the Asian Fisherfolk Conference, Songkla University, Thailand, 25–29 January 2002. However, the role of women is largely ignored by the state and other formal organisations.

27. 'Sri Lankan fishermen Under Detention', *The Island*, Sri Lanka, 18 May 1998.

28. Interview with S. Gautama Dasa, see n. 15.

29. Interview with Herman Kumara, National Convenor, National Fisheries Solidarity Sri Lanka, Negombo, Sri Lanka, 19-20 March 2002.

30. Interview with Nirmala Fernando, Munnakkara village, Negombo, 16 March 2002.
31. Interview with K. S. Dilani, Negombo, Sri Lanka, 17 March 2002.
32. Interview with W. Antony Vincent, outside Madurai Central Jail, 19 May 1998.
33. Interview with W. Wilbert, Madurai Central Jail, 20 May 1998.
34. Interview with Kumara, see n. 29.
35. Interview with Ironious Fernando, Munnakkara village, Negombo, 16 March 2002.
36. John Kurien, *People and the Sea: A 'Tropical Majority' World Perspective*, SISWU, Netherlands Institute for Social Sciences, Amsterdam, 2001.
37. On 11 March 2002, Kachchativu festival was revived after 20 years. Devotees from the Jaffna Peninsula and India flocked to it. For most of its existence as part of Sri Lanka, the island has been a no-go zone under security restrictions imposed by Colombo on its northern seas since the flare-up of ethnic conflict in the Jaffna peninsula in 1983, when Tamil militants began runs to Tamil Nadu and back using the Palk Straits. For details regarding this festival and its revival, see Nirupama Subramanian, 'To Nowhere Land', *Frontline*, 2 August 2002. Also see, 'Kachchathivu Festival After 20 Years', *The Hindu*, 12 March 2002.
38. For a detailed account, see A. J. Vijayan, 'An Overview of the Marine Fisheries and Fishers in and Around Rameswaram, Tamil Nadu', Unpublished Draft Report, pp. 3–9.
39. Vivekanandan, 'Crossing Maritime Borders', p. 77, see n. 4. One official document prepared by the Sri Lankan government says that 'prior to the determination of the Maritime Boundary between Sri Lanka and India, through the conclusion of the two Maritime Boundary Agreements of 1974 and 1976, the fishermen of both India and Sri Lanka were engaged in fishing activities in the area of the Palk Bay, Palk Strait and the Gulf of Mannar.' For details, see Legal Advisor, 'Confidential Discussion Paper on Outstanding Fisheries Issues Between Sri Lanka and India', Ministry of Fisheries, Government of Sri Lanka, 2 July 1996, p. 2.
40. Vijayan, 'An Overview of the Marine Fishers', pp. 1–16, see n. 38.
41. For details, see Asha Krishnakumar, 'Rebuilding an Ecosystem', *Frontline*, 14 March 2003. The report shows how a Chennai-based organisation launched a project to promote sustainable alternative livelihood systems using local resources for the benefit of people living off the Gulf of Mannar coast.
42. For details, see Parvathi Menon, 'A Conflict on the Waves', *Frontline*, Vol. 20, No. 6, 28 March 2003. According to this well-researched report, the bio-resources of the Gulf of Mannar can be saved only if

the conflict between the traditional and mechanised sections of the fishing industry is resolved and the economy of the local community improved.

43. Interview with K. R. Suresh, commandant of coast guards, Mandapam, 21 May 1998.

44. Ministry of Fisheries and Aquatic Resources Development (MFAR), *Six Year Fisheries Development Programme, 1999-2004*, MFAR Statistical Unit, 2005.

45. National Aquatic Resources Research & Development Agency (NARA), *Report on the Offshore Pelagic Fishery Resource Survey 1995–1997*, 1998.

46. Amarasinghe and Kumara, 'The Process of Globalisation and Sri Lanka's Fisheries', see n.26.

47. Ministry of Fisheries and Aquatic Resources Development, *National Fisheries Development Plan 1995-2000*, Colombo, 1995.

48. MFAR, *Six Year Fisheries Development,* see n. 44.

49. Ibid.

50. Amarasinghe, 'Economic and Social Implications of Multi-Day Fishing in Sri Lanka', in Kumar (ed.), *Forging Unity,* see n. 4.

51. Steve Creech and Wasantha Subasinghe, *The Labour Conditions of Sri Lanka's Deep-sea Fishworkers*, United Fishermen's and Fishworkers' Congress, Sri Lanka, 1999.

52. For details, see G. Rajaraman, 'Hobson's Choice for Fishermen', *Indian Express*, 18 February 1998.

53. Amarasinghe and Kumara, 'The Process of Globalisation', p. 20, see n. 26.

54. Interview with Steve Creech at Colombo, 21 March 2002.

55. Neomi Kodikara, 'Indian Fishermen still Poaching in Sri Lankan Waters', *Sunday Observer* (Colombo), 7 September 2003.

56. In May 2004, the goodwill mission of Indian fishermen that went to Sri Lanka found in Mannar that the local fishermen were quite bitter about the Indian trawlers and the loss they caused to their nets. The three days of the week that the Rameswaram trawlers fish are dreaded by the Sri Lankan fishermen and many take evasive action and avoid getting in the way of the trawlers or even stop fishing. As is known, boats from Rameswaram and Pudukottai fish only on Tuesdays, Thursdays and Saturdays on account of an agreement with local traditional fishermen, who fish on the other four days with their drift-nets. For details see, V. Vivekanandan, 'Historic Goodwill', *Samudra*, No. 38, July 2004, pp. 24-32.

57. For details, see V.S. Sambandan, 'Mannar Fishermen Protest their Government "Inaction" ', *The Hindu*, 11 March 2003.

58. Attacks on each other by fisherfolk and making them captive are very frequent between sea borders of India and Sri Lanka. For example,

on 11 March 2002 six fishermen from Karaikal in Tamil Nadu, who had gone fishing near Kodiakarai, were attacked by Sri Lankan fishermen. See 'Lankans Attacked 6 Tamil Fishermen', *Indian Express*, 12 March 2002. On 19 September 2002, 103 Rameswaram fishermen were detained along with their 25 mechanised boats by the fishermen of Pesalai in Sri Lanka. See '103 Fishermen Detained', *The Hindu*, 20 September 2002.

59. For details of these incidents, see T. S. Subramanian, 'Troubled Waters', *Frontline*, 11, 2003, pp. 40-42.

60. For details, see 'Colombo Arrests 75 Indian Fishermen for Encroaching', *The Hindu*, 5 March 2003; 'Fishermen Issue: Jayalalitha Seeks PM's Intervention', *The Hindu*, 6 March 2003; 'Fishermen Issue: T. N. MPs' Plea', *The Hindu*, 7 March 2003; 'TN Protests Against Killing of Fishermen', *Hindustan Times*, 29 July 1997. In this case, the nine-party opposition front comprising AIADMK, MDMK and Janata Party staged a demonstration near the Sri Lankan Deputy High Commissioner's office at Chennai and submitted a joint memorandum to the Sri Lankan Deputy High Commissioner protesting against the reports of killing of Indian fishermen by the Sri Lankan navy and air force helicopters.

61. Increasingly, deep-sea fishing vessels from Sri Lanka cross borders and get arrested by the navy or coast guards of other countries. In addition to India, Bangladesh and Maldives, Sri Lankan fishermen have also been detained by countries as far away as Thailand, Australia, Seychelles and Myanmar. For details, see Herman Kumara, 'Issues Related to Deep-sea Fishermen and Their families Due to Detention in Foreign Countries', in K.G Kumar (ed.), *Forging Unity*, pp. 90-94, see n. 4.

62. Interview with vice-admiral R. N. Ganesh, coast guard director general, Chennai, 4 August 1997.

63. Memorandum submitted to Minister for External Affairs, Government of India by ARIF, 21 February 2001, p. 4.

64. To substantiate this point, see Richard A. Mathew, 'Introduction: Mapping Contested Grounds', in Daniel H. Deudney and Richard A. Mathew (eds), *Contested Grounds: Security and Conflict in the New Environmental Politics*, State University of New York Press, Albany, 1999, pp. 1–21.

65. *Indian Express*, 4 October 1991.

66. *Indian Express*, 8 November 1993.

67. Legal Advisor, 'Confidential Discussion Paper', p. 2, see n. 39.

68. For details of recent firings and measures taken, see for example 'Firing at Fishermen: Karunanidhi writes to Manmohan', *The Hindu*, 28 February 2007; C. Jaishankar, 'Another Fisherman Hurt in Firing by Sri Lankan Navy', *The Hindu*, 1 March 2007; 'Coastal Patrol Stepped

Up', *The Hindu*, 30 March 2007; 'Karunanidhi for Coastal Patrol under Single Command', *The Hindu*, 1 April 2007; 'Fishermen along Nagapattinam Coast Boycott Fishing', *The Hindu*, 8 April 2007; Jaya Menon, 'Indian Fishermen May Have Invited Firing from Lanka', *The Indian Express*, 12 April 2007.

69. V. Suryanarayan, 'Tamil Nadu and Indian Foreign Policy', *The Hindu*, 19 December 2002.

70. V. Suryanarayan, 'Fishing in the Palk Straits', *The Hindu*, 15 February 2001.

71. V. Suryanarayan, 'Fishing in Choppy Waters', *The Hindu*, 25 February 2004.

72. Suryanarayan, *Conflicts over Fisheries*, pp. 130–156, see n. 9.

73. Ibid., p. 153.

74. Jayasinghe, *Kachchativu: And the Maritime*, pp. 123–128, see n. 9.

75. Vivekanandan, 'Crossing Maritime Borders', pp. 87–88, see n.4.

76. See, for instance, 'A Sound and Just Proposal', *The Hindu*, 9 December 2003; 'No Instance of LTTE Transgression: Coast Guard', *The Hindu*, 25 December 2003; 'Coordinated Patrolling by Indian, Sri Lankan Navies', *The Hindu*, 11 November 2005. However, coordinated patrolling is only at an experimental stage.

77. V. S. Somavanshi, 'Marine Fishery Resources and Regional Cooperation in the Indian Ocean', in V. S. Seth (ed.), *Indian Ocean Region: Conflict and Cooperation*, Centre for African Studies, Mumbai, 2004, pp. 172–78.

78. Matters agreed upon at the meeting held in India regarding the problems of detained fishermen in India and Sri Lanka, Ministry of Foreign Affairs, Sri Lanka, SA/P/IND/32, 3 July 2001.

79. Interview with Mahinda Rajapaksa, President of Sri Lanka, Colombo, 24 March 2002.

80. Legal Advisor, 'Confidential Discussion Paper', see no. 39. Also, 'Foreign Minister Convenes Meeting on Problems of Fishermen', Ministry of Foreign Affairs, Colombo, 29 November 2000, where the then Foreign Minister Lakshman Kadirgamar convened a high-level meeting to discuss the issue of arrested Sri Lankan and Indian fishermen and proposed several co-ordinated plans of action between two countries.

81. For details see, Steve Creech with Maheswari Velautham, Fr. Deverajah, Herman Kumara, Lucas Fernando, *Sri Lankan Initiatives for the Release of Arrested Fishermen*, Colombo, nd. The report describes the efforts of the network of non-governmental organisations in Sri Lanka in the 1990s regarding the release of Indian and Sri Lankan fisherfolk. According to the report, since the problem is likely to remain, NGOs on both sides will be engaged in humanitarian and legal assistance. And action needs to be taken both in Sri Lanka and

India to ensure the humane treatment of arrested Indian fishermen.
82. Vivekanandan, 'Crossing Maritime Borders', see n. 4.
83. National Fisheries Solidarity, 'Key Points Arising from the Discussion of the Arrested Fishermen Issue', held at the Ministry of Fisheries and Aquatic Resources Development on April 3rd, Sri Lanka, 6 April 1998.
84. Vivekanandan, 'Historic Goodwill', p.31, see n. 56.
85. V. Vivekanandan, 'A Unique Dinner Meeting', Email dated 29 October 2006.
86. 'Tamil Nadu, Jaffna Fishermen to Talk', *Hindustan Times*, 31 October 2002.

5.   Ironies of Identities: India and Bangladesh

1. Interview with Haribhakta Das, fisherman from Gangadharpur, Kakdwip, West Bengal, 17 June 2002.
2. Interview with Ramhari Das, Kalinagar, Kakdwip, 19 June 2002.
3. For details, see Ranabir Samaddar, *The Marginal Nation: Transborder Migration from Bangladesh to West Bengal*, Sage Publications, New Delhi, 1999.
4. Sara Curran, 'Migration, Social Capital, and the Environment: Considering Migrant Selectivity and Networks in Relation to Coastal Ecosystems', *Population and Development Review*, Vol. 28, 2002, pp. 89-125.
5. Samaddar, *Marginal Nation*, see n.3.
6. For further details, see Kathryn Jacques, *Bangladesh, India and Pakistan: International Relations and Regional Tensions in South Asia*, St. Martin's Press, New York, 2000.
7. Mohd. Khurshed Alam, 'Law of the Sea and its Implications for Bangladesh', *Bangladesh Institute of International and Strategic Studies Journal (BIISS)*, Vol. 19, No. 4, 1998.
8. M. Habibur Rahman, 'Delimitation of Maritime Boundaries: Some Pertinent Issues for Bangladesh', in M. G. Kabir and Shaukat Hassan (eds), *Issues and Challenges Facing Bangladesh Foreign Policy*, Dhaka, Bangladesh Society of International Studies 1989; M. Habibur Rahman, *Delimitation of Maritime Boundaries*, Rajshahi, Bangladesh, Dhaka, 1991.
9. O. P. Sharma, 'Delimitation of Maritime Boundary and the Question of Islands in Maritime International Law', *Sea Gull*, Vol. 4, No. 13, May-July 1998, p. 37.
10. Ibid., pp. 37-8.

11. For details, see Chapter 6 in this book.

12. Md. Ramjul Haq, 'EEZ in the Bay of Bengal: Implications for Bangladesh and Other Littoral States', in Emajuddin Ahamed and Abul Kalam (eds), *Bangladesh, South Asia and the World*, Academic Publishers, Dhaka, 1992.

13. Government of Bangladesh, *The Territorial Waters and Maritime Zones Acts 1974*, The Bangladesh Gazette, 1974.

14. Rahman, 'Delimitation of Maritime Boundaries', p. 114, see n.8.

15. This hypothesis was also supported by Harekrishna Debnath, Chairman, NFF and General Secretary, World Forum of Fisher People (WFFP). It was further proved in the interviews with the boat-owners and fisherfolk.

16. Rahman, 'Delimitation of Maritime Boundaries', p. 114, see n. 8.

17. M. Habibur Rahman, 'The Law of the Sea for SAARC Countries: A Study of Problem', in Ahamed and Kalam (eds), *Bangladesh, South Asia*, in n. 12.

18. M. R. Shyam, 'Extended Maritime Jurisdiction and Impact on South Asia', *Ocean Development and International Law Journal*, Vol. 10, No. 1-2, 1981, pp. 93-111; P. C. Sinha, 'Settlement of Maritime Claims by India: Issues and Options', *Sea Gull*, Vol. 4, No. 14, August-October 1998, p. 27.

19. Sharma, 'Delimitation of Maritime Boundary', see n. 9.

20. R. C. Sharma and P. C. Sinha, *Maritime Boundary Delimitation and India in India's Ocean Policy*, Khanna Publishers, New Delhi, 1994.

21. Rahman, 'Delimitation of Maritime Boundaries', p. 114, see n. 8.

22. Interview with Harekrishna Debnath, Chairman, NFF, Diamond Harbour, West Bengal, 20 June 2000.

23. Sharma and Sinha, *Maritime Boundary*, p. 114, see n. 20.

24. P. C. Sinha, 'Issues in Maritime Boundary Demarcation in South Asia: A Case Study of Bangladesh', *JIOS*, November 1995, p. 49; Rahman, 'Delimitation of Maritime Boundaries', p. 106, see n. 8.

25. Shaukat Hassan, 'Introductory Remarks', in Kabir and Hassan (eds), *Issues and Challenges*, p. 5, see n.8.

26. Interview with Amitabh Verma, sub-divisional police officer, Kakdwip, West Bengal, 18 June 2002.

27. Rahul Roy-Chaudhury, *Sea Power and Indian Security*, Brassey's, London, 1995.

28. Sharma and Sinha, *Maritime Boundary*, see n. 20.

29. Mohd. Khurshed Alam, 'Regional Maritime Cooperation under the Auspices of South Asian Association for Regional Cooperation (SAARC)', *BIISS Journal*, Vol. 18, No. 1, 1997, pp. 30-1.

30. K. Jayaraman, *Legal Regime of Islands*, Marwah Publications, New Delhi, 1982.

31. J. R. V. Prescott, *The Maritime Political Boundaries of the World*, Methuen, London, 1985.

32. Bangladesh Development Series, *Bangladesh 2020: A Long-Run Perspective Study*, World Bank and Bangladesh Centre for Advanced Studies, University Press Limited, Dhaka, 1998, http://www.worldbank-bangladesh.org.

33. World Bank, *Bangladesh: Promoting Higher Growth and Human Development*, Washington DC, 1987.

34. Ibid.

35. *National Workshop on Fisheries: Resources Development and Management in Bangladesh*, Madras, 1997, http://www.fao.org/docrep/X5625E/X5625E00.htm#Contents.

36. Bangladesh Development Series, *Bangladesh 2020,* see n. 32.

37. http://www.sos-arsenic.net/english/environment/shrimp.html.

38. K. Maudood Elahi, Subash C. Das and Sabiha Sultana, 'Geography of Coastal Environment: A Study of Selected Issues', in Abdul Bayes and Anu Muhammad (eds), *Bangladesh at 25: An Analytical Discourse on Development*, The University Press Limited, Dhaka, 1998.

39. Anjan Datta, 'Shrimp Culture: Expanding Farms, Shrinking Lives', *Samudra,* No. 13, October 1995, pp. 24–28. Also see, http://www.sos-arsenic.net/english/environment/shrimp.html.

40. Amitav Ghosh, *Hungry Tide*, Harper Collins, New Delhi, 2005, pp. 6-8.

41. Samaddar, *Marginal Nation*, pp. 156–7, see n. 3.

42. For further details on Sundarbans, see K. Z. Hussain and G. Acharya (eds), *Mangroves of the Sundarbans*, Vol. II: *Bangladesh*, IUCN, Bangkok, 1994; J. Seidensticker and M. A. Hai, *The Sundarbans Wildlife Management Plan: Conservation in the Bangladesh Coastal Zone*, IUCN, Switzerland, 1983.

43. Ghosh, *Hungry Tide*, p. 80, see n.40.

44. 'Orphans of the River', *Down to Earth,* 15 February 2002, pp. 30-1.

45. Prepared by the General Body of the National Fishworkers Forum 6-19 December 2001, *Charter of Demands 2002*, NFF, Thiruvananthapuram, 2002, p. 13.

46. Rahul Roy-Chaudhury, as cited in W. S. G. Bateman and Stephen Bates (eds), *Regional Maritime Management and Security*, Canberra Papers on Strategy and Defence No. 124, Canberra, Australia, 1998, p. 22.

47. D. Mazumder, Z. Samina and T. Islam, 'Freshwater Fisheries: Indigenous Knowledge and Issues of Sustainability', in Paul Sillitoe (ed.), *Indigenous Knowledge Development in Bangladesh: Present and Future*, University Press, Dhaka, 2000.

48. Sebastine Mathew, 'Fishing in the Indian Ocean', *The Hindu*, 22 September 2001.

49. Ibid.
50. Interview with Harekrishna Debnath, West Bengal, 2 June 2002.
51. Samaddar, *Marginal Nation*, p. 19, see n. 3.
52. Gilbert Etienne, 'The Process of Industrialization in India, Pakistan and Bangladesh', *South Asia Journal*, Vol. 3, 1990, p. 239.
53. Joseph F. Stepanek, *Bangladesh: Equitable Growth?* Pergamon Press, New York, 1979.
54. Gertjan de Graaf and Felix Martin, 'The Importance of Fishing for Different Social Strata in Rural Bangladesh', Paper Presented at an Internet Conference on Aquatic Resources Management for Sustainable Livelihoods of Poor People, http://naca.fisheries.go.th/dfid.
55. Bhabananda Mukherjee, 'Comparative Study of the Fisherfolk: Coastal West Bengal and Orissa', in Surajit Sinha (ed.), *Research Programmes on Cultural Anthropology and Allied Disciplines*, pp. 31–54.
56. Amitav Ghosh, *Hungry Tide*, pp. 225, 282, quoting the German poet Rainer Maria Rilke, see n. 40.
57. Interview with Manik Das, fisherman, Kakdwip, 17 June 2002.
58. Interview with Bindu Das, Secretary, Sundarban Samudrik Matsyajibi Shramik Union, Kakdwip, 17 June 2002.
59. Anne-Marie Fortier, 'Re-Membering Places and the Performance of Belongings(s)', *Theory, Culture and Society*, Vol. 6, No. 2, 1999, p. 41.
60. Interview with Haribhakta Das, Kakdwip, 17 June 2002.
61. Interview with Manik Das, Kakdwip, 17 June 2002.
62. Interview with Sunil Kumar Das, boat-owner, 24 South Parganas, Kakdwip, West Bengal, 16 June 2004.
63. Interview with Bishnupada Jana, fisherman, Ganeshpur, Kakdwip, 17 June 2002.
64. Interview with Hariram Das, fisherman, Kalinagar, Kakdwip, 17 June 2002.
65. Interview with Tejendra Lal Das, boat-owner, Kakdwip, 17 June 2002.
66. Interview with Kanahi Lal Pradhan, Manager, Sankerpur Fishermen and Fish-traders Association, 19 June 2002.
67. Interview with Nanda Gopal Das, Village Sukanya, East Midnapur, 20 June 2002.
68. Interview with Nanda Gopal's wife Radharani Das, 20 June 2002.
69. Interview with Nanda Gopal's son Nayan Raj Das, 20 June 2002.
70. Interview with Nanthu Ram Jana, Village Sukanya, East Midnapur, 20 June 2002.
71. Interview with Harekrishna Debnath, 2 June 2002.
72. '46 Fishermen held by Indian Coast Guard', *The Daily Star*, 31 December 2003.
73. Samaddar, *Marginal Nation*, p. 19, see n. 3.

74. Ershadul Huq, 'Bangladesh Opposed to Fencing Border', *India Abroad News Service,* Dhaka, 23 April 2001.

75. World Forum of Fisher People (WFFP), 'A Letter to the Governments of India, Pakistan, Bangladesh and Sri Lanka', 20 April 2002.

76. For similar arguments see Akhil Gupta and James Ferguson, 'Beyond "Culture": Space, Identity, and the Politics of Difference', *Cultural Anthropology,* Vol. 7, No. 1, 1992, pp. 6-23.

77. J. P. Augelli, 'Nationalization of Dominican Borderlands', *Geographical Review,* Vol. 70, 1980, p. 19.

78. Interview with Keshav Das, fisherman, Kakdwip, 22 June 2002.

79. Such contradictory readings of people's narratives living in borders have been noted elsewhere as well. See for example, Ulrike H. Meinhof (ed.), *Living (With) Borders: Identity Discourses on East-West Borders in Europe,* Ashgate, England, 2002.

80. Sharma and Sinha, *Maritime Boundary,* see n. 20.

81. Harun ur Rashid, *Foreign Relations of Bangladesh,* Rishi Publications, Varanasi, 2001.

82. Ibid.

83. Rahul Roy-Chaudhury, *India's Maritime Security,* Institute for Defence Studies and Analyses, New Delhi, 2000.

84. Ibid.

85. http://www.fao.org/fi/default.asp

86. Mohd. Khurshed Alam, 'Maritime Strategy of Bangladesh in the New Millennium', *BIISS Journal,* Vol. 20, No. 3, 1999, pp. 199-200.

87. Mathew, 'Fishing in the Indian Ocean', see n. 48.

88. Interview with K. K. Nag, Ex-Assistant Secretary, Marine Fisheries Department, Sankerpur Fish Harbour, 19 June 2002.

89. Interview with Utpal Kumar Sar, Assistance Director of Fisheries (Marine) West Bengal,Meen Bhavan, East Midnapur, 20 June 2002.

90. World Forum of Fisher People, 'A Letter to the Governments of India, Pakistan, Bangladesh and Sri Lanka', 20 April 2002.

91. Ghosh, *Hungry Tide,* p. 165, quoting the German poet Rainer Maria Rilke, see n. 40.

92. Hastings Donnan and Thomas M. Wilson, *Borders: Frontiers of Identity, Nation and State,* Berg, Oxford, 1999.

6.   'Unruly' Fisherfolk in the Eyes of Law

1. For a similar argument in a different context, see Ratna Kapur, *Erotic Justice: Law and the New Politics of Postcolonialism,* Glass House, London, 2005, pp. 137-77.

2. This has been expressed in other contexts as well by different scholars. See for example, D. Kennedy, *The Dark Side of Virtue: Reassessing International Humanitarianism*, Princeton University Press, Princeton, 2004; W. Brown and J. Halley (eds), *Left Legalism/Left Critique*, Duke University Press, Durham, 2002. They have also argued that the founding of international law is critically linked to colonial law.

3. R. P. Anand, 'Recent Developments in the Law of the Sea', *International Studies,* Vol. 26, No. 3, July–September 1989, p. 247.

4. Richard Hudson, 'Scramble for the Seas', *Strategic Digest,* Vol. 6, No. 1, p. 56.

5. M. Lewis Alexander, 'Geography and the Law of the Sea', *Annals of the Association of American Geographers,* Vol. 58, No. 1, March 1968, p. 184.

6. M. Channa Basavaiah, 'Victims of Development: Fisherpeoples' Movement in India', *JIOS*, Vol. 11, No. 1, April 2003. Also see, Elisabeth Mann Borgese, 'Ocean Governance and the Fishing Village', in K. G. Kumar (ed.), *Forging Unity: Coastal Communities and the Indian Ocean's Future*, Proceedings of the Indian Ocean Conference 9–13 October 2001, International Collective in Support of Fishworkers (ICSF) and International Ocean Institiute (IOI), Chennai, 2003.

7. R. P. Anand, 'A New Legal Order on Fisheries', in R. C. Sharma (ed.), *The Oceans: Realities and Prospects*, Rajesh Publications, New Delhi, 1985.

8. On UNCLOS III, see Mohamed El Baradei, *Crowded Agendas: Crowded Rooms, Institutional Arrangements at UNCLOS III: Some Lessons in Global Negotiations*, United Nations Institute for Training and Research, New York, 1981; Hugo Caminos and Michael R. Molitor, 'Progressive Development of International Law and the Package Deal', *The American Journal of International Law*, Vol. 79, No. 4, October 1985, pp. 871-90.

9. United Nations Convention on the Law of the Sea, 'Preamble', 10 December 1982.

10. See Annick de Marffy-Mantuano, 'The Procedural Framework of the Agreement Implementing the 1982 United Nations Convention on the Law of the Sea', *The American Journal of International Law*, Vol. 89, No. 4, October 1995, pp. 814-24.

11. P. K. Goel, 'A Reappraisal of International Law Applicable to Armed Conflicts at Sea', *JIOS*, Vol. 3, No. 2, March 1996.

12. Rama Puri, 'Law of the Sea: An Analysis in the Context of India', in A. N. Kakkar (ed.), *Indian Ocean,* New Book House, Allahabad, 1987.

13. Ibid.

14. See, Annexure on Articles, Article 73 in 1982 UN Convention.

15. See Part 2, Article 56, Annexure (Rights, Jurisdiction and Duties of Coastal States in EEZ), quoted in H. Mahadevan et al., *Fishworkers as 'Prisoners of War': A Fact Finding Report*, Centre for Education and Communication, New Delhi, 1998, p. 25.

16. D. F. Da Silva, 'Toward a Critique of the Socio-logos of Justice: The Analytics of Raciality and the Production of Universality', *Social Identities*, Vol 7, No. 3, 2001, p. 421.

17. See, Pakistan Letter A/CONF.62/L, 68, April 1981; 126 Meeting, 2 April 1980, *Third UN Conference on the Laws of the Sea*, Vol. 13, p. 21.

18. *Gazette of India Extraordinary*, Part II, Section 3, quoted in Puri, 'Law of the Sea', p. 121, see n. 12. Also see Rama Puri, *India and National Jurisdiction in Sea*, ABC Publishing House, New Delhi, 1985.

19. R. P. Anand, *South Asia: In Search of Regional Identity*, Banyan Publications, New Delhi, 1991.

20. See, Article 7(1) in MZI, Act No. 80 of 28 May 1976.

21. V. R. Malhotra, *The AIR Manual*, Vol. 33, 1989, 5th edn, p. 795. Also see, MZI, Act No. 42 of 1981.

22. M. Habibur Rahman, 'Delineation of Maritime Boundaries: A Survey of Problems in the Case', *Asian Survey*, Vol. 24, No.12, December 1986, p. 1307.

23. Article 7(1) in MZI, Act No. 80 of 28 May 1976.

24. See, Article 82, UNCLOS III.

25. Rahman, 'Delineation of Maritime Boundaries', p. 1306, see n. 22.

26. Satyavir Singh, 'The Maritime Zones of India: Perspectives, Problems and Prospects', *Defiance Today*, Vol. III, No. 1, April-June 1995, p. 55.

27. Special Correspondent, 'Maritime Environment in South Asia Vulnerable to Terrorism', *The Hindu*, 22 February 2004.

28. The Maritime Zones of India (Regulation of Fishing by Foreign Vessels) Act 1981, *The AIR Manual*, 4th edn, New Delhi, 1979.

29. 'Preface', in Kumar (ed.), *Forging Unity*, see n. 6.

30. William van Schendel and Itty Abraham (eds), *Illicit Flows and Criminal Things: States, Borders, and the Other Side of Globalization*, Indiana University Press, Bloomington, 2005.

31. See, Annexure, 1974, Agreement Between Sri Lanka and India on the Boundary in Historic Waters Between the Two Countries and Other Related Matters, 26 and 28 June 1974, www.un.org/Depts/los/LEGISLATIONANDTREATIES/PDFFILES/TREATIES/LKA-IND1974BW.PDF.

32. M. Channa Basavaiah, 'Fishing Along the Indian Coast: A Fishy Affair?' in Rama S. Melkote (ed.), *Indian Ocean: Issues for Peace*, Manohar, New Delhi, 1995, p. 165.

33. See, Annexure of UNCLOS III, 1982.
34. For similar arguments in different contexts, see Schendel and Abraham (eds), *Illicit Flows*, n. 30; Kapur, *Erotic Justice,* see n. 1.
35. For a larger argument on this see Balakrishnan Rajagopal, *International Law from Below: Development, Social Movements and Third World Resistance*, Cambridge University Press, Cambridge, 2003.

7. Conclusion

1. For more on this, see for example, Didier Bigo and Elspeth Guild (eds), *Controlling Frontiers: Free Movement Into and Within Europe*, Ashgate, England, 2005.
2. May Joseph, *Nomadic Identities: The Performance of Citizenship*, University of Minnesota Press, Minneapolis, 1999.
3. Arjun Appadurai, *Modernity at Large: Cultural Dimensions of Globalization*, University of Minnesota Press, Minneapolis, 1996.

Index